An
AMERICAN APOSTLE

An AMERICAN APOSTLE

The Life of
Stephen Fielding Bayne, Jr.

JOHN BOOTY

TRINITY PRESS INTERNATIONAL
Valley Forge, Pennsylvania

Trinity Press International, P.O. Box 851, Valley Forge, PA 19482–0851
Trinity Press International is a division of the Morehouse Publishing Group

Library of Congress Cataloging-in-Publication Data

Booty, John E.
    An American apostle : the life of Stephen Fielding Bayne, Jr. / by John Booty.
        p.   cm.
    Includes bibliographical references and index.
    ISBN 1-56338-208-3 (alk. paper)
    1. Bayne, Stephen F. (Stephen Fielding), 1908-1974. 2. Anglican Communion – Clergy – Biography. 3. Episcopal Church – Bishops – Biography. 4. Bishops – United States – Biography. I. Title.
BX5995.B386B66 1997
283'.092 – dc21
[B]   97-7837
                                                                 CIP

Printed in the United States of America

97   98   99   00   01   02   10   9   8   7   6   5   4   3   2   1

CONTENTS

PREFACE

When Harvard University gave Stephen Fielding Bayne, Jr., an honorary degree, thereby honoring the first Executive Officer of the Anglican Communion, it described Bayne as "an American apostle whose faith and power are called to build communion among diverse elements of a great church." In some ways it was the gargantuan task of opening a new chapter in the history of the Anglican Communion that most distinguished him in the eyes of his contemporaries. He did act as the mediator and catalyst to bring about a new sense of mutual responsibility and interdependence — communion — to churches scattered around the globe, in diverse cultures, involving all races — all related, as children to a mother, to the See of Canterbury. He gave to these churches not only a fresh sense of communion but also a vision of what that communion could mean in preparing the way to the triumph and the glory of the Kingdom of God. He was indeed a man of vision who, with judgment and blessing, helped us see beyond the news in the daily newspaper to the great sweep of history — from that which is most immediate, to the global implications of particular events, and to the future hope ever encroaching on the present. Between 1960 and 1964, the years in which he served as Anglican Executive Officer, his life — as parish priest, university and navy chaplain, diocesan bishop, national church executive, seminary professor and dean, preacher and lecturer with an international reputation for excellence and inspiration — found its most complete and satisfactory focus.

From the beginning of his ministry his vision was global; and his spirituality, the power center of his life, extended to all of history — past, present, and future — and to all races and nations, to the good and to the bad. His spirituality was grounded in the deep conviction that God created all and loved all that He created: calling forth an answering love, as a shepherd seeking those who stray; extending redemption to all through the death and resurrection of His Son; providing in Jesus Christ the means by which to love, to make our offerings in and along with His offering on the Cross. Narrow nationalism, party rigidities, racial bigotry, and sex discrimination stood condemned in the vision of God — not the optional God of post-Christian society, but the God of Abraham, Jacob and Isaac, the God and Father of our Lord Jesus Christ. The

Church in this view is more than an institution. It is that body holding "generous and devoted hands aloft in offering the world to Him
from Whom it comes, and unto Whom be glory in the Church by Christ
Jesus, world without end." Bayne thus spoke out as a prophet against
those tendencies in the Church and in contemporary society that fall
short of this biblical vision.

For this and for many other reasons, Bayne still speaks to us in the
Church and in the world, in the diverse and complex multiplicity of societies and cultures of planet earth. Bayne speaks to us in his writings,
here reviewed in some detail, but also in his life, here recounted as carefully and accurately as a fallible human being can do. He speaks to us
through his life...partly through his own fallibility and sinfulness — to
tell us of the wonderful grace that is ours in and through God's forgiveness, the power of which sustained him through years of turmoil and
moments of pain. He spoke from his heart when he wrote:

> Christianity offers no easy, neat, managed universe. It offers no
> social absolute. It offers no easily molded impersonality into which
> a man may sink himself, caring for nothing, believing in nothing,
> hoping for nothing.
>
> Christianity offers only sharp and clear selfhood, worked out in
> a myriad of choices. It offers a man only the chance to disengage
> himself from the whole. It offers him only the freedom to write
> what story he will with his life. It offers him pain, and a dazzling
> bright light on the steps he takes in this life.
>
> Christianity requires all his freedom in return.... The immeasur-
> able gift of God is that in this bondage, and in it alone, is man set
> free from the bondage of this world, from the tyranny of power,
> and from the crushing darkness of the faceless and anonymous.
> This bondage is what makes it possible for man to recognize and
> cherish his brother. It is what makes it possible for a man to be
> himself.[1]

This book contains something of the story Bayne chose to write with
his life. It does not contain the complete story. It is chiefly concerned
with Bayne the public figure, Bayne the intellectual, Bayne the spiritual
man. Admittedly, in large part because shortly before he died he wrote
about it, I have been concerned to understand Bayne's "dark night of the
soul," but that is a part, albeit an important part, of the spiritual man,
the inspirational leader. Some relevant papers have not been available
to me, such as those at Lambeth Palace and at the Episcopal Church
Archives in Austin, Texas, where papers are sealed for specified periods
of time. But I have greatly benefited from the Bayne Collection at General Theological Seminary in New York, the Archives of the Diocese of

Olympia at Seattle, the Archives of the Anglican Consultative Council, and materials in the possession of individuals.

I am especially grateful to the late Peggy Chisholm, Bishop Bayne's Administrative Assistant. Miss Chisholm has supported me most generously in my work and is the person responsible for establishing and maintaining the Bayne Collection, including materials ranging from books and articles to tapes, films, letters, and reports. *Stephen Bayne: A Bibliography* (privately printed, 1978), which has been so helpful to me and to others, would not exist without Miss Chisholm. Eileen Brady, Miss Chisholm's secretary, provided generous assistance along the way. The Reverend Bruce Bayne, the bishop's youngest child, my former student and good friend, gave generously of his time and energies to assist me. Stephen Fielding Bayne III and Duncan Bayne, also sons, were both helpful. The late Edward A. Bayne, the bishop's brother, was most attentive, providing me with materials to reconstruct the early life of my subject and much else besides.

The Right Reverend Edward R. Welles and the Right Reverend Jonathan G. Sherman provided me with reminiscences of their friend, whom they knew from the 1920s and 1930s until his death in 1974. I owe a debt of thanks to many others who supplied me with information and impressions either by letter or in personal conversations: the Right Reverend and Right Honorable Michael Ramsey, the Right Reverend and Right Honorable Donald Coggan, the Right Reverend John Howe, the Reverend Canon F. A. McDonald, Prebendary Dewi Morgan, and Mr. John Furness. Many people associated with the Diocese of Olympia, when Bayne was bishop there, provided assistance for which I am grateful, especially Ruth Jenkins, John Huston, and the Reverend Richard Garlichs and his wife, Elizabeth. I owe a special debt of thanks to the Reverend Professor Holt Graham, who knew Bayne well at Columbia. None of these people and others I have not mentioned who have helped are responsible for what I have set down in this biography.

The Very Reverend Cabell Tennis, Dean of St. Mark's Cathedral, Seattle, now Bishop of Delaware, was responsible for my being invited by the Cathedral Associates to give a series of lectures in March of 1986 on "The Global Spirituality of Stephen Bayne." This occasion not only helped me to assemble materials and thoughts relevant to this biography but to meet with a large gathering of those who knew Bayne well. I am grateful for being afforded this opportunity and for much generous hospitality.

My thanks are owed to the University of the South for a leave of absence during the academic year 1985–86; to Dean Leander Keck for providing me with a role to play as both Visiting Professor of Church History and Research Fellow at Yale Divinity School during my leave of absence; to the Very Reverend James Annand, Dean of Berkeley Divinity School at Yale, and his wife, Connie, for a place to live, a warm welcome, and continuous support; to the Very Reverend James Fenhagen and the Reverend Dr. David Green for hospitality and many favors during the time I spent working at the Bayne Collection at General Theological Seminary; the Archivist of the Diocese of Olympia for making available relevant files in her collection; to the Reverend Canon Samuel Van Culin and his staff for opening the archives of the Anglican Consultative Council for my use; and to Dr. Stephen Lee Peterson and his staff for much patience and assistance while I worked in the Yale Divinity School Library.

Easter 1996

One

BEGINNINGS

Boyhood

Stephen Fielding Bayne, Jr., was born in New York City on May 21, 1908, the second child and first son of Stephen Fielding Bayne and Edna Mabel (Ashley) Bayne.[1] His was a lineage that reached far back into the annals of Scotland, as he was fond of recalling, to A.D. 1040 when Macbeth slew Duncan the King and drove the King's sons Malcolm and Duncan Bane, into exile. In Shakespeare's play, Donalbain says to Malcolm:

> To Ireland, I; our separated fortune
> Shall keep us both the safer: where we are,
> There's daggers in men's smiles: the near in blood,
> The nearer bloody. (Macbeth, Act 2, Scene 3)

Almost six centuries later, in 1635, some Baynes ventured further to Virginia, a fearsome wilderness, but also a land of infinite promise. The Baynes farmed a large estate in Westmoreland County on the Potomac River. Then, as was the custom of the times, they pushed westward to Kentucky, Indiana, and Illinois.

It was in Illinois on December 27, 1835, that George Gladstone Bayne, Stephen's grandfather, was born and grew up to maintain the Bayne reputation for adventure, working in the cotton trade in Mississippi, New Orleans, Louisiana, and Savannah, Georgia. A first marriage ended with the death of his wife and infant daughter in 1862. By then the Southern guns had fired on Fort Sumter, signaling the beginning of a tragic war, which was anything but civil. Having moved to Kansas to be with his sister, Frances, George enlisted in the 25th Infantry, Missouri Volunteers. He became a Union officer and in time the regimental quartermaster to an army engaged against the enemy at Shiloh, Vicksburg, Chattanooga, Atlanta, and with Sherman marching in triumph to the sea.

Stephen, the younger, was enthralled and dismayed by this episode in the family history. But his innate romanticism was yet more engaged by what happened at war's end. It was then that George returned to Savannah and, when mustered out of the army, married Mary Elizabeth Yonge, the daughter of a staunch Confederate family. Looking back, Stephen recalled:

> To me as a boy, this marriage seemed romantic and heartbreaking to a degree. My grandmother could have done nothing more shameful, in the eyes of her family, than to have gone over to the enemy — and to one of Sherman's officers, worst of all. It meant the end of any living relationship with her home. Indeed, it was friends, Mr. and Mrs. Ward, who gave a little reception for them the night they were married; and I think there was never any but the most formal reconciliation with her family.

George took his bride to New York and there struggled to maintain his family, running first a grocery store on Ninth Avenue, not far from the General Theological Seminary, and then a furniture business. His business ventures were largely unsuccessful, limiting what he could provide for the education of his children, one becoming a guard on the subway and another a telegraph operator.

Stephen Fielding Bayne, Sr., was born in 1879. In time, with the financial help of a brother, he enrolled at the City College of New York. On graduating, he became a teacher and later a school principal, ending his career in education as Deputy Superintendent from 1946 until his death in 1956.[2] Known to former students as an effective teacher and strict disciplinarian, the elder Stephen instilled in his namesake a desire for and love of education. When not laboring as an educator in the New York public schools, Stephen, Sr., was using his calling and his talents elsewhere. During World War I he ran a YMCA literacy program at Camps Upton and Plattsburgh during the summers. He served as Superintendent of the Sunday School of the Chapel of the Intercession, New York, for twenty-five years, managing a school that numbered on Sundays as many as 1,200 students. In 1900 Stephen the older married Edna Ashley, the daughter of a prominent family that traced its history to colonial New England. She too was drawn to education. At the time she met her future husband, she was taking courses at Columbia University and attending the Chapel of the Intercession. Young Stephen grew up in awe of his father and with a deep affection for his mother, who inspired in him a love for art, music, and the theater.

The Baynes lived in the Washington Heights neighborhood of New York in a walk-up flat on 156th Street, not far from the Chapel of the Intercession. During Stephen's boyhood there were the three foci: home, school, and church. He grew to maturity in a close-knit family, but one that was always busy, so that its members were largely engaged in their own occupations as individuals. There were differences in temperament as well as in age among the Bayne siblings. Charlotte was three years older and Ned (Edward) was five years younger than Stephen, known as "Buddy" in those early years. Stephen was the intellectual one of the three. His brother remembers him reading virtually anything and everything available.[3]

There were moments when the family was very close. On Sundays they sometimes picnicked at Croton Reservoir between morning and evening worship at church. In the summers they went off together for family vacations. When Stephen was four they went to Nova Scotia. From 1914 on, they went by train to Essex on the shore of Lake Champlain and later by car, their first being a Ford "Model T." Essex was to be a home and anchoring place for Stephen throughout his life.

Reflecting on his boyhood, Bayne wrote: "Essex was friends, it was country, it was a time to meet people who lived somewhere else than New York. It was a time for the friendships of boyhood." It was not that Bayne found New York boring. An inquisitive child, he found the rich ethnic mix of the city endlessly fascinating. In Washington Heights he came to know Jewish people as neighbors and friends, and was enticed by "the mysteries of Friday suppertimes . . . where candles burned."[4]

Stephen went to Trinity School, an institution of Trinity Parish, which included the Chapel of the Intercession. Trinity School traced its beginnings to 1689 when William Huddlestone, a non-Juror, emigrated from England to found a school. In Bayne's time it was located on West 91st Street, where the headmaster was the Reverend Lawrence T. Cole. There Stephen played football, fenced, and acted in plays. He was a conscientious and able student, graduating in 1924 at sixteen years of age. Stephen's home atmosphere contributed to his academic success at this time. So did his zeal for reading, allied to his interest in writing. Books were for the mature Bayne the conversations of civilized life: "It never occurred to me that you ever did anything in your spare time except read."[5] While reading, young Bayne developed a fascination for words and their meanings. Later he was to develop an impatience with official documents, their misuse of words and their meaningless jargon.

The Baynes were faithful members of the Chapel of the Intercession, a part of Trinity Parish. Stephen was involved frequently in the church as an acolyte, a choir boy, and a student in the weekly Sunday School. Later in his life he remembered that Sunday School "made strangely little educational impact on me." More important was attendance at morning and evening worship services, although here his attention was often occupied by watching people, especially eccentrics, such as the woman who insisted on being first at the altar rail, and the ushers in their unsuccessful attempts to stay in step as they marched up the center aisle with the offering plates. Still, participation in corporate worship

helped him to learn more "about the ordered, balanced life of Anglican devotion" than any course in *The Book of Common Prayer*.[6] In due
time he was confirmed and began receiving communion at the Lord's
Supper. However, it was at Trinity School where he "learned about religion chiefly from my physics teacher, who for the first time let me see
that God was not a deceased clergyman but One whose mind we read
whenever we learn anything."[7]

College and Seminary

In 1924, at sixteen, Stephen began his studies at Amherst College, a
prestigious, small men's college in New England. His career at Amherst
was divided into two periods. In the first three years the adolescent
boxed, took courses, and discovered the young women at nearby Smith
College. By his own admission he was floundering. "I was just a kid
and had no self-discipline."[8] His academic record reflected this. During his sophomore and junior years he did poorly. In Philosophy 2
he received a "D" for the year and in Philosophy 4 a "C." The college suspended him, and he returned to New York where he worked
for a year on *The Wall Street Journal*. "It was 1927 and 1928, the
time of the big toot. Everybody was rich, and I felt on the fringe of
affluent greatness, writing stories about railroad dividends."[9] But then
something happened to change his life. He tells us that having left academic life he realized how important it was. At this time he determined
that he was called to a vocation as a priest of the Episcopal Church,
for which a college degree was requisite. He returned to Amherst for
his senior year "repentant and hard working." He then took Philosophy 7 under Professor Newlin and earned a straight "A." There was
one member of the Amherst faculty to whom Stephen as a student and
later as an alumnus felt especially devoted, one with whom he maintained a correspondence for years — George Ray Elliott. Wrote Bayne:
"He was a glorious teacher — Milton and Shakespeare were his strong
fields." Bayne learned much from Elliott, "not the least about style," and
came to appreciate the teacher's severe criticism of his written exercises.
During a sabbatical leave in 1929–30 Elliott was converted to "Anglo-
Catholicism from a rather pallid congregationalism" and showed great
interest in Bayne's progress toward ordination, encouraging him in his
studies, recommending that he read Paul Elmer More's *Aristocracy and
Justice* in preference to the "wordy, flamboyant, self-conscious works"
of Ortega y Gasset with which Stephen then was engaged. The combi-
nation of Anglo-Catholicism and literary talent and skill, so prominent
in Elliott, appealed mightily to young Bayne.[10]

    While at Amherst, Bayne met a Smith College student named Lucie
Culver Gould, the daughter of Maurice Philip Gould and Anna Jaffray

(Smith) Gould. Lucie attended schools in France and Switzerland before entering Smith. Stephen courted her, encouraged by the rector of Grace Church, Amherst, the Reverend Arthur Lee (Tui) Kinsolving, who wrote, "I think she is a wonder, and I hope eventually to see her in your rectory." He urged Stephen on: "Don't get humble in your wooing, you deserve Lucie and if it must be, it will be."[11] It was not to be for awhile. Stephen went to seminary at a time when marriage was not allowed in course. Lucie went to work as editor of an advertising periodical. In 1932 she went to Puerto Rico to teach in a church mission school.

In the autumn of 1929 Stephen entered the General Theological Seminary in New York at a time when it had a strong and distinguished faculty, headed by Hughell E. W. Fosbroke, dean and professor of Old Testament. Others included Burton Scott Easton in New Testament, Frank Gavin in Church History, Leonard Hodgson in Apologetics, Marshall Bowyer Stewart in Dogmatics, and Howard Chandler Robbins in Pastoral Theology. This faculty constituted a new generation of scholars destined to move the seminary from its generally conservative, Anglo-Catholic theological position to what William Manross called "liberal orthodoxy," the acceptance of modern critical scholarship and recognition of the need to recast the Church's thinking on the basis of the changed "mental outlook of the modern world."[12]

Stephen greatly admired Dean Fosbroke, who impressed Stephen with his affirmation of the grandeur of the Church in its true nature as Israel "judging, judged, intercessing, suffering, existing, proclaiming, rejoicing."[13] But he recognized Easton as "the best teacher" and his "most influential mentor and advisor... holding preeminent place among Anglican scholars in his massive introduction of form criticism."[14] Bayne benefited from the rigorous scholarship of men such as Fosbroke and Easton, and was introduced by them and others to that British scholarship that dominated the seminary curriculum of the time. Charles Gore and William Temple were the giants. Bayne acknowledged the excitement of volumes of essays, *Essays Catholic and Critical* (1926) and *Essays on the Trinity and the Incarnation* (1928), which presented Hoskyns, Rawlinson, Streeter, and Thornton as "major figures in Biblical Studies." And there were Proctor and Frere on *Liturgy and Worship* and K. E. Kirk on moral theology.[15] There were others: Barth, Brunner, and Tillich in Germany; and of Americans, Hocking, the two Niebuhrs, Bacon, and Scott. But it was British scholarship that was dominant. Partially this was because of what Bayne recognized as his growing Anglophilia, with its dangers and benefits, the danger of being a diluted Englishman, the benefit of gaining "the singular Anglican turn of mind, that humane, historical sense which is so bright a star in the Anglican constellation."[16]

During his seminary days Stephen also developed an ecclesiology much influenced by the nineteenth-century English understanding of a national church. He recalled:

We were taught to think of our ministry as that of the Church, not of a sect. . . . The notion of the whole responsibility of the Church to its community was deep in us. The religious life of our society seemed part and parcel of its total life, to us. All this was English; and I think it was good.

He was to realize that it was also unrealistic in a poly-cultural, pluralistic situation such as that prevailing in the United States. However, the fundamental understanding was right, and he learned that "it is possible to live in a society composed of many religious minorities and still keep the depth and greatness of the sense of a responsible national Church."[17] This ecclesiology emphasized the parish as the local manifestation of the national church, and Bayne early on decided that although he was attracted to a teaching ministry, or perhaps a university chaplaincy, he must first gain experience in a parish or parishes.

Howard Robbins, who taught homiletics at the General Seminary, recognized that Stephen was well suited for the parish ministry especially because of his preaching. Robbins also had the impression that Bayne's written work was more homiletical than academic. During his three seminary years, Stephen's preaching steadily improved, both his student preaching and his preaching at the Church of St. James the Less, Scarsdale, where he was assisting as a lay reader, and at places such as Christ Church, Brooklyn, where he supplied for an absent staff member. In the course of the preaching, he developed certain themes that were to be preeminent in his preaching and teaching: the love of God, the responsibility of humans, the necessity of active choice and obedience. In his first public sermon, delivered at St. James the Less, Bayne preached on "Christian Hope," using the figure of the potter and the clay, in which he acknowledged as true that "God can do what He chooses with the Clay — that doesn't matter in the slightest." What does matter is that we too are responsible, active disciples, doing the best we can, expressing the love that God inspires and directs in all the designs of life. That love is the only thing that matters; it is the ground of Christian hope. Bayne was no Pelagian, but then neither was he like those who so emphasized the sovereignty of God that human responsibility was denied.[18]

During his seminary years, Stephen began speaking in public. In 1931 he addressed the Origen Society of New York on "The Church's Mission to the Despairing," drawing on the wisdom of Unamuno's *The Tragic Sense of Life*.[19] He also addressed the Tri-Seminary Conference held in New York. In 1932 he spoke in Boston to the Church League for Industrial Democracy (CLID). In the first, he warned that Christians must live the Christian ideal in the world although conscious of the fact that they may be witnessing the destruction of society. "The Church is not a function of society," he said. "The Kingdom of God is not a socio-economic paradise." He said this with implicit criticism of the Social Gospel Movement as the Great Depression worsened. He carried this message further at the CLID meeting the next year, warning that the Church must not become so entangled in society that she becomes a mere fraction of society. Here he reflected something of the influence of Reinhold Niebuhr.[20] At the Tri-Seminary Conference, Stephen worked on the relationship between worship and social action. He was convinced that "without worship a life of devotion to one's fellows is an impossibility," and went on to say:

> I am reminded of the statement of Reinhold Niebuhr: "If men are to center their life in moral purpose, they must reassure themselves periodically on the moral purpose of life itself. That is mysticism and prayer.... " Without worship, without the constant dedication and rededication of one's self to the God one serves, without the constant seeking after God's will...ethical action, social reconstruction is an impossibility.[21]

Such an understanding accorded well with the teaching of Gore and Temple, as well as Niebuhr, and was to be a major theme in Bayne's lifework.

Bayne was known to his fellow students "for his sharp mind and his gift for communication." Jonathan Sherman remarks that it was a mystery how he gained the store of knowledge he consistently displayed. He was no recluse, participating as he did in student activities in and out of seminary. Edward Welles recalls the skit in which the students imitated the faculty. In the "G.T.S. Levites of 1930–31," Welles was Dean Fosbroke, and Stephen was Dr. Massey Shepherd. The students were so rough on the faculty that student skits were discontinued for several years.[22] Bayne was hilarious, according to Bishop Sherman, who also remembers Bayne's participation in productions of Gilbert and Sullivan. Perhaps preoccupation with such activities accounts for the event Jonathan Sherman recalled in which he and Bayne were going to a seminar with Dr. Stewart. "Steve turned to me and said, 'Jon, wasn't I supposed to report on something today?' I checked my notebook and answered, 'Yes, you are due to present a paper on ... ' — (I have forgotten the subject). 'Oh, yes,' Steve replied. When Dr. Stewart called on him, he arose and for twenty minutes, without a note in front of him, delivered an oral essay that was beautifully organized and expressed."[23]

Bayne graduated at the end of the academic year in 1932, having become close, lifelong friends with fellow students Charles Boynton, Jonathan Sherman, John Butler, and Ed Welles, all destined to become prominent leaders in the Episcopal Church. His S.T.B. thesis was lauded by Howard Robbins and many others, Robbins saying, "You seem to have summarized the salient features of several of your seminary courses, digested them, and given them to your congregation with persuasiveness and force. I congratulate you on what is really an admirable piece of work."[24] Even the awesome Bishop of New York, William T. Manning, was pleased with Stephen's preparation for ordination.

Graduate Study

Upon graduation in 1932, Bayne was ordained a deacon and in June of 1933 a priest at the Cathedral of St. John the Divine by Bishop Manning. He celebrated mass for the first time at St. James the Less, Scarsdale, in Eucharistic vestments "with full Catholic ceremonies of a low celebration."[25] He spent the summer as a part-time member of the staff of the Chapel of the Intercession and then returned to General Theological Seminary as fellow and tutor to study for an S.T.M. degree. From 1932 to 1934, Stephen tutored students, studied, wrote a thesis, and supplied churches in and around New York. He served as a weekend curate from 1932 to 1934 at St. James the Less, but on some Sundays was found to be preaching in various places, including the Cathedral of St. John the Divine, the Church of the Incarnation, New York, and St. Bernard's Church, Bernardsville, New Jersey. His preaching at this time reflected his graduate studies and his concern for the effects of the Depression, the need for social reconstruction, and the rightful involvement of the Church in politics. Preaching at the Church of the Incarnation in New York in March of 1934 in the presence of Eleanor Roosevelt, he applauded President Roosevelt and pled for the essential unity of all people, rich and poor — for what, in a later time, he would describe as "mutual responsibility."[26]

His preaching emphasized the necessity of sacrifice, of losing one's life in order to do God's will in service to those in need. To accomplish this, he told a congregation at St. Bernard's that we must pay homage to God, in awe kneeling before God, worshipping and praying.[27] Bayne also emphasized "that the Christian orbit of life, although frequently concurrent with the orbit of the world, is essentially independent of it, revolving around God; that Christian citizenship is not of this world, but of a larger world; that Christian political action, while necessary, must be an apostolic action, not a conventional one."[28] This led to a conclusion that was to echo through his life, angering some, inspiring others. "Only an atheist could say that a man's loyalty to his country came before anything else, and yet there are many people, even in this congregation, who have said that, and will say it again."[29]

For these two years, however, Bayne's life was concentrated in the work he had to do at the Seminary. He was testing the possibility of a career in academics and preparing to teach ethics and moral theology. His supervisor was the highly esteemed Dr. Easton, who guided Bayne through the complex process leading to written and oral examinations and through the preparation of an outstanding thesis. When the thesis was done and submitted to the faculty on April 1, 1934, Bayne took the written examination. This was administered by Easton and took three to four hours. It "could cover any aspect of the candidate's major field." In Bayne's case, "he was alone in a classroom in Sherred Hall; Dr. Easton came in with a brief greeting and wrote on the blackboard 'Fourth Gospel' and departed." As Bayne remembered it, "he took the first hour to plan his answer and then wrote as furiously as he could until the time was up." The oral examination occurred in the presence of the entire faculty. Donald Fraser Forrester, whom Bayne found to be less than adequate as a teacher, "was clearly lying in wait" for one whom he regarded as a brash young man. He pressed Bayne "hard on the question of St. Paul and the mystery cults. Finally Dr. Easton gently remarked that he thought Bayne had answered adequately even if not agreeably; and that was that."[30]

The crowning achievement was the thesis on "The Kingdom and the Church: An Essay in the Historical Origins of Christian Ethics." As Bayne noted, the thesis was greatly influenced by Easton's understanding of the Kingdom. However, Easton did not "tolerate slavishness in pupils, and by 1934 SFB had begun to develop some positions of his own." His aim was to provide some elements of an apologetic for a strangely defenseless Christianity in the face of contemporary secular attacks not only on its beliefs, but also on its ethical system. He examined Jesus' teaching, as found in the synoptic Gospels, with its emphasis upon the Kingdom as present reality. The motivation for entrance into the Kingdom was not acceptance of an elaborate set of doctrines, nor was it adherence to a complex system of laws. It was rather a matter of losing one's life, "a willingness . . . to give up one's life to find it again." And this radical imperative was understood in the context of God's love. Thus, although the one demand was for self-abnegation, this did not mean "that those who do not see their way clear to lose their lives are, for that reason alone, bereft of the love of God."

The primitive church, as found in Acts, Bayne believed, lost sight of this truth. Change was necessary and was achieved in the light of the resurrection and Christ's ministry of the Spirit. But Christianity was in danger. Christians became more concerned for their personal salvation than for their mission. "In Jesus' teaching, they were to represent God's redemptive love in the world."[31] But they seemed indifferent to the world. Paul, as Bayne tells it, did the necessary thing, transforming Christianity from "a religion of history to a religion of timeless authority." The key was in Paul's Christ-mysticism — "Life in Christ" — which involves not the futile quest for what Jesus would have done, but the dynamic questioning of "What does Christ in me really think?" Bayne is sure that "it is far better to come out boldly for the obedience of Paul than to attempt to bring the historic Jesus up to date." Bayne thus emphasized Paul's doctrine of Justification by Grace through Faith. That doctrine involves forgiveness and sanctification without the merit of our works. In a fundamental way it involves the surrender of the will to Christ, which Paul depicts as death, but death followed by resurrection, "with Christ, and as Christ rose, a new man." Bayne wrote, "we die and, dying, leave all our old will and heart and mind in the grave of the spirit, to accept within us the will and heart and mind of Christ, the Spirit of Christ, the Spirit of God." And the dying, what is it but repentance? "It is the repentance that the Prodigal Son knew, a change of life so complete that the Father knew no way to describe it save 'this my son was dead, and is alive again!' It is the same repentance that the Lord sent His disciples out to preach." And so, Bayne concluded, "the task of Christian apologetic is not to attempt a defense of Christ at work in the first century, but to determine the forces of Christ at work in the twentieth. This is not a fine scorn of history; in my view it is to put the breath of life into it."

Later in his life, Bayne remarked that "much of the material in the thesis on soteriology and the Kingdom was to find more developed expression in the last chapter of The Optional God — a chapter which led Dean Fosbroke to remark that it was 'pure DuBose,' which SFB took as a very great compliment."[32] In fact, the evidence shows that Bayne, who knew nothing of William Porcher DuBose when writing his S.T.M thesis, was influenced by Easton, by Albert Schweitzer, and other dominant European theologians and biblical scholars. Much of the time he was reacting against the so-called liberal theologians and their quest for the historical Jesus. Again we find ideas developing that were to be matters of concern for years to come.[33]

These were on the whole happy, productive years. As he remembered them, Bayne recalled an incident that revealed a dark side. On one July Sunday during the summer of 1932, Stephen was scheduled to preach at the Chapel of the Intercession. "Standing in the sacristy waiting for the procession to begin," he "suddenly realized that he could not possibly go on into the service — that he would faint or be sick.... Someone covered for him, and he learned thereafter the virtues of triple bromides or some other sedative. In time he learned to live with the misery of it, and even to understand something of the fear of exposure which was being expressed." He described what he experienced as due to a "deep vein of anxiety — stage fright" and spoke "of the inexorable agony of preaching."[34] According to his own memory, this was the beginning of

something that was to plague him again and again. The nature of his suffering, whether clinical depression or of some psychological root, is not
known. Bayne himself was to recognize physical manifestations resulting
from fatigue. He followed a prescribed high-protein, low-blood-sugar
diet, but "even more a better discipline against anxiety."[35] The malady
was hidden most of the time, buried deep within an otherwise strong,
jovial, brilliant, likable personality. But he knew it was there — "a thorn
in the flesh" — tormenting him but also making him sensitive to the pain
of anxiety in others. Knowing pain, he could minister to those in pain
and at strategic moments let others know that he shared their pain.

These years also provided much cause for rejoicing. He had proven
his academic ability, earning two degrees from General Theological Seminary, becoming an increasingly effective preacher, ordained deacon, and
then priest, loved by his adoring family, and successful in his wooing of
Lucie. They were married on June 19, 1934. After a ten-day honeymoon
on Cape Cod, the young couple went to Northampton, Massachusetts,
the home of Smith College, where Stephen supplied for Albion Ock-
enden while the latter was on vacation. During those five weeks they
lived with Miss Clara Allen on Paradise Road.[36] Stephen greatly impressed the people of St. John's Church for in five years, they were to
call him as their rector.

Stephen had numerous opportunities to enter the parish ministry, as
he determined he must do. There were possibilities in Massachusetts
(Tui Kinsolving inquired about the possibility of Stephen's joining his
staff at Trinity Church, Copley Square, Boston), in Spokane, Washington, in New Jersey, on Long Island, in Corning, New York, at
St. Bartholomew's, New York, and at the American Cathedral in Paris.[37]
But while at Northampton, Stephen heard from Will Scarlett, the Bishop
of Missouri, about Trinity Parish in St. Louis and was attracted by both
the bishop and the parish, both challenging in the best sense. Lucie and
Stephen returned to New York and General Seminary for August, living
"quietly in the Simpsons' apartment on the top floor of West Building.
In mid-September," Bayne reported, "we set out for St. Louis, where my
first duty was Michaelmas."[38]

Two

PARISH PRIEST

Going to St. Louis

Stephen Bayne first met the Bishop of Missouri on a rainy day in the summer of 1934. He had been summoned by telegram to meet Will Scarlett at the train station in Springfield, Massachusetts. Stephen had been warned that the bishop was "a wild man from the West, without any of the comforting memories of Bishop Seabury and the Non-Jurors and the Muhlenberg Declaration which are the staple food of Eastern Churchmen." Bayne had been cautioned not to call him "Your Grace"; moreover, he was aware that he should not kiss the bishop's ring, for that didn't exist. With trepidation, Bayne went to Springfield from Northampton. Knowing that the bishop did not wear clerical attire, he was afraid that he might not recognize the bishop. But then "a soft voiced man in a white suit" came up to him and identified himself as the bishop. They began talking, discussing the possibility of Bayne becoming the rector of Trinity Church, St. Louis. Bayne was captivated, his anxiety melted away, and he went to St. Louis devoted to Will Scarlett. He recognized that however much they differed, Scarlett would always be there to support him, and he would always appreciate the wisdom and warmth of his bishop.[1]

Trinity Church was the one Anglo-Catholic parish in St. Louis. The "low church" bishop was concerned that if it desired to be Anglo-Catholic it should have the best available young priest for its rector. Both the bishop and the new rector recognized that the parish presented serious challenges. The congregation was not large. Stephen complained to John Butler that attendance at Sunday mass was poor, ordinarily numbering around eighty people.[2] S. C. Frampton, speaking for the vestry before Stephen's arrival, told him that "Trinity is a comparatively small Parish today. It is experiencing an 'ebb tide' due to conditions. We have no so-called wealthy communicants."[3] However, with the support of loyal men and women, the new rector should find the future brighter than the present. Bayne spoke of Trinity as "a little somewhat bedraggled church . . . in the midst of the Depression."[4]

The new rector's salary was to be $2,400, raised from $2,100 by the bishop at Stephen's urging. The rental of a "rectory" was to come out of his salary.[5] The going was difficult. The bishop helped as much as he could, but Bayne had to watch every penny and bemoaned the fact that there were pay days that were payless. He understood that with all its problems Trinity did supply him with a job, whereas more than a third of the adult male communicants of the parish were unemployed. Acknowledging this fact, he persuaded the vestry to let him use a part of the church building as a dormitory for homeless men, and do volunteer work on relief projects and with union organizations.

In part, Stephen's concern for money was related to the fact that in St. Louis he and Lucie started their family. Stephen III was born in December 1935 and Philip in August 1937. The need for more income, as well as Stephen's strong desire to preach, accounted for increasing travels. He conducted a conference on "The Sacramental Life" for young people at Clear Lake, Iowa, gave lectures on "Liturgical Prayer" at the Holy Cross Monastery in West Park, New York, and studied and taught at the College of Preachers in Washington, D.C., all during his tenure at Trinity Church.

Liturgy

At the heart of Bayne's ministry at Trinity Church was liturgy, centered on the mass but including as liturgy most preaching and teaching and pastoral service, as well as prophetic witness. On first arriving at Trinity, he set to work perfecting the liturgical observances of the parish to keep them in tune with the best Anglo-Catholic practice, at times writing to John Butler and receiving advice, sometimes supportive, sometimes not.[6] In the process, liturgy at Trinity was enriched and made more accessible to ordinary folk.

From his vantage point at Trinity, Bayne began to speak out about liturgy and *The Book of Common Prayer*. He spoke with deep appreciation for the Prayer Book then in use but recommended its careful revision. He recognized that liturgy is complex, involving words and actions. He knew that around these words and actions exists a diverse and rich tradition involving ceremonies, vestments, architecture, music, and much more. In addition, there were the unspoken but real affections and loyalties of people. And, "most fundamental of all was the mystical and desperately real society which a liturgy offers and transforms." Although all of this was true, it was not to be thought that a liturgy is sacrosanct or above criticism. "It is and it must be subject to change, because the society which it reflects changes, and tradition changes, and the accidentals of life change."

Speaking at a conference of the clergy in the Diocese of Missouri in 1936, Bayne set down four criteria for what a liturgy should be. It should be (1) expressive of the creed it represents, (2) accessible to the fullest possible participation of the individual worshiper, (3) specific enough in its doctrine to be clear, but not so specific "as to be sectarian or repressive," and (4) "realistically conceived, psychologically and aesthetically, so as to be effective." In the process of his critique, Bayne found need for revision in terms of all four criteria. The language of *The Book of Common Prayer* came under attack first. Centering attention on the General Confession he said, "I wish I didn't have to ask my people to make this liturgical confession in such high-falutin' language, because I know that the chances of their getting beyond a profound admiration for Elizabethan syntax are very slim indeed."

Next he criticized the length of "the average liturgical performance." This involved him in recommending streamlining the liturgy through omission of some of its elements. He specified other such concerns as he eventually proceeded to discuss liturgical reform from the viewpoint of content. Relying to a certain extent on the wisdom of Brilioth in his work on the history of the Eucharist, Bayne made the argument that "Christian Liturgies from the beginning have carried the fivefold burden of Communion — Fellowship, Remembrance, Thanksgiving, Sacrifice, and Mystery." Using this definition as a measuring tool, Bayne was able to discern the weaknesses in the liturgy to which he was accustomed. Reviewing the history of the passage from medieval to reformation rites, Bayne found the liturgy of the Prayer Book to be strongest in respect to the communion-fellowship element, but weakest with respect to mystery. The emphasis on thanksgiving he saw as adequate but not what it should be. The element of sacrifice he found confused but still discernable, and the element of remembrance "adequately and usefully brought into play." On the whole, the Prayer Book came out fairly well in this inspection, but in need of revision. He ended by saying:

> The road to a right and just liturgical reform is not by way of piecemeal adoption and casual practice, but by a deep understanding and a delicate apprehension of the whole tradition: then a clear analysis of what the *lex credendi* is of which this is to be our *lex orandi*: then all the skill and precision of which praying minds are capable. We have all seen the unfortunate results of hasty and shallow work — all the way from 'the American Missal' to the little anonymous pamphlets which periodically appear. I say they are all out of order, because not one of them goes for its sources deep enough, or far enough.[7]

Such a conclusion, based in part on his correspondence with John Butler, arose out of Bayne's own experiments at Trinity and his realization of the dangers involved.

The Mass Is Everything

Trinity Church regarded the Holy Eucharist as the chief means of corporate worship at a time when many of the parishes in St. Louis and elsewhere emphasized "high Morning Prayer." In a sermon delivered on October 6, 1935, Bayne stated: "The Mass is everything" — that's an old Anglo-Catholic war cry. The mass *is* everything: life and the good will of men are stupid, meaningless things, without the Body and the Blood that ratifies them and makes us glad, and comforts us and makes a wordless sense out of all that is so defeating and so cruelly disappointing in our sincere desire to be good disciples. The gospel is not advice: it is Jesus, here, now."[8] He went on to acknowledge that the mass could not have such high value for people who regard themselves as "good." They might find something of worth — instructions, memories, perhaps even brotherhood. The mass is really for those who know themselves as sinners: "The sinner finds love, and he finds replenishment, and he finds transformation, and he finds God's fulfilling power." He finds Jesus, here and now. "He finds in the Eucharist the means for the constant day-by-day offering of his imperfections and his difficulties and his fears and his disillusionments. And in company with the simplest of God's gifts, bread and wine, he offers them even as all of life was once offered in the Lord Jesus. And with his comrades, sinners all, he kneels humbly waiting for the return of all their offerings transfigured and made new and strong and fine in the power that flows from God."[9]

On a yet deeper level of understanding, Bayne spoke of the communion that unites the individual to God and to fellow sinners "in a brotherhood of loving souls, who love each other because they love a God who is a companion." Acknowledging the need for such communion and the way in which the need is met in the Church, Bayne then said that when he saw that, he saw much more "of the sacramental ideal of life, with the fellowship of the mystery deepening and strengthening within me and with the Lambs of God weaving and interweaving their net of purpose and plan and goal all around me." At the very center of this communion and community there is a most simple ceremony: "When bread which is the sacrament of men's work, and wine which is the sacrament of men's joy, are lifted up and God is thanked for them, and then they are given back filled with God's own purpose and plan and ideal, and with His life and power added to them — there is a Sacrament — and I can understand it, because I have looked life in the face and seen the same things there."[10] Such an understanding reflected something of the power and the meaning of Thomas Cranmer's Prayer Book with its theology of communion, and of Richard Hooker's interpretation of the same in terms of participation — *koinonia* but also *meno, menein*. The sacraments are powerful to build up the body, the body whose members, as Bayne said, are enabled "to stand as second Christs in the world." Indeed, following Bayne's thought further, the Church is enabled corporately as well as individually as Christ in the world, for He is one with us and we with Him, to stand and to minister to the needy and the needs of the world.

The Preacher

Although for Bayne the mass was primary, this did not imply any neglect of the Word read and preached. Bayne recognized that the Prayer Book, as Thomas Cranmer claimed, is mostly Scripture, and that the sermon is an essential part of the mass. Thus he continued working on his preaching, taking every opportunity to preach and to study at the College of Preachers.

From the beginning of his ministry, Bayne concentrated much of his intellectual and spiritual energy on his preaching. He began, in accordance with Dr. Fleming's advice, writing out every sermon, indeed every utterance, including his announcements, "for the first five years of his ministry for the sake of developing the confident experience and vocabulary which would stand in good stead later."[11] Thus his first sermons were all written and preserved. Those first sermons illustrate the truth, spoken by Lucie Bayne in 1935, that they were " 'too good for the congregation' (i.e., that SB was preaching to himself or the angels or anybody except the people in the congregation)." There were in them some ideas that were not all that bad and were to be used many times again, but perhaps with greater simplicity and power.

He wrote, in 1935, of the necessity of refusing "to deal with easy definitions of what religion is," of "willingness to purify ourselves of phrases and formulas which we have inherited, when they cease to be suggestive, and become simply monuments to dead issues," and of the necessity of "understanding that it is what you suggest to people by yourself, your own life and soul, rather than what you tell them by word of mouth, that brings them into salvation."[12] These were rules for himself as a preacher, as well as for others, and in the first years at Trinity Church he was striving to live in accordance with them and to achieve at least a limited degree of success in reaching his people through preaching God's saving word.

In his first sermon at Trinity Church, Bayne spoke empathetically to his people who were suffering the harsh realities of the Depression. He could justly speak thus, for he shared their plight — at least to some degree. He also referred to the concern that they shared to eliminate the sufferings of those around them. Then he strove for a deeper wisdom, claiming that the wounds of those who were suffering could not be healed until there was the realization that they were symptoms of a greater disease, "a disease that is as large as society is — a disease that *is* society itself, warped and twisted and matted with the sickness of despair."[13] To many in his congregation the young preacher sounded too dour, too pessimistic. A month later he spoke of being laughed at for his pessimism. He did not intend that his entire message sound pessimistic. The challenge was to lead his people to discover that beyond his realism there was a gospel. So he persisted, saying:

> When I see a world shot through and through with disunity and war and nationalism and secularism, and when I see men all around me playing at disbelief, making a luxury of religion, pampering the whims and fancies of uneducated men and women who choose not to believe this or that or the other thing, when I put these facts side by side, I know from the bottom of my heart that he who would find his life must lose it — that unless a man puts all his faith in God, he will have no faith to put in himself. And modern man by and large has proved that beyond any question.[14]

The radical commitment of faith in God above and beyond all else is what is required, and what is promised is "the comradeship of Christ. We have Him — we give Him — and He gives the rest." In a sermon on Ephesians 2:13–14 he stated:

> We will start at our altar, where the walls are always down; and, shoulder to shoulder, welded together in Christ our peace, we will learn deeply and truly what the comradeship of Christ is like. As Christ our peace invades the bread and wine, so does He invade us, and we will live that out so that from beginning to end, our life in our parish is one long communion, tested and constantly fed by the day-by-day enactment of that communion, which is our spiritual fare. The peace of Christ — Christ our peace — will come down from the altar and break the wall between friend and stranger, between rich and poor, between worker and bosses, not only at the altar rail, but all the way through. And all of our religion will be filled with Him, in whom we have first found our faith.[15]

This is the gospel — communion with God in Christ and with one another in Him. Bayne would have people's attention fixed on that communion, for it is through such communion that despair is overcome and defeat becomes victory. This is no easy gospel. It will not fill the churches. It is demanding. This thought led him to assert: "The religion that is strong is the religion that is unpopular. Ever since Calvary that has been proved to be so. No, victory is not in numbers. It is in the strength of pure hearts and consecrated lives."[16]

Nor did he encourage people to believe that the turning point from despair to hope, from death to life, was in some isolated "religious" experience, extraordinary and exotic. The arena in which the battle for the soul occurred was that of day-to-day ordinary life. Jesus taught that it was in the commonplace things of life that the real glory of life lay. In a sermon on John 4:48, Bayne exhorted his people: "Don't keep your religion for the Grand Canyons in your life. Pray without ceasing. Thank God every time you eat a meal. Pray for His help every time you get a pain. He stands waiting at every insignificant commonplace wicket gate in your life."[17]

On the Sunday before his institution as rector of Trinity Church, Bayne spoke of laziness in spiritual things, spiritual pride, and spiritual dullness — the curse of the Christian — and of his expectations concerning his people and himself. "I don't ask or expect miracles," he said. "But as long as I am your rector I shall ask without any relenting that our Parish shall put first things first. Absolute devotion to God's will, absolute self-forgetfulness, absolute courage, those are the things that Christ demanded of His disciples, and they are the things he demands of us now."[18] Obedience was a central theme in all of his preaching, such obedience as sets people free to be what God created them to be, and to do what God would have them to do.

The Christianity he recommended was stern, realistic, pessimistic when considering the ability to save oneself, and demanding — demanding obedience to Christ's commands and to the call to lose one's life if one is to find one's life. But Bayne drew a line beyond which he would not go. On the Second Sunday in Advent 1934, "Bible Sunday," he defined Fundamentalism as "a state of mind wherein religion becomes a closed book — a secret and separate chamber in one's soul — having no relationship with an unkind and hostile world outside."[19] He would have nothing to do with such religion, yet he also refused what he saw as liberalism's confusion of the Kingdom and the "unkind and hostile world outside." For the rest of his life Bayne was to struggle with an understanding of a Church in but not of the world, with a mission to that world, and yet with knowledge of God as active in the world. He was undoubtedly convinced that there was no salvation to be found in the society of his time; he was equally convinced that God gave His son for the sake of the redemption of that same society.

During his time at Trinity Church, Stephen Bayne labored over his preaching. In 1936 and 1937 he spent two months in each of those years at the College of Preachers in Washington, D.C. There he submitted sermons to the criticism of those qualified to judge. From October 21–28, 1936, he led a conference with the Reverend Charles Feilding on "Preaching the Parables."[20] He was becoming known as an effective preacher; indeed, perfecting his preaching ability may have been his chief accomplishment in those years. Others began to single him out as both an exemplar and a teacher, something that made him very uncomfortable. Through his preaching he was working out a theology that was equal to the times in which he lived and to the gospel he was ordained to preach. As he became more sure of his own theological understanding, he could concentrate more on the communication of the gospel in terms that people could comprehend, with understanding that could effect people's "affections" and influence their manner of life.

The Teacher

Teaching was for Bayne as it had been for Richard Hooker, a liturgical function. Teaching, or catechizing, was for the Elizabethan a form of proclamation or preaching (*Lawes,* V.18.3). When Bayne was teaching he was proclaiming the faith, and when he was preaching he was teaching. More narrowly, Bayne was early on drawn to classroom teaching, including lecturing.

During his years in St. Louis, Bayne maintained his interest in and fascination with teaching. From John Butler's point of view, Bayne did too much formal teaching in his parish; it would have been better to have concentrated more on pastoral calling. Bayne wrote a set of lectures and asked Frank Gavin for advice, a request granted by Gavin in a lengthy letter.[21] In 1937 Bayne gave a talk designed to help church school teachers provide the "Elements of Christian Character" to their children.[22] In all these writings he sought to avoid shortcuts or simplistic and misleading techniques. He bemoaned the fact that "there is a great tendency in our day to reduce religion to rules and to reduce faith to formulas: to try to can the holy life in a convenient package for ignorant people." Yet he wanted to be clear and simple in his teaching, as clear and simple as was proper in the "teaching of the central doctrines about God and Christian living, and the Church."[23]

In his parish one of Bayne's more successful instruments for teaching was the parish paper, called *The Tractarian.* He was to make good use of such communication for the rest of his life: the parish paper, the diocesan paper, the different forms of periodic newsletters and papers designed to suit the need apparent wherever he happened to be exercising his ministry. He chose the title of the Trinity Church parish paper for two reasons: (1) because "a 'Tractarian' was a person who knew and taught the Catholic religion of the Prayer Book," and (2) because, "knowing it, he went out and did something about it, besides prayer all by himself." Bayne then set out to teach the Catholic faith, inviting the congregation to join him as editor in making the paper truly effective. "The Parish," he wrote in that first issue of *The Tractarian,* "sets its own gait. Chiefly at Mass. The Parish is the normal Church family. The Eucharist is the normal Church life. Therefore, the Parish Eucharist is the touchstone of everything else. It is the family offering."[24]

As can be seen in a perusal of *The Tractarian* from 1937 on, one of Bayne's major educational thrusts had to do with the keeping of Lent in preparation for the celebration of Easter. In 1938, the people received in the parish paper a Lenten Calendar, "with a page arranged for you to use to write your Rule for Lent. This page may be torn off and handed in at one of the services on Ash Wednesday. Then all the Rules are blessed and kept together at the Altar until Easter." Bayne especially emphasized Holy Week. In an editorial in *The Tractarian* he spoke of that sacred time as a "time of joy, sorrow, and then deeper joy. That is the meaning of Liturgy in Holy Week." He went on to say, "Our hearts follow the Liturgy. And it seems a perfectly natural and sensible thing to go from joy through sorrow to joy again — spiral-wise. There is a sense in the Liturgy which meets an instinctive sense in us. The Liturgy follows life." Then Easter, for which time all of the days from Ash Wednesday on were a preparation, is the truly great day.[25]

In preaching on Easter Day in 1935, Bayne affirmed his faith in the resurrection. He believed that the apostles saw not an apparition but Christ himself. "They saw Christ Himself and they knew, with a certainty that is appalling even now, that he would never leave them, that forever and forever, the Church of Christ and the risen and ascended Christ Himself were bound together in a bond more solemn and lasting than life itself." He then gave an eloquent testimonial, exhibiting his power as a teacher:

> I am confident that when I pray, Christ is burning His prayer inside me. I am confident that when I give a cup of cold water to one of His brethren, it is Christ again feeding His disciples. I am confident that when I hold in my hand the Bread of Life, I am not handling a promise for the future or a remembrance of the past, but I am standing face to face with the Lord of all created things. That is the faith of Easter.[26]

Implicit here is Bayne's understanding of faith and dogma as "Christian believing." In a sermon preached at Trinity Church, Bayne explained what he understood and years later identified as "Standard SB on dogma."[27] Equating dogma with a statement of faith such as "We believe that Jesus Christ is true God and true man," he argued that dogma could be looked upon "as a monument: as a finished product." He preferred another viewpoint, looking upon dogma as "a channel buoy: as a bell or a light anchored over a spot in the channel where there is shoal water or a rock or a snag that could tear the bottom out of your ship. Beyond this point there is danger." He insisted that the statement of faith he cited did not say all that we know of Jesus Christ. It provides an anchoring, a safeguard against misbelief. Furthermore, it does not stifle faith but rather releases it. "It gives faith a strong foundation for the

building of its own beautiful tower; your faith starts with the sure beginning that all Christians share." On Trinity Sunday in 1935 he discussed
the doctrine or dogma of the Trinity in terms of what St. Paul (and the
rest of the apostles) wanted to say when setting down these words: "The
Grace of our Lord Jesus Christ and the Love of God, and the Fellowship
of the Holy Spirit be with you." Bayne, in keeping with his understanding of dogma suggested that what St. Paul was saying might have been
expressed: "I believe in God. I believe that Jesus Christ was God in action. I believe that God is the heart and life of this fellowship to which
I belong." It was as clear and as simple as that. As Bayne remarked,
"It's a lot more complicated if you start to think what they *didn't* want
to say."[28]

Bayne distinguished between common knowledge and faith. Knowledge such as that gained in the study of arithmetic is easily gained,
compared to faith that comes out of the depths of a person's being and
changes the person. Faith is a deep kind of knowledge born of a personal
relationship, such a relationship as the disciples had with Jesus, one that
took time to develop. Bayne said in the first of a series of sermons on
faith preached in 1935:

> His power — and the power and the grace of a life lived as He
> lived it, lived in Him and through Him — that was the Light of the
> World. Because He lived in a certain way, men searched their own
> spirits and found deep down in their hearts a kind of knowledge
> that was deeper and richer and truer than anything they had ever
> called knowledge before. This man was right. What He said, what
> He did, was right. They couldn't prove it any more than you or I
> can, but they knew in the wordless knowledge of faith that it was
> right, that it was worth dying for. And that wager of faith was the
> way salvation came.[29]

Faith as such Bayne knew to be costly and dangerous. It could cost
one's life. There were martyrs who died on account of their faith. Others
had given up families and fortune for the sake of faith. Lives had been
radically, sometimes painfully, changed, but the fruits had been glorious.
By faith people had been made humble, and brave, and loving, where
before faith they had been prideful, cowardly, and full of envy and hatred.[30] In another sermon Bayne labored the point that faith concerns
personal relationship. He distinguished between the person who sees his
primary duty in terms of doing what Jesus told people to do, and the
person who lives by faith, in a personal relationship of trust with Jesus
Christ. Salvation comes by faith, not works. The ideal Christian is the
person of faith:

> He is too busy loving to have any time for fear. He speaks little of
> himself. He tries to see things as they really are. He is humble. He

is a realist because he admits the possibility of God. He is able to worship Perfection because he doesn't have to bother trying to protect his own perfection. He is the sort of person other people want to trust with their secrets. There is a kind of envelope of interest and concern that meets you when you turn to him. It is that kind of soul which worships Christ. Love has taken the place of fear. Worship and adoration have taken the place of self-seeking and the race to keep himself always in the front rank. He will do good things too not because he wants to prove himself to be as good as Christ was but because his soul is so sweet with the worship of Christ that it will only bear good fruit.[31]

Faith changes people, it can also change society. In a sermon preached sometime in 1935, Bayne charged that American Christians have been guilty of "a national apostasy from our faith." They have said that *whatever* is done should be done in the name of Jesus: "to Him nothing was foreign to God — no field of human action or of human thought could operate without God," and they professed themselves to be his disciples. Bayne then stated: "Just as soon as Christian people get over being bull-dozed by agnosticism and begin to fight for what they believe, the whole map of our society will change overnight." It would happen because Christians, when they are true to themselves, live not by a code but by faith, in fellowship with Christ, through whom the power of God works to reform and renew not only individuals, and indeed not only societies, but all that is and is to be.[32]

In such sermons, Bayne was thinking through knotty problems, problems he believed to be important for his people as well as himself. In preaching he was teaching his flock as he proclaimed the gospel.

The Pastor

It was at Trinity that Stephen Bayne learned what it was to be a pastor... thinking it through, experiencing what it involved, writing about what it meant to be a pastor. He learned the relationship of the pastor to God, to liturgy, and to the people of God. He defined a pastor as a shepherd. "He has his flock in his care; he is hired to feed them," to guard them, and "to help them to grow to be the best they can be." He does this as a faithful minister of God's word and sacraments, as that ministry extends from the altar to the pew, to the home, and to the marketplace. He acknowledged the seeming triviality of all that the pastor does day by day: "talking about business with men..., typewriting in his office... moving a poor family from one hot flat to another, coaching an operetta."[33] These were all things that someone else not ordained might do, but he did them because they helped him to be where his people were.

For Bayne the pastor lived and worked as a shepherd with the Great Shepherd always near, directing him in his vocation, the agent of reconciliation. The essential task of the pastor did not change with the passage of time, but he learned to "know the details and techniques which will make it possible for him to stand in the shadow of the Divine in his own generation."[34] He described the pastor as a leader who not only helps people to interpret their experiences but also prescribes direction in concord with the Church's purposes. The pastor is concerned for the notoriously lost souls, bringing them to a deepening relationship in the body of Christ's Church and standing "in the place of God" to the parish. "Not between them and God, but that they may know and love God better for knowing him."[35]

Such focus on the ordained minister is misunderstood unless we take into account Bayne's insistence on "the ultimate unity of the whole process of pastoral work," which involves all of the people of God, laity as well as clergy. He spoke of the work of "Christ the Pastor" represented by the ordained ministry as "reproductive," carried on "through the pastor to the Body which he serves. The body too stands equally as a recipient and a minister of God's pastoral care."[36] He objected to the professionalizing of the ordained ministry and to the hierarchialism associated with Anglo-Catholics. "We have been ignorant of certain fundamental truths about priesthood. In particular, we have been ignorant of one truth — the truth that the priesthood is a community affair. It is an exercise of common right that is the property of all Catholic Christians."[37] Bayne realized the implications in this teaching, telling his congregation that what he had said

> means that when I baptize a baby, you do it, really. When I absolve a congregation, you do it really. When I celebrate the Eucharist, it is you who lie on the altar, and yourselves, in Christ Jesus, whom you receive. I quote a phrase to you, "You are the body and the members of Christ." If that be really true, then you are offered, and you are sacrificed — you in the Lord and He in you — offered by my hands, which are your hands. To your own sacrifice you say Amen — "we who are many are one bread and one body."[38]

His agenda was to help build up a disparate people into a body, the body of the Lord, whose ministry to one another and to those outside the congregation could be recognized as Christ's ministry. Their rector would be seen as the shepherd of the flock, the representative of the people, chosen by them "to serve as her minister, as the Ambassador of God to God's people. What witness he may have, what skills he may have, what kind of person he may be — those are entirely incidental questions."[39]

As an Anglo-Catholic who thought theologically, Bayne believed that ceremonial was useless or worse if the people were not dedicated to ministry. Ministry by the body was his overarching concern. In May of 1935 he preached a sermon in which he analyzed the reasons why people go to church. "They are attracted by social teaching, by intellectual understanding, by the beauty of the services."[40] None of these is sufficient. In another sermon, he spoke of that which is sufficient, even essential — the individual quest "for a personal relationship with God," arising out of a profound sense of loneliness, even when in the midst of people. This loneliness is rooted in a failure to understand the value of physical things. The lonely man is not at ease with his own body. Furthermore, "he is not very obedient — not very humble, not very receptive to the claims of other people or the claims of life.... He never understands how hard it is to believe in a common faith when you don't believe in a common life." The people who compose the parish and are the body of Christ are meant to minister to the lonely, providing a holy, creative, nurturing common life. "If the lonely man is lucky," Bayne said, "he will find a parish where all these things are true — where the sacraments are held high for men to see, and where the fellowship of the mystery shines out in every particular of parish life." Admitting that, most likely, the lonely man would find a parish possessing only a limited knowledge of these things. He exhorted his people, "I hope, when the lonely people come here, they will find a little" of such knowledge.[41] So it was that Stephen Bayne as pastor was concerned to be an instrument for the development of the full potential of a parish, such a parish as Trinity Church, St. Louis.

The Apologist and Prophet

As pastor, living day by day with a diversity of people, Bayne looked hard at and gave much thought to the human condition. His people lived in a society that was confronting crisis after crisis; many people were in pain, suffering through the Great Depression. Much of his reflection at this time took place as he prepared his weekly sermons. His high yet realistic view of humanity was expressed in a sermon wherein he asserted that "the Prodigal Son is Jesus' idea of manhood — free, sinful, and yet somehow touched with greatness, because by God's help he can grow and mature in Grace and in the companionship with God."[42] Bayne centered much of his attention on human freedom, by which he meant being yourself, who you are as God created you. Such freedom is "developed through choosing" and is "an inner poise rather than an outer state of affairs." He stated that "the free soul, expressing itself through a series of choices, finding itself after each decision a little more poised, a little more active...a little more creative—this free soul finds its true spiritual climate to be obedience."[43] In a sermon preached at Christ Church Cathedral, St. Louis, he argued that "the amount of a person's creative freedom—his ability to be a person—is directly proportional to his ability to obey." He then stated: Life cannot exist in a vacuum. Whether it is religious life or political life or social life or economic life, it must start from an acceptance of what is, of what exists, before it can go on to new things. And obedience is the technique of the acceptance of one's own tradition."[44]

Freedom involves being *for* something or someone—belonging. To be truly free is to belong, and belonging involves obedience. Bayne understood the value of aloneness. Aloneness involves the freedom of the will. "No man is really free until he is alone in this fundamental way." It can be at times painful when it means separation "of the most delicate attachments of your own heart." But aloneness of the fundamental kind "supplies its own satisfaction—first in the freedom of the will and of action that it brings, and second, in the companionship with God which is the matrix in which it is set." Thus fundamental aloneness is freedom experienced as we separate ourselves from those things that hold us captive, those relationships that bind us to anything and everyone less than God, and as we draw or are drawn nearer to the throne of God, and companionship with God, which is that obedience that makes us free for fellowship with God and with one another in God.[45]

Bayne acknowledged the human need for companionship, true companionship "over against the shadow of it that we call society." That is to say, people "need worship—an ideal and standard before which they bow their knees."[46] In his Lenten series of 1937, he spoke of "freedom in worship." There is such freedom because worship "lets you most be yourself to the fullest capacity of your being." Worship "encourages you to make choices on which your freedom depends," "makes you free *inside* where it counts," and "gives you a person and a fellowship and a belief supremely worth your obedience."[47]

He saw the modern dilemma to a large extent in terms of the loss of freedom, such freedom as he believed to be fundamental. How is one to account for such loss? In his Lenten series of 1937, Bayne repeated a statement made in a sermon preached two years earlier. The enemies are such "ideas and feelings and habits that tend to do one of four things:

1. Limit man's opportunities for self expression....

2. Make his personal choices seem less important in his own eyes....

3. Lead him to think that the important forces in life are the ones which work on him from outside rather than inside....

4. Induce him to imagine that his own nature and destiny...is
something inherently independent of anybody or anything else.[48]

Bayne believed that society was in dire straits in the 1930s largely because of the loss of freedom and the working of freedom's enemies as
he understood them.

Intimately related to the freedom that comes from obedience to God
is cooperation. Bayne spoke of cooperation in terms of the Church — the
cooperative society, seeing in Jesus' Body the ideal, for in Jesus' Body is
comradeship and help.

In a Lenten series preached at Trinity Church in 1935, Bayne labored
to develop Christian perspectives on property, labor, peace, and patriotism.[49] He advocated duty and responsibility, and acknowledged the
complexity of the modern world. One's duty and responsibility first to
God and then in relationship to fellow human beings is of necessity
worked out in a flawed world, a world of money, a world in which
much labor has become mechanical and uninteresting, but a world that
nevertheless strives, imperfectly, for peace and justice. In preaching on
"Peace and Patriotism" he rejoiced that by entering into the "Kellogg
Treaty" the nation had renounced war. Through all of the peregrina-
tions of his thought, Bayne held up Christ as the ideal, the exemplar. In
Jesus he saw the four qualities of freedom realized fully: "the quality of
self-expression, the quality of free and responsible choice, the quality of
inner poise and balance, and fundamentally, the quality of obedience."
He concluded:

But we see...that these qualities arrange themselves in a certain
order....The free man 1. expresses Himself 2. by His decisions
which arise 3. from an inner spiritual poise and balance which
4. comes from a fundamental responsiveness to life. In other
words, the basic attitude is obedience, and from obedience comes
the inner peace and poise, and that poise permits choices to be
made, and the choices determine the self-expression which is the
surface indication of freedom.[50]

It was with this in mind that Bayne spoke eloquently of Christ the
King. In acknowledging Christ as King, God is rethroned at the center
of things and all things are interpreted in terms of our acknowledgment.
Bayne put the cause in various ways. At the end of the 1935 Lenten series he said, "If we shall bow our knee to Him first, then we shall find
ourselves in his service." In a later sermon, he put it this way: "Our
Lord says that we should love our neighbors. In spite of the fact that life
is against us? No — because life is built that way. We *are* members one
of another....When some tiresome, dirty old man needs our help, do
we give it because of a future reward, or do we give it because there

is a fundamental kinship between him and ourselves that we cannot deny?"[51] Later he argued: "The power of God to heal you physically, and to make you better spiritually, is not an ideal which you can help create: but it is an ever present thing, if you will only use it. Christ is not *going to be King;* He *is* King. Heaven is not in the future; it is now."[52] Bayne's conviction centered upon Christ's embodiment of humanity as God meant it to be and on the power in the Church to enable communion with Christ, to obey God's will as embodied in Christ — such obedience as restores the humanity of sinful, enslaved persons and cultivates their growth in freedom until they come to the fullness of their humanity. In the end, for the sake of a better world and a better life for all peoples, Bayne emphasized something deeper than religion viewed as "a way of dealing with social problems," not because he was disinterested in social problems, but because he was so concerned for them. He was bold to say that he cared most for "the human souls in God's Hands" and that he cared more for them than for "orthodoxy in liberal social thinking." He explained: "Society — governments — masses of people — *that is what we live in, not what we live for.* Man loves his neighbor best when he loves God best."[53] This, as Bayne well knew, could be misunderstood, or it could be very well understood and provoke anger in a patriot's breast. But he said it, and he said it not only with a realization of human frailty and perversity, but also with a growing concern for what Nazism in Germany and atheistic communism in Russia represented.

Finances: A Nagging Problem

Not everything went well at Trinity, at least not in the eyes of the rector. There were low points as well as high. One Sunday he reported, "Fine day — good attendance and excellent music." But another Sunday he noted, "Poor attendance — sleet at 10 A.M." There was the Sunday when the choir didn't appear, and another when "there were only 50 people to hear one of the best sermons ever written." In one issue of *The Tractarian,* Bayne told his people:

> A lot of things we wish we didn't have to cope with — a tiny, stationary Church School, a leaky roof, sad imitation of a Parish Eucharist at 9:15 on Sundays, a general ignorance even of the hour of the daily Masses, so unbelievably few who ever volunteer to do the endless jobs around the Church — lots of things we wish we didn't have to cope with.[54]

Finances were a constant concern for rector and people. People, some of necessity, defaulted on their pledges; budget goals set by the vestry seemed at times unattainable. Stephen's salary in 1934 was set at $2,400. In 1938 it was $2,100, the amount initially offered to him. He accused Episcopalians in general of not supporting the Church adequately with necessary finances because of "Selfishness, Ignorance, and Thanklessness."[55] People complained of his harshness in making such accusations. He responded:

> I say a lot of hard-boiled things about money and especially Church money. I have been accused more than once of being very unspiritual in the way in which I look at the problems of church finance. I presume that that means I don't talk about money needed for postage stamps and floor-cleaning compound and my own salary as if it were alms for the poor. There is no sense in confusing the issue — there is plenty of room for almsgiving too — but I do not like to talk and think about the bread-and-butter needs of our Parish under a guise of pious anonymity.

He then set forth a rule that every active member of the parish was charged with responsibility to see that the parish "is supplied with its reasonable needs, decently and fittingly, and without the condescension and snobbery with which so many people deal with 'the poor Church.'" Anything less than the best is not good enough for the Church, properly understood. When the responsibility is met, with people giving generously from the heart, what then?[56]

It is not true to conclude that such dissatisfaction represented his entire time at Trinity. He saw growth in the parish, he was on the whole well liked, his bishop was supportive. He had a growing family, there were vacations to the Grand Canyon and Essex, and there was a growing demand for him as a conference speaker and teacher. But he was restless and began to feel that the time to move had come.

Northampton Again

In the spring of 1938 Bayne was thinking of leaving Trinity to find a place where he could test his vocation to be a college chaplain. His father talked with Frederic Fleming, the rector of Trinity Church, New York, about this, and Fleming visited the Baynes in St. Louis to discuss a vacancy at St. John's, Northampton, Massachusetts.[57] This was the parish Stephen had supplied briefly in the summer of 1934. The rector of St. John's was also chaplain at Smith College, thus it would provide the opportunity Bayne sought. Visiting the parish in the late fall of 1938, Bayne learned that he was well remembered, that he was the one person the congregation really wanted, and that the Bishop of Western Massachusetts, Appleton Lawrence, supported his call to St. John's Church. Bayne knew that there was much that needed attention, that among his friends there were those, such as Karl Block,[58] who thought he would

make a mistake in accepting the call. Also Fleming, although supportive, recognized the difficulty in being rector of St. John's *and* chaplain
to Smith College.[59]

Bayne accepted the call and began his ministry at St. John's, Northampton, on Ash Wednesday, February 22, 1939. It was a large and
complex parish, "half faculty people with a temperament," the rest
townsfolk. In addition, there were "600 students taking some part in the
parish's life."[60] The rector had to minister to his parish flock and also do
what was needed as chaplain to Episcopal students at Smith. He managed this in large part by involving the students in the life of the parish
and enlisting the assistance of parishioners in his college ministry. And
he did all of the normal things associated with parish life: preaching,
teaching, visiting, managing, and all of the rest.

The three and a half years Stephen Bayne spent at Northampton were
overshadowed by war. He was there through the desperate times of
the beginning of war in Europe in September 1939 to the disaster of
Pearl Harbor in 1941 — "through the tense years," as he himself recalled, "from Hitler's rape of Czechoslovakia to the Pacific war." War
was on the minds of his people, and he attempted to minister to them
in their anxiety and to understand better himself what was happening.
In a sermon on the parables of salt and of light, Bayne identified war
as "an intensified form of peace. The same evil conditions prevailing in
peace time are intensified." He sought to engender a national, realistic
understanding, arguing that "nobody wins from a war. . . . Underneath
the open conflict, the flags, the armed forces, there is at work a deeper
plan, a deeper purpose, a deeper sense to be served. There is something
to be born in suffering." He understood the Church's role to be that of
focusing upon the deeper purpose and of maintaining attention to things
that matter above and beyond war. Then too he was convinced that "the
world has a right to expect from the Church the answer to the question,
'Why?' " He said:

> I listened to an address over the radio last night, like addresses of
> many others with simple minds who see things in the black and
> white. It is not enough to put the democracies over here and the
> totalitarian states over there. . . . What answer can you give to a
> man who says, "My totalitarian state works more effectively than
> yours"? There is an answer to that. You have got to be able to
> answer why. There is a value to the individual human life; there is
> a value in freedom; there is a value to a government that reflects
> freedom of human nature. Our government reflects most clearly
> the things we believe about God and humans.[61]

As the war developed, Bayne did not lose his conviction that no one
wins in war. But he believed that Christians could not avoid the con-

flict with Nazism and that the defeat of Hitler was a matter of justice. His nation was right in this conflict, although he reserved the right as a Christian to make that judgment. He was as opposed as ever to blind, unthinking nationalism.

Bayne's years in Northampton were not without pleasure. He found his bishop to be an admirable man: "Appleton Lawrence had noble qualities as a diocesan," he recalled. Though Lawrence had not yet mellowed to the extent he did later, "he knew every clerical family in his diocese. I remember his passing through town about eleven one evening, seeing our lights on, and stopping to ask, 'Why weren't you and your Lucie out riding around in the moonlight?' "[62]

Bayne on the whole was satisfied with his preaching and was well received. He remarked later that "he had come a long way in understanding preaching and learning how to use a preacher's tools. Even though much heaviness, turgidity, pretentiousness remained to be burned out, there was communication and seriousness and depth too, still to be refined but capable of bearing weight."[63] He must have been gratified when receiving a letter from a famed member of Smith's faculty, Mary Ellen Chase, in which she wrote: "I do not for a moment assume that you, like college teachers! — need cheering on your way; but simply for my own sake I want to tell you that your sermon this morning did more for me than any of the hundreds I have heard during a rather generous number of years! I walked home after church with three of my colleagues on the Smith faculty; and we were all with one accord thanking God for you!"[64]

His preaching was not always well received. On occasion he was critical of his congregation, such as on Easter Day in 1939, when he pointed out the actual reasons why most people were there, reasons far removed from the true meaning of Easter.[65] In Advent 1940, Bayne began another parish paper, this one called *Prologue*. Here he conveyed something of his enthusiasm and his gratification. In the issue for Lent 1941, he wrote, "With a magnificent unanimity, the parish has started Lent this year. The congregation on Ash Wednesday were over half again as large as last year's, as it has been for almost every service thus far." Reflecting on Easter in the nation and in the parish that same year, he wrote, "It was a quiet, deep, moving Easter. Unprecedented numbers of people went to Church, somewhere. Here at St. John's there was as rich an outpouring of spiritual interest, indicated by an overwhelming attendance, as there has ever been."

The parish paper was an instrument for education as well as communication, education focused on the church year, especially Lent, and on the Church, its nature and its work. He taught that the Church exists for many purposes, but first it must be admitted that it exists for no purpose at all. It exists because God is, "and we are drawn irresistibly to love

Him and long for Him and fear Him with all our hearts." Having understood that, he noted, it may further be understood that fundamentally the Church exists for prayer:

A man, standing by the side of Christ, facing the world's misery with the Christ's compassion, girding himself with the tranquil purposefulness of the Christ's will, trying to see through the world's darkness with the directness of the Christ's clear gaze, offering himself, haltingly and imperfectly, because of and in company with the serene, free love of Christ's perfect offering, straining to think out life's somber puzzles in the light of the Christ's steady truth, straining and thinking and offering and willing because of Christ and with Christ and through Christ — a man standing by the side of the Lord Jesus and trying to be like Him — that is the great work of Christ's Church. That's prayer.[66]

Bayne's departure from Northampton for Columbia University occasioned a summing up in the June 1942 issue of *Prologue* of his ministry over the past three and a half years at St. John's Church. He had viewed his first task to be that of engaging people in the Church's life — its services, meetings, parties, and at the rector's office — making the Church home "a real home where people liked to come and stay." He then wrote: "People have often wondered why I spent so much time here in my office, early and late. There was a reason.... People have often commented on the amount of conversation there was here, the amount of coffee drunk, the general air of informality.... I want you all to know that that was not accidental." He then explained: "This is not just God's House at 11:00 o'clock Sunday morning. This is God's house, and our best home, twenty-four hours a day." He succeeded in impressing this upon many in Northampton. His second task was "to discover and use to the full all the richness, gravity, freedom, balance of our inheritance in the Prayer Book." He managed to achieve much in this area, too, and was content to be called a "cautious Catholic," if that meant putting first things first in matters of liturgy and ceremonial. The third task was that of building up the student congregation, especially reaching out to those Episcopal students who did not attend church. "I believed (and still believe), that we needed to break down a lot of barriers between us and the community we live in." And he was convinced that the parish needed to be more responsible in its support of the work of the Church, the diocese in particular, providing more not only in terms of finances but also in terms of leadership. Although much was achieved in all of these areas, there was much yet to be achieved under the leadership of his successor, the Reverend Robert Noel Rodenmayer.

On July 1 Bayne left Northampton for "a somewhat peripatetic existence, commuting between Essex, New York, where he and Mrs. Bayne and the infantry will be based — and various points on the Eastern seaboard." By that time their family included not only Stephen III and Philip but also Duncan, born September 27, 1939, and Lydia, born November 26, 1941. Bayne was to preach on Sunday mornings during July at Bard College and on Sunday evenings at the Cathedral of St. John the Divine in New York. He planned for August to be a month without such engagements and to be in residence in New York for the beginning of the winter term at Columbia, September 21, 1942.[67]

Three

THE COLLEGE CHAPLAIN DURING WORLD WAR II

Chaplain of Columbia University

Bayne arrived at Columbia University, in the New York he knew so well, to be chaplain of the university and to be chairman of and teach in the Department of Religion. From the outset he changed the direction of the job. Raymond Knox, his predecessor, had viewed the chaplaincy chiefly in relation to the Department of Religion. He did not like to preach and encouraged the use of the chapel mainly for academic occasions. Bayne, with the support of President Butler and of Dean Hawkes who had hired him, centered his attention on the chapel, on services designed to attract a wide spectrum of people, and on preaching.[1]

This did not mean that he ignored his responsibility to teach and to chair the Department of Religion. He had, after all, felt a strong call to teach as an apologist of the Church. Indeed, he labored hard to improve the curriculum for undergraduates, to enhance teaching in the department, and to overcome widespread indifference to religion among students and faculty. By the time he left Columbia a new curriculum was in place:

> A basic course in the English Bible will serve as the foundation; then in alternate years, Primitive Christianity and Contemporary Religious Movements will be studied. Also in alternate years, courses in Judaism since the Diaspora and in Oriental Religions will be offered. Two seminars, one in the Philosophy of Religion and another in Religion in Modern Life, complete the curriculum.[2]

Bayne pointed out the possibilities inherent in expanding offerings in Judaism and Oriental Religions to include other traditions, if these initial courses proved to be successful.

But the chapel was paramount and occupied an increasing amount of time. Eventually Bayne was relieved of teaching responsibilities, an occurrence that must have aroused mixed emotions in him as well as in those who benefited from his classroom teaching. He increased the number of services held in the chapel. In addition to the traditional brief, noontime services on weekdays, Bayne added Eucharists on Tuesdays and Fridays. A second celebration was added on Sundays, and a small Sunday School was begun. The daily schedule of noontime services involved, besides procuring student leaders, inviting guest preachers: some from Union Seminary, such as Reinhold Niebuhr and Paul Tillich; some from General Seminary, such as Cuthbert Simpson and Norman Pittenger; and some from prominent city churches, such as W. Russell Bowie and Robert McCracken. Faculty at Columbia and Barnard College were also included, persons such as Virginia Harrington, Helen White, Harry Ayres, Joseph Blair, and Ursula Niebuhr. The chaplain was ordinarily the preacher on Sundays. In building up the chapel family, Bayne was assisted by Shunji Nishi, a rising theologian, Holt Graham, a student assistant who was to become a New Testament scholar of note, Lowell Beveridge, director of the university choir, and others.

Attendance at chapel services on Sundays "was never spectacular," Bayne recalled, but "it did grow and the Sunday congregation included a wide variety of people. The daily services were less responsive — perhaps fifty students and faculty, plus the fifty students in the superb choir."[3] In 1947, Bayne reported that on the Sundays on which Morning Prayer was held the average attendance, excluding the choir, ranged from "218 during Lent to 172 during January."[4] The choir was Bayne's pride and joy. It was, he remembered, "the heart of the congregation," and it was to these young people led by Lowell Beveridge, a choir half of men and half of women, that the chaplain more and more directed his preaching. "On critical occasions," he reported, "it was SB's habit to wear a particular pair of argyle socks, with bright red diamonds, and the choir learned to look for them and avenge their spirits accordingly.[5]

In addition, there were marriages, baptisms, funerals, and memorial services. There were concerts, and at one time T. S. Eliot's *Murder in the Cathedral* was presented in the chapel. The chaplain was also there to support the work of the denominational chaplains: Eugene Carden, William Cole, Donald Hieges, Henry Snyder, Mowbray Tate, counselors to the Protestant students; as well as Isidor Hoffman, counselor to the Jewish students; and John K. Daly, counselor to the Roman Catholic students. The center for religious activities was Earl Hall. This too was in the chaplain's portfolio. Earl Hall's various activities included open houses, meetings, informal and formal classes, counseling, meals served. In 1947 Bayne reported a total of 553 scheduled events in Earl Hall involving 40,000 students.[6]

Bayne's attention in all areas of his responsibility was more intensely on the chapel and its worshiping community of faculty, students, and others who were attracted to its worship, its music, and its superb preaching. At the end of his first academic year, Bayne wrote that the task of the chapel was that of "giving worthy praise to God; and with our magnificent choir and organ and the leadership of the Director of Chapel music we are greatly blessed." Another task was that of interpretation, not of the Episcopal Church, but "of Christianity and of the Gospel in terms of the age in which we live and in terms of that most central and representative tradition of Christianity to which this university belongs." A third task concerned pastoral care. " 'Chapel is a cold place.' How many times that has been said! Really, it is not so. I hope and pray that... the years to come may see Chapel become a loved and familiar hearth for many souls, and a place where the love and truth of God is known and given." On another occasion he asserted that the chapel is not a parish Church. "It is place of worship, yes, above all... a place where there is, as God gives us to see it, that 'habitual vision of greatness' without which education is a senseless and circular vanity... a place, finally, where the comradeship of men and women engaged in a common task may be seen in its clearest and highest terms."[7]

In his final report as chaplain, in 1947, Bayne noted progress toward the fulfillment of these goals, but he also recorded his disappointment. He thought of the multitudes that passed by the chapel daily and never entered. He recognized that this was because of various factors, including the crowded schedules of faculty and students and the pervasive indifference to the Church and religion. He also blamed himself, especially the fact that his tenure of thirty months as chaplain of Columbia University, divided by the time he spent away as a military chaplain, was "too brief to establish the kind of relationship one hoped for, at what seemed to him the ministry he had been born and trained to do."[8]

The Teacher

Stephen Bayne did not leave behind the lectures and other materials prepared for use in his formal teaching at Columbia, but he did preserve much that provides evidence of his teaching at Columbia and elsewhere during the 1940s. There were the daily meditations prepared for use in a Lenten edition of *Forward Day by Day*. Of all his writings, these were among those few that he considered totally inadequate. Indeed, Gilbert Symonds, his editor, had to rewrite much of what Bayne wrote.[9] There were devotional addresses written for delivery at the Triennial Meeting of the Women's Auxiliary of the General Convention in 1943. These were so well received that such addresses were perpetuated in subsequent years. Yet Bayne "never really liked" the addresses he gave, published under the title *Gifts of the Spirit*. They indicated that freedom, life, joy, and selfhood form gifts that are really one — Christ himself.

"The gifts of the Spirit," he wrote, "are not things or graces or arts or qualities; God's gift was and is a Person who supremely ennobles and transforms all life.... The gifts of the Spirit are ways of talking about Jesus."[10]

As in the past, much of his teaching was by way of the sermons he preached. In Lent of 1943, he gave a series of five sermons on science and religion, two ways of knowing and living — the one dominated by empiricism, the other by faith. Later he stated that he was never satisfied with these sermons, and indeed they seem to reflect something of a personal struggle through which he was going at the time, expressed in his anger at the Church. While a global war was claiming innocent victims and faith was perishing in the face of inhumanity and destruction, too many Christians were busying themselves with trivia. He was angered when he thought of the pettiness, the selfishness, the superficiality of so many in the Church — of too many at Columbia. The conclusion of his sermon was infused with pain and anger:

> There is sweeping around this world something far more terrible than war — a "sickness that destroyeth in the noon day," a sickening knowledge...that there is no God, no Truth, no Man, no Reason — that there is nothing but war, war, war and death.
>
> There is a medicine for that sickness, a medicine of the mind and the heart and the will. It is what we ought to know about in this Chapel, instead of spending so much time wondering how to get people in it. It is a bitter medicine, but life-giving. What religion does concern itself with, too often, is kindergarten stuff — a little ethical idealism, some pleasant aesthetic experiences, lovely music, an interesting sermon, a few paper goals as to membership and budget, a little tampering with the normal life of the community. What we should concern ourselves with is precisely this deep search for the foundation of belief, and the strong affirmation of Faith.[11]

On the following Sunday, he argued that the scientist and the Christian are much alike: "We both have gone to the door of that dark cave where madness lies, and despair: we both have looked the facts in the face: both skeptics: both discontent with half-truths: and both accepting the ultimate mystery of life and knowledge and deliberately choosing the nobler feast, on faith, for hope's sake." The chaplain was here thinking of a particular kind of scientist, of course, the sort of person who was humble in the face of data, devoid of arrogance, available, as is right, to whatever the truth may reveal.[12]

In the midst of such considerations there was the question of human nature, whether it was all that the Old and New Testaments claimed or whether it was meaningless or worthless, as some moderns seemed to think. In the third sermon, Bayne addressed this area of his abiding concern to know and to believe. His skill in raising the central question was shown when he said: "Here he is, man, a bundle of desires and fears and influences and temptations and opportunities. We want to know not how successfully has he fulfilled his desires or adopted his influences or resisted his temptations, but how far has he welded all those separate and imperfect selves into one self. How far is he a person; how far is he a man; how far is he free?"[13]

Bayne concluded: "What counts and what costs is how far we have gone in passing those separate fragments through the fire of sacrifice and discipline, and joined them into one." There is continuity here with what he formerly taught, there is evidence of the influence of T. S. Eliot's *Little Gidding,* and there is the stark challenge: "The desperate question before men is whether there will be any self left to be judged at all, or whether in saving our life we may not lose it altogether."

In the fourth sermon Bayne explained and defended the truth in the theory of projection, carrying a principle through from what is known to what is unknown, from what is given to what is believed, that is, to the end. He cited Thomas Aquinas as explaining: "The subjective impressions and determinations of an intellect are not the direct objects, the contents of our thought. These mental forms are rather the means through which we are led to a knowledge of the reality external to us." Bayne concluded: "That is a very deep and thoughtful way of expressing the truth that there is in the theory of 'projection.'"[14]

Some of Bayne's most effective teaching at Columbia came through his homilies printed on the fourth page of the St. Paul's Chapel Bulletins.[15] These were short essays — literary gems — concerning people, places, and events, all with the intent to teach something straightforward and simple about Christian faith and life. For instance, there was an essay sarcastically lauding "the commercial Christmas. . . . It brightens up the stores immeasurably; it supplies the remnants of our Puritan conscience with an excuse to adorn the streets; it redeems the city, thanks to the late Prince Consort, with blessed reminders of the country, if only for a week or two." He saw in this and much more a kind of yearning for something alluding us. To discover that something, that to which we are led in life, to be freed "from the bondage of 'me' and 'mine' to the wide liberty of 'thee' and 'thou'" is not going to happen easily. "But somehow," Bayne concluded, "man has got to be made ready to see the world as God sees it — pretty small and not very satisfying except for its one superb privilege of being a birthplace for the children of God. It's about at that point that you remember the Stable and the Child, and wonder at the patience of God."[16]

In another homily Bayne mused over an occasion when at a tea party a casual remark by his hostess caused him to daydream, remembering his boyhood, "lying on the lawns in the dark sunlight of the past, chewing blades of grass and dreaming the long dreams of innocence." Reflecting on the experience, he viewed it as signifying "the bitter and the sweet." He concluded:

> It may even be...that manhood depends on our remembering, that the pain as well as the delight come only because it is the same self now as then, that the lost innocence was *ours,* and so were the blindnesses by which we lost it, and so is the wisdom and the gentleness gained, if memory will only keep the gentleness alive. The same self, the single self, then as now, and the straight road between — it is a book that a man writes with his life, and not a magazine.... It's memory that makes and keeps us whole, not for the sake of the dead past, but for this moment's sake and for the new self always waiting to be known.[17]

One homily stuck in Bayne's mind and was used again, as a Christmas greeting in *Puget Soundings,* December 1959. He told of a woman who, hearing a reading of Dickens' *Christmas Carol,* said, "Wouldn't it be wonderful if there were something in real life as lovely as Christmas?" Bayne viewed her as fairly typical of most moderns for whom "the world of illusion is perilously close to being the only real world." Over against this woman's yearning question Bayne puts his question, which is his Christmas greeting: "Wouldn't it be wonderful if there were anything in our dreams or hopes or aspirations half as lovely as the reality of life?" He explained what he meant:

> We will stack St. Luke up against Dickens any day. We cannot wish you a Christmas half so joyful as the one already provided. We cannot wish for you a hope half so high as the reality already accomplished. We cannot wish for you a future half so bright as the life which day by day enfolds you. All we can wish you — and this we do with the greatest enthusiasm — is eyes to see and ears to hear the real people (meaning most of all the Real Person), and a heart and will to love them (particularly Him), and the freedom to dream dreams which will do justice to reality.[18]

The last of his "fourth page" homilies was on "clearing out your desk," "a magnificent exercise in humility."[19] As he was doing so, in preparation for leaving, he found a list of possible "fourth page" topics: one to be an exploration of "that most vexing choice, whether to eat the bacon or the egg first," another being "a mournful reflection on how neither coffee nor cigars taste as good as they smell." There were unanswered letters, plans not pursued, unwritten sermons, pamphlets unread, "and our private and miraculous filing system which never quite got up to date." These suggest many more: "the visits unmade, the clarion calls unsounded, the tocsins unrung." He supposed that he was not unusual in this regard, and the reality caused him to marvel at the affirmation on the Cross, "It is finished." It is man's fate to start more than he can finish and to learn through his unfinished business what he ought to do and what he must leave to others.

Views on Education

Situated as he was in the midst of a great university, Bayne reflected on the meaning of education and the idea of the university. Shortly before leaving for service in the Navy, Bayne spoke to a gathering of Barnard College alumnae on "Education in the Post-War World." He talked of the problem of defining education and indicated that in his bewilderment he found himself "coming back to that classic definition of education as being 'a student at one end of a log and Mark Hopkins on the other.'" He found this appealing, for its simplicity and purity, in contrast to technical and pseudo-technical definitions, and because he could put anyone he chose on the log in place of Hopkins: priest or philosopher or astronomer or medicine man. Such an image led him to this formal definition:

> Education as I see it is society's way of reproducing itself spiritually. The old and the wise who are the trustees of society . . . want to be sure that the young men and women who are coming up to take their place will be able to start where they leave off. . . . They want to be sure that a living tradition and a living history is passed on. They want to be sure that the young and foolish will be ready to carry on in the same living tradition.[20]

What they pass on concerns three things: (1) what we understand of the universe we inhabit "and our skills in manipulating and exploring" that universe; (2) "customs, habits, mores, manners" that have been determined to be "the necessary means by which" people manage to live together in society; and (3) "the beliefs by which society lives, not the technical formulae and religious beliefs particularly, but the deep, usually unspoken, radical, fundamental attitudes which are the life blood of any civilization." This last, the most important, has to do with "convictions about man, his nature and destiny, convictions about society, convictions about nature and the kind of world it is."[21]

In developing this definition, Bayne expressed the conviction that education at its best, and thus essentially, is wholistic. It is not a private enterprise, not limited to students and teachers, but belongs to society. Nor is it limited to one or to several disciplines or specialties. He was confident (perhaps more hopeful than confident) that postwar education would emphasize "unity and completeness in the curriculum." At the core of this education would be "the question of the fundamental belief about man." He argued: "Democracy is the way men live when they perceive a certain dignity in themselves and each other, a dignity not of their contriving nor of society's but a dignity derived from their status and function in an intelligible universe." Education at its best will cultivate such a perception of dignity.[22]

Bayne concluded, perhaps most controversially, considering the setting in which he spoke: "I am convinced that all education in a free society is religious education, because I am convinced that unless men are taught to see themselves as children of God there is no way in which the ideal of freedom can be long sustained, and it is only under God that the total and social education in which we believe can ever be safely administered. No earthly power can keep us from Fascism but only the deep and true ideas of the dignity of man and of human society under God.[23]

As with so much of his thinking about education and contemporary society, Bayne's attention turned toward human nature. Baccalaureate sermons at this time seemed inevitably to turn to this central concern. In one given in 1943 he identified the questions "What is man?" "Why was he made?" "What does he live for?" as the most important questions in the world. He claimed that the present Western civilization was built on one great answer: "Man is a child of God, like Jesus Christ: he was made to be heroic and self-sacrificing and humble and loving, like Jesus Christ: he lives for God, like Jesus Christ."[24]

In a commencement address given in October 1943, Bayne spoke of a college existing "to teach us to see man whole," "to teach us how to tell the important values from the unimportant ones in human life," and "to teach us to take sides." "To be educated," he said, "means that you have studied man and have begun to discriminate between more and less important things."[25] In another baccalaureate sermon at Columbia, given in May of 1943, he told the graduating seniors that he hoped that out of their education they would remember three ideas: "Freedom, which you have shared in the company of free men which a University ought to be; the Idea of what a man really is; and Belief, passionate and enduring." Speaking of the university further on in the sermon, he defined it as "a company of free men to whom, in the words of the Great Myth, 'the tree in the midst of the garden is a tree to be desired to make one wise.' " And he said, "The University ... exists, at heart, for no other purpose than that men should know the truth; and the truth, as the greatest of teachers told us, the truth makes men free."[26] Such constant reiteration of humanity as free in obedience, as recipient of truth, and committed to responsible action on the world's stage, making decisions courageously in the teeth of lesser truths, places Bayne squarely in the tradition that from the time of Erasmus and Colet and More has been identified as

Christian humanist. In the same month that Bayne gave this sermon, he participated in a symposium at Kenyon College on academic freedom, stressing the important relationship between freedom and authority. He was becoming known as someone who had important things to say on education.

Preacher to the University

Bayne was called to Columbia University because he was known to be an effective preacher. He knew what was expected of him and carefully crafted his sermons, regarding himself as the instrument of God, constantly remembering "that his task was to make himself invisible and God all-pervading."[27] He was accustomed to asking the pertinent, pressing question of the day. At this time he and his congregation found some of their most pressing questions prompted by an intensifying world war.

In a sermon preached on November 8, 1942, "on the heels of the North African landing"[28] Bayne began by saying that he could not preach as planned; he then referred to the enemy, "the *real* enemy." German and Italian fascism represent not only foreign, threatening movements, he said, "they have been revelations of what was true about ourselves. We have seen in them an ugly mirror of the depths of blindness and selfishness which have also been true about ourselves." In characteristic fashion, Bayne refused to join in the frenzied campaign of self-righteousness and hatred sponsored by the government and embraced by many, not only bigots, but also "decent folk."

Bayne's preaching possessed a theological coherency that was centered upon the major concerns of those who came to hear him preach. The essence of that theology was constant, inherent in every sermon. In a sermon on the meaning of Advent, Bayne recalled the Advent hymn "O Come, O Come Emmanuel," and he said: "These are holy and terrible words." They are holy because they are a prayer; they are holy and terrible because on the lips of some they are a prayer summoning the one, true God, and on the lips of others, "the God-with-us is...no more than a paraphrase" of disbelievers' "best hopes."[29] In another sermon, preached January 24, 1943, on the patronal feast of the chapel, Bayne spoke of the basic, simple needs of the refugee, the soldier, of all people:

> *Man needs a new spirit,* because codes and systems and treaties and Leagues don't mean a thing if men's hearts and wills are not right....
> *Man needs a new vision and new understanding of society.* He has outgrown the old structures, nations, classes, economic systems, he needs a new world.

Man needs a new estimate of himself and his brother. He has
outgrown the old estimates, based on color and race and tradition:
the new world must be a people's world, a world of the common
man.[30]

For Bayne, those simple needs are met by the Christian faith, which is
no complex system of thought, but a person: Jesus Christ, who stands
at the place where the old world and the new world meet; Jesus Christ,
truly God and truly Man; Jesus Christ, who does not simply leave us in
our human predicament, but shows us the way out of our predicament,
the way into the new world where our needs are met. To pray "O Come,
O Come Emmanuel" in the right way, in the context of fervent faith, is
to be made ready for sainthood — to live by the discipline, the joy, and
the freedom of the saints.[31]

Chaplain in the United States Navy

By November 1943, Stephen Bayne was determined to enlist in the Navy
as a chaplain. He gave as his reasons (1) the fact that he could "see the
end of the first stage of administrative unentanglement which has been
the commanding obligation of my work here this last year," (2) the fact
that the chapel was "considerably overstaffed," and (3) the conclusion
that "I do not think I can go along much further as I am distracted by
the feeling that I am not where I ought to be." The last reason spoke
of his needing to be where the greatest involvement in the war effort
would be found, the greatest demands and the greatest sacrifice, as he
saw it.[32] It also concerned his vocational quandary and the frustration
he felt at Columbia. On January 22, 1944, he was informed of his being
recommended for appointment as reserve chaplain in the U.S. Navy. His
rank at the outset was to be Lieutenant (junior grade), ChC(S), U.S.N.R.
He had his last service at Columbia on February 6 and reported for
active duty on February 19, 1944. He received his training at Chaplains' School, William and Mary College, and was sent, on completion
of that course, to be chaplain of the United States Naval Air Station,
Fort Lauderdale, Florida, where he began work on May 8, 1944. Bayne
left his family in New York. He decided against taking them with him,
although many officers and men on the station lived with their families in Fort Lauderdale. As he put it, "my wife and I decided not to,
partly for financial reasons as rentals for suitable accommodations for
us and our four children are prohibitive, and partly because, as the only
chaplain on the Station, it seems wiser to be continuously available for
emergency calls as well as simple availability." Finances continued to
be a pressing problem for Stephen Bayne. On December 31, 1944, he
labored over his budget, plaintively asking, "Where did it go?"

The chaplaincy was demanding. The station existed to train pilots and aircrewmen for torpedo hauling and other such tasks. There were about 2,500 officers and men divided into three classifications — "those who operate and maintain the base, instructors, and student officers and aircrewmen." From his office in the Recreation Building, the chaplain organized the religious services of the base, conducting services in various locations, including a hanger, arranging for Roman Catholic and Jewish services, counseling men in distress, acting as history officer, taking his turn at watch, writing a column for the base newspaper, assisting with services at other nearby naval facilities, preaching at services in town on Sundays, helping out at local Episcopal Churches, serving on the Welfare Board of the U.S.N.A.S., and participating in community affairs.

Counseling was an important aspect of his work. There seemed to be fairly frequent air crashes involving men of the station, memorial services to conduct, families to be comforted. He wrote of "an unending stream of boys coming in and out [of his office] with their problems — some of them quite severe, some paltry." He encountered much perturbation and suffering from "the dislocation, the loneliness, the sudden new isolation, the secret injury of mass discipline and mass life, the separation from home, the instability . . . of life." Then there were the family problems that all chaplains faced. Bayne spoke of one wife who wrote to him to complain that her husband did not send her enough of his pay to support their family. When Bayne talked with the man, the chaplain was appalled to learn that the airman held back sixty dollars a month to spend on himself. "A little imagination," Bayne wrote, "was all he lacked; and how great a difference it made that he did not have it! It had simply never occurred to him that it was not his money alone, that it had its source in other people's lives, that it was a stewardship for him, that it was a mark of his freedom and his responsibility, that he could not keep on splitting his self between his wife and his new independence and be any kind of self at all."[33]

At the outset, Bayne was eager to preach and teach in ways meaningful to the personnel of the base. In his column "Chat with the Chaplain" in The Avenger, the base paper of May 13, 1944, he compared his work as chaplain at Columbia with his work at the base. "It was my work to plan services for teachers and students of different faiths, to teach, to counsel, and to do in general what a chaplain is expected to do in the Navy." He could hope that his past experience would stand him in good stead in his present ministry as a military chaplain. But in a letter he spoke of the problem he faced,

the ever-recurrent problem of teaching and exciting the Christian faith among these men, so many of whom are completely illiterate

religiously. At our air station, it seems, we are so completely sur-
rounded by evidences of man's power and man's ingenuity that we
need doubly hard to think clearly about man's ultimate dependence
on God. It seems so much to be our world and our resources and
our history; the power and delicacy of the fragile massive weapons
which we are trained to use seems often to take the place of God.
And the principal job of the chaplain here, I should think, is to
counterattack, not with the intent of weakening the effectiveness
of our training or our weapons, but to set them and man's whole
power in the great setting in which alone it makes sense.[34]

He confessed that in some ways he was "not well-equipped for the
job." His years of experience working among students on campuses
made "it very difficult" for him "to speak effectively in the terms of
this more generalized segment of people." He also felt limited by virtue
of his lack of combat experience. He felt ill at ease preaching to and
admiring "men of long and bitter experience in this war," officers who
"have forgotten more than I ever knew about the problems facing us."
In a letter to Henry Knox Sherrill, Bayne complained of his assignment,
dearly desiring combat duty afloat or ashore. He knew that his defective
vision (8/20 right eye, 8/20 left eye) could be used to prevent assignment
to combat service. Knowing that he was due to be detached from the
air station in a month or so, he was frankly worried and unhappy. "It
is hard," he wrote, "to feel that the Navy pays any attention to a man's
training and experience, or that there is any rhyme or reason to its assignments." He hastened to explain that this was not a complaint, "but
there are jobs I could be a lot more useful at than I am at this one; it is
a little hard to justify leaving the work at Columbia, and the sacrifices
my wife is making, in terms of the relatively superficial job I am doing
here, and my conscience troubles me no little."[35]

When he left Fort Lauderdale, an editorial was printed in *The
Avenger* which recalled that when he first arrived, Bayne was regarded
as important, the chaplain of Columbia University on leave for the du-
ration. But he quickly became "OUR chaplain. He took on our troubles,
became our friend, earned our respect by his industry, dignity, humanity,
and geniality. We fell for him like a ton of bricks and without his making
a single strained overture to win our confidence." The editorial went on
to note: "Never once has he burlesqued his calling or found it necessary
to feign coarseness in order to get along with us run-of-the-mill people.
We have appreciated the compliment he thus paid us. We have grown to
like him so much as a person that we feel almost as though 'they' were
doing us wrong in taking him away."

Stephen Bayne was then assigned to duty as chaplain of the U.S.S.
Salerno Bay (CVE-110) then nearing completion at the Bemerton Navy

Yard, near Seattle, Washington, an assignment that met some of his needs. He gave the invocation at the commissioning of the ship on May 19, 1945. On June 1 he was promoted to Lieutenant, ChC(S), U.S.N.R. He did much as he had done at Fort Lauderdale, but was engaged in what he could honestly regard as active duty.

All through his tour of duty, Bayne kept contact with his family. Letters to his growing children, Stephen Fielding Bayne III (Tert), Philip, Duncan, and Lydia, survive, illustrated letters, written in a manner to amuse, but also to instruct. The letters are full of praise for good things and chastisement for bad things the children have done. He told them of his experiences and on VE Day wrote telling them, "We are celebrating VE Day by taking our ship down [the Columbia] river for a trial run today...I walked around her yesterday, even down into the engine room. She is practically all finished, all painted and shined up.... I'll be glad when we finally get our ship commissioned, and gladder still when we get our planes (Did I tell you we are going to have *Marine* officers?) and get to Japan and get the war over with." But the final touches took time, and the Commercial Iron Works did not turn the completed ship over to the Navy until June 1945, with not enough time left for combat against Japan.

With the surrender of Japan, Bayne was eager for demobilization. The process was begun on October 15, 1945. On February 10, 1946, his commanding officer commended him: "Appreciation is indicated for a job well done." His separation papers were dated February 12, 1946. Net service for pay purposes: 2 years, 13 days. He was awarded ribbons for service in the American and Pacific theaters, and for victory.

Columbia's Chaplain in Residence Again

As has been noted, Bayne's second period as chaplain of Columbia University, beginning February 15, 1946, was relatively brief and was overshadowed by his election in midcourse as Bishop of Olympia. From December 9, 1946, he was "bishop elect" and to all intents and purposes less a chaplain than a bishop. Of necessity, much of his thought and time were given over to the major responsibility he was to assume when consecrated on June 11, 1947. Nevertheless, in that period he carried on the duties of chaplain, administering the chaplaincy services of the university, conducting the services in the university chapel, helping to devise a new curriculum for the college, counseling students and faculty, keeping engagements outside of the university. He was more and more involved in external matters: chaplain of the Church Mission of Help, chaplain of the Orphans' Home and Asylum, New York, trustee of Youth Consultation Services, of Windham House, and of Pomfret School, member and then secretary of the Joint Commission on Holy Matrimony of the

General Convention of the Episcopal Church, member of the Executive Committee of the Church Congress, and chairman of the College Commission of the Second Province of the Episcopal Church.

From the time of his rectorship at Northampton, Bayne had been engaged in the work of the national church's Joint Commission on Holy Matrimony and had been developing an understanding of marriage and the family that was to result in his being acknowledged at the 1958 Lambeth Conference as a master of this vital subject. In addressing the Women's Auxiliary on *Gifts of the Spirit* at the 1943 General Convention, Bayne had stressed the vital importance of the marriage vows for the development of human freedom, and thus the realization of humanity as it was created to be. In the Joint Commission, Bayne was engaged in the difficult work of revising the marriage canons to maintain continuity with the past teachings of the church and to take into account marriage and divorce in contemporary society. In July 1946, along with Frederick A. Prattle, also a member of the Joint Commission, Bayne defended the proposed revision, in an article published in *The Living Church,* against an editorial in that same journal attacking the proposed revision.[36]

In his preaching, Bayne continued to speak about the essential character of human nature, of freedom, and of society. In one sermon Bayne warned that American society, which is a "technical society," was on the road to destruction. He recognized and bemoaned the fact that the universities and colleges of the country were crowded beyond capacity by so many people who want, or have been informed that they want, "not knowledge and faith and the freedom of a reflective mind, but formulas and technical tricks and competitive skills." They are truly members of technical society, learning how to do things with their hands instead of with their hearts. This is what "technical society" means. "It means the cold, cynical horse-sense of a culture that literally has no more sense than a horse does, who will work blindly and stupidly and formlessly until he drops in his tracks." The pathetic and dangerous mindset of technical man Bayne illustrated by reference to a friend of his "who makes atomic bombs for a living. He is very fond," said Bayne, "of leading up to a certain point in the conversation and then pointing his finger at me...and saying, 'What we do with atomic power is up to him. All I do is make the stuff.'" Technical man seems dedicated not to inquiry concerning ends and purposes for doing what is done, and not for the morality of it all, but rather to "the inevitable senseless increment of power." What is to be done? Bayne answered, in part, this way:

> The medicine for society is going to be found when society finds something to serve which is greater than itself. But society is people. And if men don't find meaning and purpose in their lives

then society won't find it. You can't add nothing and nothing and get something. *And men will not find meaning and purpose in their lives until they learn once again to be whole men living in a single world.* They will not find it as long as they keep life broken up into compartments. It is not simply that one man is a scientist and another man is a preacher — and that both act as if we lived in separate worlds with different languages and different kinds of truth. That is the terrible fission at the very heart of our life.[37]

The answer is Christ, "who is Whole and Single and who sees life Whole and Single."

In a related, succeeding sermon, Bayne launched another attack, explaining that a choice must be made "between a civilization which puts man first and a civilization which puts a diabolical abstraction — the state — first. And if you think I'm talking about Russia and the United States, you are wrong. I am talking about the United States and the United Nations, and the only possible basis that there is for hope and peace in this world." In the course of his sermon he asserted:

The State is *not* good. [God is good.]
The State can*not* make anything or anybody good. [God has made man good.]
The State exists to serve men — not important men, not even "good" men — it exists to serve men. [And men exist for one another and for God. That is the Christian faith.][38]

In an issue of *The Witness,* Bayne reiterated this conviction, a conviction that became stronger as he became more and more aware of and alarmed by "that monstrous anachronism — absolute national sovereignty" as a major threat to the Christian faith and to humanity.[39]

In a substantial address delivered at a Round Table Dinner of the Church Club of New York, Bayne elaborated on both his critique of modern American society and on Christianity as providing a way out of a destructive situation."[40] As he later said, he gave the hundred or so members "a generous dose of Drucker, Tawney et al."[41] Before speaking on business and economics, his topic for the evening, Bayne suggested five moral principles as providing the necessary basis for his address. (1) Man, by creation, adoption, and grace is a child of God — all men, good and bad, Christian or other. (2) He emphasized the fact of the human family and the natural caring that characterizes that family as created by God. (3) The end or purpose of humanity, as created by God, is to grow in "freedom toward God, in the fullest possible fellowship" with our neighbors. (4) Humanity takes precedence over all that is created to serve it. And (5) "the natural society of men, the children of God, has absolute priority over the State, which is an instrumentality allowed

by God because of the sins of men." Society, as he viewed it, did not
live by these principles. Religion had been privatized, and society had
been organized as if there were no God. He pointed, for example, to the
"moral irresponsibility of modern corporations," the impatience people
have with the capacity of industrialized society to furnish needed security, and our mindless attitudes toward competition, mergers, cartels,
and the size of industry. He stated:

> I know that if we are going to stay sane in this world we have
> got to find ways to restore to life the meaningfulness, the sense of
> moral order, which it does not have now. I know that the profit
> motive will not stand alone; it is nothing more than organized
> avarice, sin, when it is not checked and balanced by the love of
> God and the love of a good job well done, both of which are far
> more important motives, and strangely silent in this world of ours.

He ended by speaking at some length of some aids to correcting the
situation: the altar, the Bible, and "serious conferences." The Holy Communion, he said, illuminates Christian society as found in the act and
the sight of the Sacrament — "as the fruits of this generous earth are
raised in offering and worship and then restored to us for the nour-
ishment of our corporate Body, as the Brotherhood kneels side by side
in the presence of that transcendent parable of Society." Bayne saw in
the Bible medicine for those discouraged "at the abject dismal secular
world" they live in: "the careful, dedicated life of the Jew, whose every
step and gesture was prescribed and measured by the law of God; the
possessed and fathomless godliness of St. Paul; the love of St. John; and
having all through it the steady constant obedience of our Lord. Even to
read a verse or two a day makes you forever dissatisfied with the stony
barrenness of a life planned without God."

Bayne also gave thought to the Church and its vocation. Shortly
before leaving Columbia, he gave the Alumni Essay at the General Seminary. "In the address," he later recalled,[42] "several germinal ideas, to
which SFB returned many times, are brought into focus." He began
by expressing discomfort with modern ecumenical discussions and their
tendency to avoid conflict, and thus avoid substance. He was annoyed,
for instance, when the episcopate was under discussion, at the tendency
to focus on "the administrative Episcopate." Another theory sometimes
proposed is that of the reproductive episcopate "in which the bishop is
retained, and supported, in the manner of a queen bee, complete to the
distended abdomen and the buzzing cluster of attendant presbyters, for
the sole purpose of perpetuating the Line."[43] The need, as he viewed
it, was for the honest assessment of very different traditions. As to the
Episcopal Church, realistic questions ought to be asked concerning the

real nature of the Church and what contribution it would bring to a reunited Church.

In this way he began a serious quest for an understanding of Anglicanism, a quest that was to last the rest of his life and to prove at times frustrating but in the end helpful and even inspiring to many in the Anglican Communion. What constituted Anglicanism's uniqueness? It is often said that worship according to *The Book of Common Prayer* is Anglicanism's greatest treasure and greatest gift. Bayne questioned that assumption.He said: "The forms of the Prayer Book have great excellence; I am used to them and nourished by them; but the forms themselves are not particularly useful or relevant to our world. Morning Prayer looks silly, and it is silly when you analyze it without knowledge of its history or the shadowy choirs of the past who say the office with you."[44] The truth in the assumption lies deeper than the forms and the techniques of Prayer Book worship. "I rather think," he said, "it is a certain humane and antique wholeness and grace, which permeates our ordered worship, an objectivity, a sense not so much of the 'otherness' of God as of our capacity, with his help, to offer Him the best of human words and thoughts." There are, however, dangers in this, such as that "of the starved and stunted imagination, which expresses itself in the stumbling performance of the liturgy" and the "lack of a vivid sense of the supernatural in worship." But it is magnificent, this sense of order. We believe in the use of language people can understand, but we believe also in using a language appropriate to the praise of God, in "music and stone and vestment and gesture alike; so that, if we will, man's whole creaturely environment, and the best of his mind, can be brought into the obedience of Christ."[45]

Anglicanism he understood as being characterized by "maturity" as well, maturity that attached equal importance to freedom and responsibility. Freedom in the realm of belief he regarded as coming "very close to the heart of our whole way of life," and he said:

> All the way from Chillingworth, with his abrupt "we call no man master on earth," to the present Archbishop of Canterbury who sets out our three great authorities of Scripture and Tradition and Experience and finds there is no absolute authority but rather an area of judgment within which we freely move — in all that was we have shown more consistency than anywhere else.
>
> At the heart of the Church, at the heart of the Faith, there is an infallible authority, but as Laud pointed out, "This comes to no more than to say that there shall be always a Church." Indeed it comes to hardly more than to say there is a God who entered and enters in human history. Beyond that, in truth, we do not look for an infallible authority nor would we accept one.[46]

There is too in Anglicanism an emphasis on the incarnation and on history. Anglicans resist abstractions. "The Liturgy is not a separate and universal type of worship; it is Christ in action in His Body. The Christian life is not a series of techniques and aphorisms; it is the disciple and his Lord. Prayer is not an exercise of the human spirit; it is our answer to the gift of His Spirit."[47] And finally there is an emphasis on the ministry of the laity, of the entire body. The whole pattern of life in Anglicanism — "humane, mature, free, and above all centered on the Incarnation — combines to make sense out of the whole Church and the whole ministry, not just one official segment of it. I can see," said Bayne, "no importance whatever in the perpetuation of bishops, or of clergy, as an isolated class. Without them, the laity are as sheep without a shepherd. Without the laity, the clergy are a completely odious fungus on the body politic."[48]

In addresses such as those made before the Church Club of New York and the faculty, students, and alumni of the General Theological Seminary, the chaplain of Columbia and Bishop-elect of Olympia was emerging as a major thinker and an inspirational voice in the Episcopal Church. It would be true to say that by the year 1947, his chief convictions were formed and in place, and he was ready for leadership. Through pain and frustration he was coming to grips with himself, with the age in which he lived, and with the Church he served. Something of the spirit of the man, of the complexity and reality of Stephen Bayne, came through in the last sermon he preached at Columbia.

A skull, a skeleton... death hides just under the surface of life. This fragile moment of our consciousness is like a bubble; we come from the darkness and in the end we go back to the dark, and the dark surrounds us and presses in on us at every turn. Defiantly man snatches his evanescent life away from the dark and affirms it, constructing something in the face of the dark.[49]

The Rev. Stephen Fielding Bayne, Jr., was ordained into the priesthood in the Chapel of the Intercession, Parish of Trinity Church in the City of New York, June 11, 1933. *Courtesy of archives of the Episcopal Church, USA.*

During World War II, Chaplain Bayne was commissioned as a Lieu-
tenant in the United States Naval Reserve and served at the Naval Air
Station in Fort Lauderdale, Florida, and aboard the aircraft carrier
Salerno Bay. May 7, 1945. *Courtesy of Stephen F. Bayne, Jr. Collection.
St. Mark's Library, General Theological Seminary, New York.*

The Rt. Rev. Stephen F. Bayne, Jr., Bishop of Olympia, blessing the city of Seattle after his consecration, June 11, 1947. *Courtesy of Archives of the Episcopal Church USA, Austin, Texas.*

(Left to right) Dr. Stephen F. Bayne; the newly instituted Rector of the Parish of Trinity Church, the Rev. Dr. John Heuss; Canon Edward N. West; the Rt. Rev. Horace W. B. Donegan, Bishop of New York; and Rear Admiral Reginald R. Belknap, Church-Warden of the Parish of Trinity Church. June 3, 1952. *Courtesy of Parish of Trinity Church.*

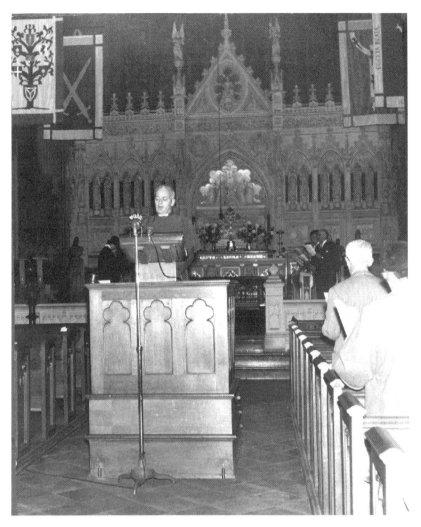

The Rt. Rev. Stephen F. Bayne, Jr., preaching at Trinity Church, November 4, 1955. The sermon was part of a series, "The Mission for Christian Action," and was broadcast by WQXR on the program "Old Trinity on the Air." *Courtesy of Parish of Trinity Church, New York.*

On January 1, 1960, the Rt. Rev. Stephen F. Bayne was appointed to the newly created post of Anglican Executive Officer of the Anglican Communion, making him the second most influential Anglican figure in the world. Bishop Bayne (top row, second from left) is seen here with the Most Rev. and Rt. Hon. Arthur M. Ramsey, the Archbishop of Canterbury, and other leaders of the Anglican Communion, circa 1962. *Courtesy of Stephen F. Bayne, Jr. Collection, St. Mark's Library, General Theological Seminary, New York.*

The Rt. Rev. R. Ambrose Reeves, Bishop of Johannesburg, meeting Bishop Bayne (right) at the airport, circa 1960. As the Anglican Executive Officer, Bayne traveled over 150,000 miles per year in the service of the Anglican Communion. *Courtesy of Stephen F. Bayne, Jr. Collection, St. Mark's Library, General Theological Seminary, New York.*

Bishop Bayne (right) made it a point to visit Trinity Church as often as his busy schedule allowed. In this image he is seen with the Vicar, the Rev. Bernard C. Newman. Bishop Bayne had come "home" to celebrate the 28th anniversary of his ordination to the priesthood and 14th anniversary of his Consecration as Bishop. June 11, 1961. *Courtesy of Parish of Trinity Church, New York.*

The Rt. Rev. Stephen Fielding Bayne, circa 1970. Photographer, Fabian Bachrach. *Courtesy of Parish of Trinity Church, New York.*

The Class of 1973, General Theological Seminary, New York City. Bishop Bayne had returned to teaching at General Theological Seminary in the fall of 1970. He also served as Acting Dean and then Dean of the Seminary until he retired in 1973. Bayne is in the front row, right of center. *Courtesy of Stephen F. Bayne, Jr. Collection, St. Mark's Library, General Theological Seminary, New York.*

Four

THE BISHOP OF OLYMPIA

Being a Bishop

On December 9, 1946, a special convention of the Diocese of Olympia ignored the report of its own nominating committee and elected Stephen Bayne as its diocesan on the fourth ballot. Bayne was personally known to many of the delegates, who met him while he served as chaplain of the U.S.S. *Salerno Bay* at the Bemerton Navy Yard near Seattle. Bayne had made himself known to Simeon Arthur Huston, the Bishop of Olympia, and other clergy, volunteering to assist as needed and as he could. In his interview with Bayne in 1963, Sam Welles reported that at about the time that the chaplain arrived in Bemerton, St. Mark's Cathedral, Seattle, which had been closed due to financial difficulties, reopened. "By helping out temporarily at the Cathedral while he was in naval uniform, he unwittingly took a hand in his own future." On that day in December, as the Special Convention met, Bayne knew nothing of their consideration of him as a candidate. When informed of his election, he was surprised and perplexed. He consulted a number of people and reported that it was the only time in his career "that the bulk of the advice" from friends and mentors "was negative." He flew out to Seattle during the Christmas vacation at Columbia and "visited most of the parishes and missions of the diocese." In the end, he felt that it was right that he should accept the election, in spite of the advice he had received. "I knew the job was there to be done," he said. "My wonderful predecessor had left peace and love — no split diocese. The energies were all there to be tapped."[1] On January 11 he announced his acceptance, adding: "I have been honored most profoundly in being asked to come to Olympia. In my decision I can only pray that God will accept my imperfect ministry and make us all, clergy and laity alike, the disciplined and witnessing Church He wills us to be."[2] His consecration was scheduled for June 11, 1947, at St. Mark's Cathedral. Bayne attended Commencement at Columbia on June 3 and then flew to Des Moines, where he joined his father, his three sons, and a nephew. From there they drove to Seattle, which they reached on June 8, three days before the consecration.[3]

What were his feelings? There was excitement surely, and perhaps some misgivings about the decision and about his ability to do what was expected. On May 8, 1947, Bayne's mother wrote: "God never gives us a bigger job to do than He has the help to do it right there. Mary Steel said she thought you were worried. I know just how you have butterflies in your stomach. I get them so often too; after a while they fly away and the task that looked so formidable is behind us. Just like the rochets. I was so tired and forlorn when I was making the first one, it seemed as if it was all wrong. Now it is beautiful in its box of pink paper and the ruffs are perfect."[4]

The consecration was a grand occasion. Bayne was attended by old friends John Butler and John Craine, rector of Trinity Church, Seattle, where Bayne had assisted. Among the acolytes were the three oldest Bayne children, Stephen III, 11 years old, Philip, 9, and Duncan, 7. They also assisted in vesting the new bishop. The consecrator was Henry Knox Sherrill, the Presiding Bishop of the Episcopal Church. Co-consecrators were Bishops Gray (Coadjutor of Connecticut) and Huston (the Second Bishop of Olympia). The preacher was Clinton Quinn, Bishop of Texas, who reminded Bayne that he should be a "Father in God" to his clergy, that his churchmanship should be comprehensive, truly catholic. Quinn warned him of the dangers of "Episcopitis" — pride, overconfidence, aloofness, slothful thinking — saying a bishop "should grow, not swell." He concluded, "Your life and your home and all you do are examples to the flock. Work hard with the clergy, through the clergy, and with the people; keep close to God and you cannot lose."[5] Two hymns, especially meaningful to Bayne, were sung in procession: "Crown Him with many crowns" and "Glorious things of Thee are spoken." In his address the Presiding Bishop warned the people of the diocese: "Do not expect your Bishop to make bricks without straw. Do not destroy the enthusiasm and zeal with which he comes to you with any petty things. Rather, give him the tools with which to work; throw yourselves unselfishly into the task."[6]

How did Bayne regard episcopacy and thus himself as bishop? During his time as diocesan, Bayne preached at the consecrations of Richard Watson for Utah, Edward Welles for Western Missouri, John Craine for Indianapolis, and Dan Corrigan to be suffragan of Colorado. He also preached on the occasion of Lauriston Scaife's tenth anniversary celebration as Bishop of Western New York. In these sermons he wrestled with an understanding of the episcopacy and affirmed that a bishop is *called:* "Our action is all response; all initiative is with the Lord."[7] A bishop is sent, as the Church is sent, as apostle: "The Church is the people who are 'sent'; the Bishop is the man who is 'sent,' the Apostolic man." He is sent as *pontifex* — "bridge builder" sent pre-eminently into the future. He is sent as *episcopos* — "overseer, watchman, raised above our shoulders so that he can tell us how we are doing and where we are going, and most of all can see the faces of those who are yet outside our company."[8] The bishop is one who exercises power, "the power that comes to a man in the Household of God to define, in his own life and words, the very nature of the Christian fellowship itself, the aspirations and necessities of humanity, the true character of Christ's discipleship; and to define those things not in terms of a brief and passing ministry, but in terms of a bishop's lifelong marriage with his diocese."[9]

Bayne strove to retain a proper balance between the bishop's rightful sense of leadership, power, and authority, and the bishop's equally necessary sense of imperfection and therefore his utter dependence upon Christ, whose steward he is, and upon the people who are Christ's body in the world. In part, his success in achieving something of this difficult balance is reflected in a statement made by one member of his flock in the diocese of Olympia who said, "You expect formalities when he enters a meeting, but all of a sudden there he is, easy and conversational, yet still a personage." Probing the personality of the man as bishop, Sam Welles wrote that "the directness, drive, and informality of this native New Yorker delighted" the people of Olympia: "His stiff schedule included some 600 sermons and addresses a year, plus endless individual and group meetings. Laymen were astounded but gratified to find that he made theology as warm and immediate as politics or baseball. He was — often almost simultaneously — crisp, canny, trenchant, imaginative, stern, and loving."[10]

On the tenth anniversary of his episcopate, Bayne reminded his people that when he was first chosen and decided to accept his election as their bishop he searched for words to describe his "hopes and ideals for the Church." Two words had come to mind, "disciplined" and "witnessing." "I felt that if the Church were disciplined within herself, and intent on bold witness to the world outside, no harm could befall her."[11] During the ten years, he had patterned his course, remembering those words, convinced that a Church "which is not afraid of hardness and austerity in its own inner life, can be trusted on any frontier, with every freedom in preaching the Gospel and ministering to the needs of men, without fear of sentimentality or romanticism." One instrument, representative of much else, for cultivating the necessary discipline in himself and in his clergy was a book of prayers he compiled for daily use. Of this book, sent out to all the clergy and to postulants and candidates for ordination as well, he said in a preface:

These prayers are put forward to be included in the prayers of the clergy, in the hope that by this brief common prayer we will find deeper comradeship, the assurance of continual intercession for one another, inner serenity from knowing that we stand together in a common task under a common judgment, with a common hope. I will suggest other and different prayers from time to time and include them in my letters to you.... These are just a beginning.

These prayers (as part of our own)...the daily offices and five hours a week of study...the Prayer Book fasts and feasts...a weekly self-examination...at least two days of retreat a year... this I pray will be the least rule we shall want to keep in our clerical family.[12]

Among the many prayers for morning, noon, and evening, for all the clergy named by name, for all sorts of people and things in the Church and in the world, is this one for dedication. It is expressive of the bishop's hopes, ideals, needs, and prayers:

O Holy Spirit, Lord and giver of life, redeem us from dead works to serve the living God. Consecrate us anew, bishop, clergy, and laity, to love mercy, to do justly, and to walk humbly. Help us to learn the discipline of Christ. Give us a soldier's virtue to do our duty with cheerfulness, and to bear our honest witness with courage, day by day. As Thou hast given us a fair country, and strong and eager hands, give us also eyes to see beyond today and its needs and fears, to God's Country which lies ahead. We ask Thee not to take us out of life but to prove Thy power within it. We ask not for easy ways, but for a clear road and a right will and comradeship in the way. Give us a pure intention and patient faith and sufficient success, and now and always the joy of serving Thee, Who livest and reignest with the Father and the Son, one God, world without end.[13]

The Diocese and Its Bishop

The Diocese of Olympia includes all of that territory of the State of Washington that is west of the Cascade Mountains, or an area of about 25,000 square miles. Bayne regarded all of this great area and all of its life, sacred and secular, to be of intense concern, a field for missionary endeavor. At one time he said that he would "like to see more clergymen down at the Boeing plant, off in the lumber camps, at sea, building bridges." He himself served as chairman of the Seattle Housing Authority, Chairman of the Child Welfare Advisory Committee of the State of Washington, a member of the Advisory Board of the Seattle Council on Aging, a member of the Advisory Board of the Seattle Research Foundation for Alcoholism, a member of the State Public Assistance Advisory Committee,[14] and was honored as a humanitarian by B'nai B'rith. He traveled extensively, visiting every parish and mission,

confirming, preaching, teaching, consulting, listening, watching and being watched, intent upon being, to the fullest extent possible, the Chief
Pastor to all the people of the Episcopal Church in western Washington,
and the Chief Missionary too.

Bayne served Olympia all through the 1950s, when the church was
enjoying the fruits of a postwar boom. In his thirteen years, the church
in that diocese grew from 18,000 members and 13,000 communicants
to 40,000 members and 24,000 communicants. In the twelve years
prior to his final convention in 1959, the number of clergy, forty-six
in 1947, more than doubled, and twenty-five new congregations were
added to the twenty-six parishes and thirty-three missions existing in
1947. Resident clergy were placed in some sixteen communities, which
had been without priests previously. The record was equally dramatic
when measured in terms of buildings and dollars. "We have bought,"
Bayne reported, "thirty parsonages alone. Fifty-six new church buildings
or parish halls have been dedicated. And the dollar value of our buildings and property (for whatever the figure is worth) has increased 600
percent, to more than $12,000,000. In receipts, our budget for Diocesan
and missionary work next year alone will exceed the total of what was
given in all our congregations, for all our operating expenses, twelve
years ago."[15] Church growth was a constant concern of Bayne's during these years. In 1949 he reported confirming just over one thousand
persons in the previous year. By 1955 he passed the two thousand per
year mark.

In obedience to canon law, Bayne made a statement on the affairs
of the Church at each annual convention of the diocese. He took this
seriously, as he later recalled, "and wrote long reports/addresses/sermons
which were inflicted on the convention at the opening service, which was
evensong, in a crowded cathedral, with 'Lord Christ, when first thou
came to men' as the invariable pre-address hymn."

In 1953 he spoke of evangelism and a new sense of outreach evident
in the churches of the diocese: "It is an evangelism of attraction rather
than pressure; much more depends on what we are than on what we
say, or on easy promises easily extended." He preferred this approach
believing "that in the long run people are drawn to a deep faith at a
deep level; and that you cannot short-circuit freedom indefinitely."[16] In
1948 he spoke of his concern that the laity recognize their responsibility
for ministry in the Church and for the cultivation of and witness to a
faith that attracts people at a deep level.[17]

In 1949, Bayne talked about Anglicanism and the Episcopal Church
and the ways in which each parish should emphasize that atmosphere
and attitude that welcomes people into community. Referring to the
difficulty involved in trying to define what it is to be an Episcopalian,
he said:

There is almost no doctrinal test; you don't have to do anything
except be baptized; the way you become an Episcopalian, by our
laws, is by going to an Episcopal Church and paying your freight.
You will be asked no questions about your morals or your mind. It
is not a school of thought or a party or a set of orthodoxies which
you are joining, but a *community* of people, presumably a whole
community.

This is the feel of our Church. We did not make it so; that spirit
is ours by inheritance; it is part of the Church-spirit [as opposed to
the sect-spirit].[18]

Bayne was convinced, as he said in his address to the convention in
1950, that the parochial ministry was and will remain at the heart of
the Church, "where the flock of Christ gathers and finds its true community around the altar." The cultivation and growth of this community
was the bishop's major concern, not for the sake of cultivating some sort
of exclusive club, but that the Church might be more fully the Church,
the devotion and faith born and nurtured in the parishes generating the
spiritual power needed to invade and capture the battlefields of faith
"in labor unions, in college classrooms, in social agencies, in industrial
plants, in business offices."[19]

The Episcopal Church in western Washington was booming. Building
programs were in progress all over the diocese. At the outset there was
a new diocesan office to renovate and pay for, a new church and parish
hall at St. David's, Shelton, a new church for Epiphany, Seattle, a parish
hall for Emmanuel, East Sound, a new church for St. John's, Gig Harbor, new buildings for St. Elizabeth's, Seahurst, and All Saints', Seattle,
and much more. There were missions to found, diocesan programs to
establish and finance, the quota for the national budget to meet. The
pressures were unrelenting, the challenge awesome. In 1950 the bishop
found himself questioning the dedication of the people of his diocese.
The average communicant, he figured, gave "$2.00 a year — four cents
a Sunday — to the mission of his own Diocese," and it was difficult to
get that much. "Why do we not give more?" he asked. "Is it because we
are stingy? I do not think so. I think it is because we do not know or
think deeply enough about what we are giving for. A budget in terms
of dollars means very little. A budget in terms of human personality
means infinitely more. If we could only hold up before ourselves the
people whom we are helping — the clergy and the congregations, the
world around — I think our generosity would reach its rightful expression." This was a point he attempted to make in the House of Bishops,
and it was an idea that was to develop in his mind until it blossomed
at the Anglican Congress in Toronto, in 1963, in a program named
"Mutual Responsibility and Interdependence." He wished he could turn

things around, upside down, and instead of stressing money and money quotas — which was really not at all successful — stress the support of "personalities and causes which we know and which become part of our life."[20]

Bayne spent much time and energy raising funds to assist the steady growth in the diocese. In 1955 he spoke of numerous building programs, of capital funds drives, of the Centennial Fund, of the completion of the Cathedral without the incurring of debt. He attempted to stress the meaning and purpose of it all:

> If our duty is a humble one, building churches and organizing missions and making surveys, it is also and always a very exalted duty, none other than to live Christ's life in this world...to teach, to heal, to love, to forgive, to offer, to reconcile, to be in the world and yet not of the world — this is the Church's work for it is Christ's work. And this work is to be done in this present world — confused, broken, homesick and fearful, and eager for religious security as few generations have been.[21]

The building of churches, organizing of missions, and making surveys were done for the sake of this ministry, which is Christ's ministry. Furthermore, he indicated that he was not overly impressed by the "success" suggested by all the signs of growth in numbers of people, in building, in funds. He did not countenance complacency.

Money raising and building programs, as necessary as they were, were not sufficient, however. Much like Newman in sermons preached at Oxford, Bayne had a vision:

> If all the Episcopal Church means is a decorated Protestantism, or a group of inherited prejudices, or a small society of quarrelsome people who like to pretend they are Catholics but do so painlessly — then we had better shut up shop now and save the money.
>
> But if we have the vision to see the commonwealth of the future pressing to be born, and see the Lord, biding in the shadows watching over His own — if we are willing to bind ourselves into the loyal discipline of His Church and stand up for Him with all our hearts — then, my brethren, what a great dream and hope there is! To build the household of God and man among these green peaks of ours, to see springing into life a new city of men free from the dead hand of past mistakes and failures, to build a new and better democracy for the new children of the West, to make and keep this God's country as He wills it to be — that is our vocation in this Diocese, and may God give us pure hearts and clean hands and tireless wills to bring these things to pass.[22]

After 1952, Bayne's convention addresses involved "themes of more general character . . . patriotism, public responsibility (about Dave Beck), evangelism, et al."[23] As early as 1948 he was speaking of a dangerous mood in the nation. He pointed out that toward the end of World War II Americans were oversold on Russia but have veered toward the opposite extreme. There were signs of panic. Legislation like the Mundt Bill was very dangerous. "It puts a premium upon suspicion and on fear precisely at a time when we need above all things confidence and openness." The passage of the bill, he argued, "will succeed in doing exactly what we do not want done, driving underground and out of sight the very forces that threaten us only when they are hidden. It is panic legislation." He had no love for communism. He saw its weakness "in the simple fact that it treats men as if they were animals instead of sons of God. And Communism fattens on every evidence that democracy gives that we think men are really just animals, too."[24]

In 1953 he was attacking McCarthyism and "the malaise and fear which still grips so many in our nation, which indeed continues to threaten the very existence of a civilized and free community, and to which the Gospel is in direct and clear opposition." He was firm in his conviction: "Any nation which has lost its confidence in itself; which distrusts its own people and their ideas; which puts a premium on security; which paralyzes the free exploration of the truth; which has forgotten its own buoyant, confident trust in its own mission; which puts its own existence as its final goal — any such nation has jeopardized its existence, and is in peril of denying its own faith in God."[25] In 1954, mindful on the one hand of continuing McCarthyism in some places and on the other hand of the decision in the case of *Brown* v. *Board of Education of Topeka,* legally ending segregation in the schools, he discussed true patriotism, or love of country, whose purpose it is to "give birth to something far greater and far truer." The true patriot knows "that true love of his land and his people must irresistibly lead to an inner love and a greater society" — the Kingdom of God. It is God's Kingdom that is ultimate.[26]

The report that a very prominent labor leader, Dave Beck, was involved in a violation of tax laws by mishandling his union's funds brought forth from the bishop in his 1957 convention address some serious thoughts on moral responsibility in high places. The irresponsibility in the affairs of leaders of management as well as labor, evident to all, pointed to a most serious moral weakness or flaw in the nation. The peccadilloes of labor and management underline "the fact of irresponsible power — power wielded by labor tycoons as well as by management tycoons, wielded by cynical men who are above any moral law. To deal with the working man," he said, "as if he were a commodity to be bought and sold used to be the privilege of 19th Century capitalists. The privilege is apparently now shared by some 20th Century labor leaders. And there are equal problems on the side of management."[27] According to a report (*Washington Daily News*, March 28, 1969), Dave Beck, the Teamster boss, protested, reminding Bayne of Beck's help in raising funds to pay off the mortgage on St. Mark's Cathedral. Beck protested that the bishop had not spoken to him to get his side of the story before launching the attack. Bayne did not and could not retract what he had said. He saw it as his responsibility as a bishop of the Church to speak out against moral irresponsibility wherever he encountered it. He had, after all, not confined his attack to Beck or labor leaders in general. He was equally incensed about management "when it is divorced from ownership and from any sense of social responsibility, and interprets its function as if the only end to be sought was an uninterrupted dividend record."[28]

Of a less inflammatory nature, but still of vital social concern, was the increasingly grave plight of the poor in western Washington and in the nation. As president of the Seattle Housing Authority, Bayne was knowledgeable about and deeply concerned for the adequate housing of those over sixty-five. He acknowledged that the Church alone could do little in this area, by itself, but he had hoped that the diocese might be able to provide some housing, and he expressed his disappointment that there was so little support for the idea. Housing was not the only issue, however. The mental health of the aged he viewed as being largely dependent upon the elderly having a sense of usefulness, and this was an area in which the Church could do much and perhaps more than any other institution.[29] In his 1956 address he noted that the Seattle Urban League made the statement that there was more racial discrimination in the urban area at 11 A.M. on Sunday morning than at any other time. Bayne supported the diocesan Department of Christian Social Relations' request that a committee on Inter-racial Relations be established to deal with the problem. In that same address he spoke, too, of "the prodigious heartache of alcoholism." He was intent upon establishing and nurturing programs to provide healing for alcoholics, and he endorsed the work of Alcoholics Anonymous.

Bayne did much in his thirteen years as Bishop of Olympia, through his addresses and through his actions, to raise the consciousness of Episcopalians in matters of social concern on every level, from the parish to the nation. He had often expressed his strong conviction that Christianity was not to be confined to the fringes of natural life but was rightly concerned with politics and economics and indeed with everything involved in human existence. To any who might object, Bayne would refer to "obedience." "We are not our own masters here," he said in 1958. "Our parishes do not exist to serve their priests.... Clergy and laity alike are men under authority, obedient to the Lord Whose Body is the Church."[30]

The life of the bishop was a busy, at times frenetic one. In connection with his concern for education, he started a faculty study group at the University of Washington and at its first meeting in January 1956 presented a paper on "Christian Anthropology" for discussion.[31] In 1948 he had begun an annual Lenten series of "Bishop's Evenings" — something he spoke of at one time as a "diluted preachings mission" designed "to provide for the Church a simple, adaptable medium for a teaching evangelism."[32] He paid close attention to the supervision of diocesan institutions. The Annie Wright Seminary for girls in Tacoma received special attention from Bayne. Tacoma had been the see city of the diocese, but with the rapid growth of Seattle, Bishop Huston had relocated the see. Conscious of hurt feelings, Bayne attempted to spend one day each week in Tacoma. He made the Annie Wright School his headquarters and at the beginning taught a class of senior girls. Over the years he maintained close contact with its greatly admired headmistress, Ruth Jenkins.[33] The bishop was also involved in the reorganization of diocesan structures. He paid close attention to theological education, the selection and calling of clergy, and the health and welfare of clergy and their families.

Bayne's involvement in the ecumenical movement was marked during this period by his attendance in Geneva at a Faith and Order meeting, where he substituted for the Right Reverend Angus Dun, Bishop of Washington, D.C. It was also marked by his subsequent involvement in Seattle in a Faith and Order study group on baptism, by his correspondence with Cuthbert Simpson concerning baptism, and by his attendance in 1954 at the Evanston meeting of the World Council of Churches.[34] In the House of Bishops he was a member of the Committee of Nine, a committee headed by Angus Dun, which was begun in 1947 "to consider in brotherly conference the areas of difference and of conflict within our Church and to recommend ways and means of setting forward peace, understanding, and unity among us." Initially, they focused on differences in public worship and liturgical use, in public doctrinal teachings, in the matter of church discipline, and in the administration and government of the Church. Bayne was a very active member of this select and at times powerful committee.[35] At the Anglican Congress in 1954, Bayne organized the work of discussion groups and the presentation of the findings of the groups at plenary sessions, and earned the gratitude of senior bishops all through the Anglican Communion.[36] He was in attendance as a newly consecrated bishop at the Lambeth Conference of Bishops in 1948, where he delivered a paper on confirmation.[37] Ten years later, at Lambeth 1958, he was an acknowledged leader, chairman of one of the five core committees, as will be noted later.

In addition, there were books and articles to be written, conferences to be led, and a young and boisterous family needing attention, now five

children with the birth of Bruce on March 20, 1948, the year following the bishop's consecration. In the thirteen Olympian years, the three
oldest boys, Stephen III, Philip, and Duncan grew to maturity through
adolescences ranging from benign to painful. The family lived at first
at 1305 East Prospect, in Seattle, but in 1952 moved to a replica of an
English manor house, at 1147 Harvard. In a basement room Bayne had
his hideaway and there did his writing in peace. One might also mention Bayne's close alliances with those who helped lead the diocese, staff
and others, and friendships made, people ministered to in their pain,
happy occasions, music (the bishop developed a liking for Brahms) and
laughter, much fun, as in the exchange of telegrams with the Bishop of
Oregon, and some tears. His interest in Gilbert and Sullivan continued
during the Seattle years.

In 1950 the bishop was designated by the Presiding Bishop to
represent the Episcopal Church in the U.S.A. at the Church Congress celebrating the centennial of the Diocese of Christchurch, in New Zealand.
It was an honor. Bayne delivered three talks there, preparatory to some
of his most important writing, and made many friends. It was a happy
event. But, as Bayne recalled years later, before going he "had had a difficult time physically, with what appeared at first to be simple fatigue —
and in some measure was — but also was a need for a high-protein low-
blood-sugar diet, and even more for a better discipline against anxiety."
He went to New Zealand "still wrestling with all this, and even asked
the privilege of making one or two of his talks sitting down, pleading his
'spaghetti legs.' "[38] The acute sense of vulnerability, the recurrent anxiety
and depression, that he had first known in 1934 would not leave him, no
matter how successful he was, no matter how frequently or how much
he was appreciated by others. This, as well as the strength, the courage,
the laughter, the brilliance, was a part of the man too and contributed
to his sensitivity, his acuteness, his ability to empathize with those who
suffered, and to his attitude of dependence on and obedience to God.
Manly as he was, he knew that he could not do what he had to do
alone. With such knowledge, gained through painful experience, he was
the greater man.

He received abundant affirmation. In celebration of his tenth anniversary as Bishop of Olympia, a Congress on Life and Work was held.
Theodore O. Wedel, William Pollard, and many others were there. On
March 28, 1957, there was a Service of Witness with a great crowd gathered in St. Mark's Cathedral and a massed choir drawn from parishes
and missions all over the diocese singing: "The Son of God goes forth
to war," "Crown Him with many crowns," "Jesus shall reign where'er
the sun," and "The Church's one Foundation."[39] There was a lengthy
procession with civic and public dignitaries, officials of the diocese, min-
isters of Seattle churches, visiting clergy, and many others. All were

gathered to honor Stephen Bayne. The preacher was Angus Dun, whose sermon was entitled "The Church and the World in Mid-Century." In the course of his sermon Bishop Dun said:

> In our world and time at this mid-century, Christ's people are a great company. They have fanned out over most of the continents and islands and nations of the earth. They have broken into many companies which bear many names beside the one which is above every name....
>
> Christ's people are a people on mission sent. They are called to walk with restraint and without panic the narrow way between human suicide in atomic war and the acceptance of intolerable tyranny.[40]

After the service a man came up to Bayne and said, "I cannot tell you what this has meant. I never knew the Church thought and talked about these things at all." Bayne was grateful for the tribute that the Service of Witness embodied, but he was thrilled that the three days of the Congress ending with the service had been so effective in reaching people on a deep level. He said, after telling of the man and his gratitude: "To have touched one man — indeed many men and women — with some sense of urgency and the relevance of Christ to the whole of our life is the finest privilege we could ever know."[41]

This was, according to the testimony of many who knew him, the happiest, most fulfilling period of Stephen Bayne's life. Year after year he expressed his gratitude to his diocese for their having called him to serve them. In 1957, he said: "A year, when I look back on it, is a wonderfully generous, confusing, joyful feast of memories. The 'Bishop's Evenings,' the endless wonder of Confirmation, a preaching mission, the breaking of bread and the prayers in one congregation after another, the heartbreaking problems we have to face sometimes, the affectionate comradeship that makes it possible for us to face them...all these blessings are so freely given, and come in such abundance, that the years slip by without noticing them."[42]

The Bishop at Lambeth

While Bishop of Olympia, Stephen Bayne was much in demand outside of the diocese. He attended meetings of the House of Bishops and of General Convention, and lectured in New Zealand, at the General Seminary, at Seabury-Western Seminary, and elsewhere. Often his lectures resulted in books. During his tenure in Olympia he did some of his finest writing and produced his most memorable book. These will occupy our attention in the next chapter. Here we will concentrate on Bishop Bayne's participation in the Lambeth Conferences of the bishops of the

Anglican Communion in 1948 and 1958. These conferences and his participation in them were of great importance for his future and the future of the Anglican Communion, for in them he emerged as an international statesman, a leader of the Anglican Communion worldwide.

We begin with the Conference held in the summer of 1948. That which most impressed and moved him, he told his diocese, "was the sight of all those bishops, from the ends of the earth, White and Black, Chinese, Japanese, Indian, American, British, all the spiritual children of the great family of our Anglican Communion," meeting together "at the ancient throne of Augustine, and held together, not by law or dogma, but by the common blood of the Prayer Book in our veins." There were great differences of opinion, differences in style and manners, but a very real collegiality as well. "Sometimes," he said, "we American bishops have to remind our English brothers that there was a little unpleasantness in 1776 or thereabouts, but we get along all right." The conference met for five weeks, one at the beginning and two at the end as a committee of the whole in the old library at Lambeth, and two weeks in the middle in separate committees, some at Church House and others at Lambeth in London. When the bishops met together there was an endless string of addresses. Bayne reported his impressions as they met daily.

There were the giants: Kirk of Oxford, "massive and iron," Bell of Chichester, "careful, precise, intellectually austere, to a degree," Grey of Armagh, Wand of London, Strong of New Guinea, Yoshiro of Kobe, and the rest. The remarkable thing was that through it all the Church emerged. "The vexations and the superficialities alike disappear, and the steady reality of the Brotherhood remains, clearer and surer for all of this."[43]

Bayne was assigned to Committee V(B) on Baptism and Confirmation, chaired by Callen of Grahamstown. "It was a dreary committee, almost paralyzed by the protestantism of the Bishop of Sodor and Man, and the report was nothing to exclaim about." Bayne presented an address on the rite of Confirmation during the first week of the Conference. He recalled that he read from a manuscript, which was "not Done...at Lambeth Conferences."[44] This was his baptism of fire. He rehearsed the history of the initiation rite, from a two-part but unified act, to fragmentation, to the present ritual. He spoke of the pros and cons of the ritual in use in 1948 and urged revision. In the course of his address he spoke of what he, a new bishop liked about confirmation:

I like the sense of young boys and girls at the beginning of the mature life coming to affirm their intention to live up to their baptismal vows and to take their freely chosen places as members in the priestly body of the Church: I like the sense of grown men and

women turning their backs once for all on the world and asking
for a final and definitive rebirth as Christians and as Churchmen:
I like the sense of the Lord Jesus coming as close to mortal men
as He can and as I believe He does through the Bishop in Confirmation and accepting our promises and sealing us in His Kingdom
until the end of the world. It is those vivid impressions of what is
surely either a preposterous farce or else certain spiritual reality,
which, I am frank to say, count the most with me.[45]

This careful statement lay behind a popular tract Bayne wrote, *Now You
Are Confirmed*, published by Forward Movement in 1953.[46]

Stephen Bayne, as Bishop of Olympia, was also in attendance at the
Lambeth Conference of 1958. By now he occupied an important place
in Anglican affairs, being chairman of the Conference Committee on
the Family in Contemporary Society and a member of the Anglican
Consultative Body. As the conference began at Lambeth Palace in July,
he was at once aware of an atmosphere different from that of 1948,
a quicker realization of collegiality and a more rapid development of
that confidence necessary if people are to be utterly frank in their conversations with one another. Bayne attributed this in large part to the
meeting of the Anglican Congress in 1954. "Those marvelous ten days,"
he said, "of thought and discussion did more to make the Anglican
Communion a reality than any other thing that ever happened to us."
At Lambeth in 1958, "it was barely three days from the opening service before Indians were waggling their fingers at Americans and asking
how we knew so much about overpopulation, and did so little about
our wheat surplus, and Africans were admonishing Englishmen to remember that time was running out in the once dark continent."[47] In a
report to his diocese he put the case somewhat differently: Lambeth is
in a curious mood this year — everybody likes everybody so much that
we all seem reluctant to get involved in divisive issues, and it is hard
to get much radical thinking done unless you are willing to take strong
and sometimes passionate sides. I don't know that it is necessary to issue a world-shaking pronouncement every time we meet, actually. The
meeting itself, and the knitting-together of the immense, scattered brotherhood of the Church is really the thing that matters."[48] Indeed, he was
convinced that "Lambeth is like an iceberg; eight-ninths of it invisible
(being the conversation and relationships of 320 bishops from all over);
and one-ninth (the reports) doesn't give too accurate an idea of the true
depth of our meeting."

A large part of Lambeth 1958 for Bayne, and for Lucie and Lydia
who accompanied him, was social. Besides time spent with the Cuthbert Simpsons at Christ Church, Oxford, a preconference meeting at
Sheffield, and a trip to Dublin, Bayne was caught up in colorful, mov-

ing opening and closing services, luncheon with the Duke of Edinburgh, a Royal Garden party (attended by the Duke of Edinburgh, the Queen Mother, and Winston Churchill, though because of a sinus infection the Queen was not there), a great festival of choir music in the Albert Hall, a weekend with Archbishop Fisher and his wife at Canterbury (at the "Old Palace," "so called because it's conspicuously newer than Lambeth Palace, on the same principle that the bugler in the Grenadier Guards is called 'a drummer,' I suppose"), informal and formal dinners with bishops from all over the world, an Episcopal trip down the Thames to Greenwich, speaking engagements at Oxford, Canterbury, Westminster, and on the BBC, and much else, including at the last a reception held by the Queen for all of the bishops.

There were two weeks of very heavy work for Bayne as his committee met, either in plenary or in subcommittees. Their work was devoted to the drafting of a report, including resolutions requiring action by the Conference in its final sessions. Their meetings ran from 10:30 A.M. to 4:45 P.M. each day. Various drafting groups met before or after, and then, "if there is some particular point to be looked up or written, that has to be done at night after hours. So it means pretty unremitting work for nearly all; and after ten days, our tempers get short and we would give anything for a night's sleep." The work went well, however, and Bayne presented the report:

> The better part of three days I had to be on my feet on the plat-
> form, presenting, interpreting, defending our report, and trying to
> guide our eighteen or so resolutions through the debate. I was ex-
> hausted when Friday night came. . . . But I remembered some of the
> lessons I had learned in 1948 Lambeth, about how to fight hard
> when it was needed, and we managed to come out fairly well.
> In fact we accomplished a minor miracle, I think, in producing
> a report on family life and planning, in which we did not once
> use the words "birth control" or "contraceptive." (I had decided
> at the outset to avoid any phrases which were heavily charged
> emotionally; and the committee fully agreed.)[49]

On August 10, Archbishop Fisher bade farewell to the bishops af-
ter the final service. " 'I know that I shall never again see many of you, in this life. We shall never be together again, many of us. But we have learned a great truth' — and the tears were on his cheeks and on ours too, as he spoke — 'we have learned how deeply we are always together in the Spirit.' " Musing on this the same day, Bayne thought of the bishops returning to their sees, to treason trials in South Africa, to the heartbreaking problems of Southeast Asia, to a new United Church in Ceylon, to racial strife in Detroit, to wheat farms in Saskatchewan, to steel mills in Birmingham, "but," he wrote:

The unity of the Spirit is very great in us, and we pray that it
may equally be so with the forty millions whose shepherds it is
our honor to be.

Never underestimate the Anglican brotherhood. Forty million
is not many among the teeming hundreds of millions in the world.
But when we are faithful and obedient, and especially when we are
loyal to each other in the brotherhood, God can use us as He wills,
and make of us what He wills. I thank God daily, for the blessing
of being part of this great family, and I hope I shall always try to
live up to it.[50]

Two things were happening in relation to Lambeth 1958 that were
to be determinative in Bayne's future. One was his own concern for
the Anglican Communion, publicly expressed in the *Episcopal Overseas
Missions Review.* In his article, the critical nature of the times for the
Anglican Communion was indicated by numerous factors: "One is the
tangled world situation, and our need to rethink the whole grand strategy and significance of the Christian mission.... Another is the startling
change in the dynamics of our world society whereby the weak things of
the world are confounding the mighty — as in the new self-consciousness
and confident assertiveness of the indigenous peoples of the world, no
longer willing to accept their sometime role as wards of the West. And
there are yet other factors."[51] He then examined the situation in detail and emphasized the ecumenical development in world missions and
the challenge that this fact posed to those responsible for missionary
strategy. He concluded:

Missionary strategy and ecumenical strategy are inseparable —
that is the sum of what I have tried to say. The part our Communion will play in the world mission of the Church cannot be
understood apart from our part in ecumenical life. Our mission is
to help establish, among "every people, tongue, and nation," the
Catholic Church of Jesus Christ, fully rooted in the local community, yet fully sharing in the life of the whole Body. We shall not
do this alone, nor would we wish to. Therefore, missionary and
ecumenical strategy must be inseparable.[52]

Bayne was becoming known as one deeply committed both to the Anglican Communion and to the necessary development of missionary and
ecumenical strategy for the mid-twentieth century.

The other determinative happening was at the Conference itself.
While Bayne was absorbed in the considerations of the Family in Contemporary Society, others were considering the future of the Anglican
Communion. Resolutions 60 and 61 provided for the hiring of a full-
time officer, to be the executive officer of two existing inter-Anglican

bodies — the Advisory Council on Missionary Strategy and the Consultative Body of the Lambeth Conference — and through these agencies
the chief liaison officer of the entire Anglican Communion, to be known,
after some debate, as the Anglican Executive Officer. Bayne knew of this
action and wrote approvingly of it but could not have guessed that in
October following the close of Lambeth, Archbishop Fisher would be
sounding him out as to his availability for the job.

The Final Months

When Lambeth ended, Bayne went to St. Augustine's College, Canterbury, to give a series of talks. He then caught up with Lucie and Lydia
on the continent, eventually going by plane to Vienna and from there
to Moscow for a few days, leaving Russia and arriving in Helsinki,
Finland, at the beginning of September. He reported on his trip to the
diocese and in a series of dispatches to the *Seattle Times*. He mused on
the streak of violence among Russians, who seemed to erupt suddenly
over seemingly inconsequential matters; however, they also expressed
themselves in "mystical, joyous, studious, gloomy" streaks as well. They
could not be expected to be like twentieth-century Americans, Bayne
agreed, but he hoped they could be "good, 20th Century Russians, given
self-control and a rediscovery of the love of God and of the need for
humility toward life." He did not believe that the "present structure
of the Soviet State" would help in this, and he came out of Russia
more certain than ever that there is no way to short-circuit freedom.
"Mankind has only one way to learn how to be free, and that is by
practicing freedom and gradually learning the lessons of self-control
and responsible choice in which freedom rests."[53] He was impressed
by the many signs of the existence and life of Christianity in Russia:
"At the monastery of St. Sergius, at Zagorsk, where we worshiped and
spent several hours, it was difficult to find standing room, and the lines
visiting the shrine of the saint, or waiting for holy water...were inter-
minable. Perhaps fewer men than we would expect but many young
people, even a soldier or two."[54] He was impressed also by the "spar-
tan" character of life in Russia and the sabre rattling, but the latter
was true on both sides of the iron curtain. "I was prepared to be reminded at every hand of Soviet military might (including Sputnik); but
I don't know that I felt any more impressed by theirs than I would
have been at home with daily reminders in newspapers and radio of our
growing military capacity, 'massive retaliation,' and so on." On November 3, Bayne spoke to the Monday Club in Seattle and urged dialogue
and competition as keynotes of American policy toward Russia in the
years ahead.[55]

By that time, Bayne was thinking about the possibility of leaving

Olympia. The details concerning his becoming Anglican Executive Officer are discussed in Chapter 6. Here note must be taken of the fact that these thirteen years as Bishop of Olympia were Bayne's happiest years. From then on he was to be at the centers of power in the Anglican Communion and the Episcopal Church, where there was confusion and frustration. He was to be near the top but never at the top, Anglican Executive Officer but not the Archbishop of Canterbury, First Vice President of the Executive Council of the Episcopal Church, but not President, not Presiding Bishop. In 1958 there were many bishops prepared to vote for him for Presiding Bishop, but he was too young. What happened in the 1964 vote for the Presiding Bishop will be discussed later. Furthermore, his health was to deteriorate in large part because of exhaustion, anxiety, and eventually emphysema. He was a heavy cigarette smoker.

In accounting for the years in western Washington being the Camelot, halcyon days, the love affair of bishop with clergy and laity was primary. He could be demanding. In his convention address in 1951 he reflected on his reputation as a "tough bishop" specifically with regard to his demand that seminarians have a working knowledge of Greek, not be married in course, with some exceptions, and serve as deacons for an entire year.[56] But he was highly respected. The diocese had a bishop recognized as a leader not only in Olympia, but also in the nation and in the Anglican Communion, and the Episcopal Church in western Washington had an astounding record of growth under his leadership. Above all, he was a man of exceptional warmth, pastoral care, sympathy, and empathy.

Something of the personal character of Bishop Bayne's involvement with his diocese is reflected in his editorials in the diocesan paper, *The Olympian Churchman,* but more so in his instrument for personal contact with his clergy and others, *PIE.* It was "a generally weekly communique... begun by SFB in 1955." As he explained, the title "comes from the medieval Pica, the name given in England to the book of directions for saying the various services." He cited the Prayer Book in 1549 as speaking of "the number and hardness of the Rules called Pie... that to turn the Book only was so hard and intricate a matter, that many times there was more business to find out what should be read, than to read it when it was found out." "This," said Bayne, "seemed an admirable time-honored designation for a bishop's newsletter."[57]

PIE kept people in touch with what was going on in the diocese and with what the bishop was doing. It was also a means by which the bishop could remind his clergy about certain things, encourage them, and amuse them, raising sagging spirits when needed. There is, for instance, his description of a photograph of the clergy taken at Diocesan Convention in 1955. He said that it was an excellent photograph:

There are one or two sour balls only, and the radiant sun of the Bishop of Utah redeems us all. The Dean yearns from the midst, Charles Forbes is bashfully hiding behind Hugh Barnes, Matt Bigliardi is remarking, "I can lick any man in this outfit." Eng is the inscrutable Oriental, the Archdeacon is sternly virtuous, Price is sticking his tongue out at somebody, and a passing acquaintance has just handed Vincent Gowen a piece of Limburger cheese. In other words it's a darn good photo.[58]

PIE gave the bishop a place for expressing his frustrations and anger and a place for some educational promotion. Also in 1955 he wrote:

The inevitable mush-headed Vicar has put in his appearance in the Princess Margaret furore, I see. There could be a slightly Gilbert-and-Sullivanish flavor to the whole affair — royal background, star-crossed lovers, episcopal blunderbuss, aging clerical sap, now for the mustard and cress — if it weren't all so desperately troubling, no matter how you look at it. The lives of two people...her duty and his...a chaotic moral theology...a Church impotent to deal with an urgent contemporary problem...romantic individualism masquerading as the Gospel...is there anyone not moved to the deepest and most penitent intercession for all concerned? I hope there are many who pray with me for God's mercy and justice to prevail.[59]

In December 1955 there was the famed, oft-republished diatribe against Christmas in post-Christian American society, an Advent thought beginning, "I wonder how much longer people's nerves can stand it, the pre-Christmas orgy, I mean. Every carol in the book, nearly, has been sobbed, tinkled, whined, moaned, glamorized, inflated with tintinnabulus hot air until it has exploded."[60] In November 1958 he wrote of separation of church and state with regard to public education and reported that according to present policy his prayer at the inauguration of the new president of the University of Washington should have landed him "in the pokey. Mercifully, it didn't."[61] In the same month he had some sharp things to say about political parties in Washington State, ending his editorial with a "Harumph."[62]

In PIE, during Bayne's last months in the diocese, there were indications of the impending change: his acceptance of the Archbishop's appointment to be Anglican Executive Officer, the call for and election of a new bishop for Olympia, his resignation accepted by the House of Bishops with provision made for him to retain a seat, voice, and vote by virtue of his new office. Also there was great activity: the post-Lambeth discussions and post-General Convention reports given all over the diocese; election to the National (later Executive) Council of the Church and attendance at its first meetings; planning for the new office, for moving to London, for a smooth transition to the new bishop, and always the regular work of the bishop, in the last weeks assisted by Bishop Lewis, his successor.

As Bayne was struggling with the decision that resulted in his leaving the diocese, the Standing Committee spoke for everyone expressing pride in the fact that from among all the bishops of the Anglican Communion theirs should be chosen to be the first executive officer of the Communion. They saw the call as a testimony "to his capabilities as a devout and dedicated Christian minister, an energetic and resourceful organizer, and a profound teacher and disciple of our Lord." It was also testimony that his "unique talents and abilities . . . are needed in the new program for further expansion of the Church throughout the world." They concluded: "The Diocese of Olympia should be honored to be able to release its Bishop."[63] At his final diocesan convention, Bayne spoke of resentment at the idea of leaving:

> I can't say that I look forward to laying down my ministry with any easy contentment. When the Archbishop first asked me to do the new work, I must be frank to say that my first reaction was resentment. It was a fruitless reaction because I know that such decisions cannot be made with one's feelings. . . . But resentment was there, and it remains: I do not see how anybody could give up all this without heartbreak.[64]

He ended with these words:

> When I speak of the honor and privilege of these twelve years, I mean much more than simply the excitement of a growing diocese. That part of it has been child's play. What has mattered has been the ever-deepening sense of holiness in everyday things. Thousands of communicants or millions of dollars mean very little. A faithful family, fighting for its unity against odds, by the supernatural grace of God — a man bearing his faithful witness in his office — a woman giving herself in difficult and costly service to her community — boys and girls who are straight and true when all around them there is compromise and meanness — this is the ministry that really matters. And for this, and for the ideal of the single, holy body of Christ, which is the deepest treasure of this Diocese, I give the deepest thanks I know.
>
> I go now to a new work, perplexing, uncharted, mysterious. There have been many times, and there will be more, when my heart fails at the thought of the so great hope and dream, and of my utter incapacity for it.[65]

Five

THE BISHOP AS THEOLOGIAN

The Optional God (1953)

During his very busy days as Bishop of Olympia, Bishop Bayne did some of his best writing. As was noted in the last chapter, much of what appeared in books was hammered out in lectures given over several years. The work was done because he felt called to write and teach. Here was his vocation and his avocation. "Writing is a pleasure," he said, "because it's such a wonderfully disciplined way to get one's thoughts organized. In my writing I try to float ideas, and try to avoid both too much bounce and too little."[1] It was during these years that Bayne wrote *The Optional God* — "the only book I ever liked writing and then afterward too." The immediate genesis of the book was in his writing the Paddock Lectures, delivered at the General Theological Seminary in New York during February 1952. "The invitation," he said, "was a flattering one, for the lectureship was as imposing as any in the Episcopal Church" and had been "adorned by as great a Christian thinker as William Temple." He recalled later that the lectures were roughed out during ten days at Palm Beach, California, made possible by the Hodges, "two Seattle friends." He then had "the better part of three weeks at Chelsea Square [The General Seminary], finishing and delivering them."[2]

Harvey Guthrie, who heard the lectures and wrote an introduction to the 1980 reprint of the book, was deeply impressed and rightly observed that "*The Optional God* addresses itself to the phenomenon of the 'post-Christian world,' the world Christians began to be aware of as the setting for their life and thought as the twentieth century moved past its halfway point. It is concerned with the same set of realities to which Dietrich Bonhoeffer spoke, and indeed appeared at just about the same time as English translations of Bonhoeffer's writings began to appear."[3]

The basis for the entire book was presented in a paragraph at the very beginning. This statement was a distillation of much of his thought in past years and provided the theory that was to be explained and tested in the succeeding chapters.

There is a belief, held commonly enough in our world, that the religious issue — the question of the reality of God — is a side issue. We do not readily deny God's existence (at least Western man does not); but we look at the possibility of God as at best a helpful supplement to the real dynamics of life. It makes no fundamental difference whether he exists or not. It is useful to Western society to believe in Him, and such belief is to be commended; on the other hand, the basic activities of our democracies must be constructed to get along without Him. In the words I use as a title, God is optional.[4]

In the first chapter, Bayne expanded on this paragraph. In Chapters 2–5 he expanded his theory, as Guthrie says, not "theoretically, but in terms of four realities": (1) the state, (2) the educational system, (3) human vocation and work, and (4) the freedom and individuality in which human selfhood must be grounded. "As a flare suddenly illuminates the dark," Guthrie states, "so that things can be seen clearly for a moment in the night, the book clarifies what it means to live in a secular world by illuminating basic realities and activities of human experience."[5] The final chapter, "The Church and the Kingdom," is a fit conclusion, eloquent and challenging.

Bayne insisted that twentieth-century Christians live in a post-Christian world. It is a world in which words such as freedom, man, and individuality are Christian words, but divorced from their context. He wrote: "The tools, the words we use in this world of the optional God are tools that still bear the Christian form and fit the Christian signs. . . . They involve meanings and choices that often confuse issues and darken counsel; they presuppose beliefs no longer understood; they are too big for secular man alone for they assume a stature in man which, without God, he does not have."[6] Furthermore, Bayne insisted that this optionalism involved the Church, confined by the society to the arena of "religion" and excluded from the main issues of daily life.

Thus the Church is secularized. He commented, "A curious consequence of this is that the more purely 'religious' we become — the more of the world we leave out of the Church — the easier it is to leave out God too." He mused on how many sermons there are that could be preached without any mention of God and how susceptible Anglicanism is to optionalism. "More at home in the world than other companies of Christian people, we are too often of the world, too." He viewed the irrelevancy of much contemporary Christianity, fringe sects and charismatics, neo-orthodoxy: "Great segments of both Protestant and Catholic thought now practically identify the Gospel and a liberal-Republican interpretation of the free-enterprise system, to the advantage of neither." In this Bayne located "the heart of the problem of the Church's mission to society."

It is a society dominated by a myth — that the question of God is a secondary question. That myth has an effect on the Church as destructive as its effect on the State, the school, industry...indeed everything in our lives. Is the answer to the myth of Optionalism simply to damn the secular society as "bad" — to say that it is an enemy and that the Church's job is to destroy it or flee from it?[7]

In the chapters that follow Bayne intended to answer this question, but here he claimed that one must not be too quick to condemn, knowing "how great are the gifts that Christian faith has made the modern society" and remembering and using "the words still lambent with Christian meanings." Thus the critic who is quick to condemn secular society "will accept and understand the institutions around him....He will understand that ours is, in the phrase a 'post-Christian society,' living on inherited wealth." And he will be sensitive to the great harm the Church, imbued with optionalism, has perpetrated on secular man and secular society.[8]

In a chapter on "Community and Communion," Bayne attempted to determine the proper role of the Church in a post-Christian world, in relation to the State. He rejected the notion that there is any form of the State that can realistically be called "Christian," and he rejected three possible attitudes toward the State: withdrawal, partnership, or identity. The Church in his view is *"a community in communion."*

She is the type of community from which other communities should draw their strength. She is the vessel of judgment, of the perpendicular Word which keeps a narcissistic society from idolizing itself. She is the truly radical body in society, eternally vigilant for the free minorities, eternally inventive to improvise new social and political solutions to timeless needs. She is the medicine against a State that tries to be its own justification because she asks always the question, 'To whom are you offering what you do, and who will value it and use it?' She is the household where men are accepted as they are, and where they meet one another in dignity and gentleness, and in a common hope which carries them all together.[9]

This is the Church's mission in a post-Christian society.

Bayne emphasized (1) the fundamental importance of education in a free society for the transmission of knowledge and for the preparation of responsible citizens capable of knowing when and how to choose and to take sides; (2) the failures of our educational institutions in doing

what they are meant to do; (3) the falsity in concluding that state education is good in itself; and (4) the importance of independent schools.
He attacked the flabbiness of most teaching and learning, especially the
method of mediocrity cultivated in the name of some vague concept
of egalitarianism. The Church's mission in relation to education in a
post-Christian world he described by elucidating two words, two key
concepts — *penetration* and *partnership*. "At every point and in every
way it is the Church's duty to society to leaven the lump." This means
reinforcing teaching as a "Christian ministry," "the writing of books,
and the planned and coherent invasion of graduate studies," and involvement by Christians in P.T.A.'s and the like. By penetration he meant
Church maintenance of independent schools and the Church's cultivation of her own teaching, understanding more clearly what she ought to
teach. "Partnership," he said, "means . . . the creative fermenting conflict
of a better idea and a fuller understanding of the truth, with the partial
truth and the half-understanding of the secular view."[10]

In the fourth chapter of *The Optional God,* Bayne began by quoting from a World Council of Churches pamphlet: "In modern society
the divine purpose of work is distorted and *the dignity of work is not
respected.* This has been the cause of much of the present moral and
spiritual chaos." Modern man is uneasy and discontented. In the natural order of things he expects to find his dignity in society through his
work. In actuality, his work denigrates his human dignity. The problem
is then a very deep one and is located in the moral structure of the community. "Either man is the master of his work, or its slave; and whether
he will be the master or not depends not on industrial or economic factors but on theological factors. Man is a theological problem. Work is
a theological problem. And an impersonal industrial community simply
cannot create meaning or assign value."[11]

Apart from God, or in a situation of optionalism, the good life has
been defined "entirely in terms of producing, buying, and selling. It is
the 'egoism' of the industrial society, which arrogates to itself, sucks up
into itself the value-giving functions of society, that has cheated man out
of one of his fundamental joys." Over against such a view, Bayne speaks
of "a society to which the act of oblation is the final and concluding
act of the whole inventive process." As to the Church's mission in this
sphere, he refers again to penetration, to vocation in the fullest sense of
that word, to a recovery of the lost unity of prayer and work, and to
"the rediscovery of an ancient wholeness to life."[12]

In his chapter on "Freedom and Individuality" Bayne developed his
subject matter differently. It may have been because as he was preparing
his lectures in his room at the General, someone in the next room was
playing a recording of the *St. John Passion*.[13] His attention was focused
on the Cross — "the story of freedom." Here, he said, "enthroned at

the heart of life, is the free man; and in some extraordinary way we find ourselves explained and justified in Him. Even if the end is tragedy, foolishness, still the writing of the story of the Passion in every man's heart is the only way to peace and to a secure selfhood for him." The crisis of modern times is found in "the deliberate attempt to choke out of man that part of him to which the Cross speaks and which the Cross illuminates," his freedom and individuality, his selfhood. He viewed the critical struggle in the opposition of the barbarian for "whom freedom and individuality are ridiculous" and "the civilized man, the child of the Cross, to whom the precarious adventure of selfhood and society itself is always a story of the particular and individual man choosing his way into selfhood, choosing his way toward excellence, and wearing civilized life as he goes in the very fabric of his arduous choices. The civilized man is the one to whom freedom and individuality are the most precious things he knows. For them he is prepared to sacrifice all other gifts." Bayne's ultimate point is that liberalism, the bulwark against the State and statism, without commitment to God leads to totalitarianism and that "without the Cross, freedom would be impossible."[14]

He has more to say on the matter here in this chapter and elsewhere, but he has emphasized what is to him central. He concludes:

Christianity offers no easy, neat, managed universe....

Christianity offers only sharp and clear selfhood, worked out in a myriad of choices.... It offers him only the freedom to write what story he will with his life....

Christianity requires all his freedom in return....

The immeasurable gift of God is that in this bondage, and in it alone, is man set free from the bondage of the world.... This bondage is what makes it possible for man to recognize and cherish his brother. It is what makes it possible for a man to be himself.[15]

What is the Church's task in all of this? The Church's task here, as in all else, is to be the Church and nothing else, the people whose lives — all of their lives — are informed by the Cross.

In the final chapter, "The Church and the Kingdom," Bayne discussed the Church and the weakening of its own interior "witness and integrity by the alien spirits of the world." Among such spirits he numbered and discussed the spirit of the sect, as opposed to the spirit of the Church, the loss of a sense of the supernatural, and optionalism. Once more he found in penetration and partnership words descriptive of the mission of the Church in a hostile and indifferent world. Penetration of contemporary society involves the Church in painful relativities and ambiguities where difficult choices must be made. In the Kingdom and in the Church choices must be made in response to God, who in his love called into creation out of nothing the world and all that is in it and calls us still toward perfection, eliciting the response of love in freedom and communion — created love answering creating love in offering all to God from whence all things come. He said:

> As in the Kingdom, so is it in the Church. The heart of the Church is an offering. Creed and Bible and ministry and sacraments all minister to something quite outside of themselves. They are meaningless as ends in themselves.... We say, "I believe in God. — I stake my life on God; and I offer my life to Him whom I trust." The Church is the locus of the universal offering that fulfills Creation and opens the door of the Kingdom. The Church is the Creation, offering and being offered. The Church is the breaking crest of the wave of the Universe returning to Him from whom it comes. The Church is existence itself, fulfilled and being fulfilled in the endless and inexhaustible liturgy of the time.[16]

His plea from the midst of a post-Christian world that treats God as optional is that the Church be the Church. There is in this a strong insistence that the "Kingdom and the Church are continuous with all of life" and that "the Cross is not a religious fact," but, "part of humanity ...the massive symbol to which all life conforms, believing or not believing." God was not optional for Bayne. The question of God was no side issue. In all of this discussion he stimulated those who heard him and those who read his book to see both their lives in post-Christian society and the Kingdom and the Church in new, challenging, hopeful ways. The gospel became once more, as it always is, "the heaven and the Light."

Bayne, the theologian, was constantly teaching, and as he taught he was organizing his thoughts. There were lesser occasions, at confirmations, when speaking before service organizations, and at Bishop's Evenings, but there were also greater occasions. We have noted the lectures he gave at the congress celebrating the Centennial of the Diocese of Christchurch in New Zealand. There were also lectures given at the fall convocation of Hobart and William Smith Colleges, November 8–9, 1957. They were on creation and monotheism and are noteworthy in part because in them he identified his theological stance as incarnational (hence the doctrine of Creation) and Anglican.[17] He was dealing with a theological stance that involved overcoming the sacred-secular dichotomy without, however, obscuring the struggle that must go on between the Church and post-Christian society.

He began, in his first lecture, with insistence that Anglicanism is creedal and incarnational, and in this, free from bondage to any particular systematic theology or philosophy. This can be and sometimes is regarded as a weakness, but, said Bayne, we like it that way.

We like good Anglican books which have the theological consistency of a good, nourishing, French peasant soup, starting with a sound stock, and added to day by day with whatever happens to be left over — a dash of Platonism, some Aristotelian greens, a Calvinist bone or two, a Lutheran turnip, a spoonful of Kierkegaard, a pinch of Temple, then brought to a quick boil with group dynamics, and pushed to the back of the stove to cool a bit! This is the kind of thinking we like to do, but it is infuriating to the orderly mind.[18]

Bayne recognized that such eclecticism had its dangers. It could represent "intellectual laziness and a refusal to cope with the persistent problems of our time." He concluded: "Anglicanism's restless refusal to accept any universal, over-riding philosophy is a very fine thing if it bears its fruit of intellectual leadership and aggressive thought. But if it ends simply in a series of historical relevancies, it is no true child of God at all."

The Anglican emphasis on the doctrine of the Incarnation he attributed to "the peculiar fascination history holds for us." There is the strong conviction involved in this "that human history is the theatre in which the leadership of the Holy Spirit is expressed. It is small wonder that we are by temperament inclined to center our thought around God in history." Bayne pointed to the appeal, at the heart of the sixteenth-century Settlement in England, to history and to the insistence on expressing the "Church" idea in an age of sectarianism. Another reason for the Anglican's peculiar theological stance he identified in "the timeless suspicion" that "no speculation and no theory can usurp the place rightfully held for moral conduct and Christian life." All intellectual adventures must stand the test of conduct. Bayne concluded:

"Man's unity, certainly the unity of the Christian body, will not be found in any theory. It will be found only in the simple charity of the common acts and common brotherhood of the followers of Christ. Therefore at the heart of any teaching of Christianity there must stand the unique and unexampled figure of Christ and His authoritative teaching."[19]

Bayne the theologian was certainly eclectic and not bound to any specific systematic theology or philosophy. His inspiration came from many places: from T. S. Eliot, *Little Gidding* and *The Rock;* from Lancelot Andrewes, whom he cited often; from Nicholas Berdyaev and Ortega y Gassett; from Peter Drucker and J. H. Oldham; from all those he mentioned when talking about education at General in the early 1930s; and in particular from his teachers, Burton Scott Easton and Frank Gavin, to whom he dedicated his book, *The Optional God.* It is probable that he was also influenced by Karl Barth on Romans, by Reinhold Niebuhr, and possibly by existentialist theologians. At the outset of his Hobart lectures he mentioned Gore and Temple and DuBose.

Thus far we have been observing the development of Stephen Bayne's key ideas and doctrines in relation to his concern to expose the falsities of modern society, to uncover God's will for the post-Christian world, and to engage people in the kind of dialectical processes of analysis and thought that avoid both sentimental optimism and despair-ridden pessimism. He wanted to focus attention on reality — the reality of our error and our pain, our impending suicide as a civilization, and the reality of the Cross as both judgment and actual hope. His thought was systematic, but he, rather like F. D. Maurice in some respects, eschewed systems. He explained himself this way:

> All Christian doctrine is more akin to biology than it is to philosophy, for all Christian doctrine is organically related to God's supreme revelation of Himself in Christ the Incarnate Lord. There is, therefore, a unity to Christian doctrine like the unity in the body of Christ, a common life which holds all members together and keeps them alive and healthy. And, with this, there is also a clear subordination in Christian doctrine, for all must be tested and proved by the supreme revelation. We speak of this as the test of Scripture, for it is in Scripture that the supreme revelation is recorded. But the ultimate test is not one of words but of a Person; and in Him all the life and thought of the Church must be rooted.[20]

How was *The Optional God* received? By and large the reviews of the book were simply descriptive and laudatory. Roy Elliott wrote to say, "It is all human, in the very best sense, vital and beautiful in a fine way, brilliant."[21] The *Church Times* identified the author as an "American Liberal," praised the chapter on "Freedom and Individuality" as "a noble piece of writing, in which the 'liberal' gives of his best," but considered the final chapter less satisfactory. "It is true," the reviewer said, "that few are found nowadays to defend anathemas and excommunications, but there should be limits even to comprehensiveness." What irritated was Bayne's reference to the historic creeds as "our war songs...our family saga." Said the reviewer: "A rhetorical peroration leaves the reader with a sense of vagueness and uncertainty, unlike the clarity of the Gospel message. The Church is to 'give thanks for all truth and for the indomitable purposes of all men of goodwill': to 'bear her witness...in company with any who will talk with her.' "[22] In such statements Bayne was echoing the sentiments of many leaders of Anglicanism and expressing a conviction that would be questioned in the late 1970s and 1980s. But as will be seen, Bayne was himself concerned to

promote the theological enterprise; he despaired of theological sloppi-
ness and mindless action in the Church. He resisted theological rigidity,
but he was not a vapid liberal.

Christian Living (1957)

Bayne's major contribution in the field of Christian Ethics and Moral
Theology was published in 1957 as a part of the "Church's Teaching
Series." That series had its origin, as Bayne recalled at Bookbinders
Restaurant, Philadelphia, at the time of the 1946 General Convention,
when Bayne and John Heuss "were brooding over the extraordinary (as
it then seemed) state of disunity in the church."[23] They came "to the
conclusion that one thing needed, of many, was a try at setting some
unitive norms — indeed the first official, general statements the Episcopal Church would ever have had — of what its central beliefs were."
John Heuss, as the chief executive for the National Council's Department of Christian Education, also saw the advantage of having such a
series as a basis for a new church school curriculum. He began work on
six volumes ranging from Scripture and History to Theology and Ethics,
culminating in volumes on Liturgics and "The Episcopal Church and
Its Work."

Authors' Committees were established for each volume, and as Bayne
recounts it, the committee for the volume on Christian Ethics and
Moral Theology had a particularly difficult time. At least two authors attempted the task without success. In 1955 Bayne was asked to
undertake it.

> Over the closing months of that year and most of 1956, the book
> was written — in trains, planes, the Bishop's House, wherever an
> hour or two could be found. As manuscript for a chapter or two
> was ready, it was sent to Margaret Lockwood for transcription.
> Then in a day or so of conference with the Authors' Committee
> at 281 [Fourth Avenue, New York], the draft would be discussed,
> criticized, subjected to every possible challenge — then remanded
> to SFB for rewriting, as his own judgment dictated. The Committee
> differed sharply about many things, but in the end it was agreed
> that it must be the author's book, not the Committee's. Perhaps
> the only abiding major decision in the Committee was as to Part I,
> which seemed to a sizable minority to be too theoretical, difficult,
> abstract . . . and so it remained, no doubt. The Preface was carefully
> written with this in mind.[24]

The committee was composed of a prestigious company: John Coburn,
Powel Dawley, Robert Dentan, Joseph Fletcher, John Heuss, David

Hunter, Leon McCauley, John Midworth, James Pike, Norman Pittenger, Massey Shepherd, C. W. F. Smith, William Sydnor, T. O. Wedel,
and Moran Weston.

Bayne described his book as concerned with the "what" of Christian
living, rather than the "how." He explained that the first part, the part
the committee tried to alter, was a kind of prologue — "a connected
and thoughtful essay about Freedom" — setting forth a theme that runs
through all of the rest of the book. He allowed that the reader need not
read the chapter on freedom first, but it is clear that he would prefer
that a reader come to grips with this fundamental theme before launching into the chapters on more specific, practical topics. Part II concerns
"Personal Life, Family, and Work," Part III, "Church, Community, and
Nation," and Part IV, "National and International Life." The book ends
with an epilogue, — which Bayne called "a brief summary."

Part I begins with the assertion that "the heart of this book is exactly this faith that *responsible freedom is the secret of man's existence
under God.*" This assertion is based on the conviction "that when God
became man, He did so completely, not evading or shrinking the necessity of freedom but assuring and fulfilling it.... This freedom itself, with
all its puzzles, its costly and confusing choices, *is the very means of our
communion and partnership with God.*" Freedom is, then, a fact, but it
has limitations in terms of time and space, knowledge, and what Bayne
called "the divided self," or "the impurity of our own motives." There
is also the imperfect nature of the possible choices themselves, the "frustrating grayness of most of our problems." And finally, there is the truth
that an awareness of freedom *"simultaneously awakens in us a sense of
obligation and personal responsibility."* He wrote:

> The conscientious person who faces the fact of an inescapable
> choice and thinks deeply about it perceives that there is a clear and
> haunting sense of obligation about the choice he is to make. It is
> not simply that, because he is human, he must therefore choose be-
> tween the alternatives life offers. It is something deeper than that.
> It is the discovery that, when he makes a choice, his own deepest
> self is somehow involved.[25]

We are sensitive to the realization in our depths that "we are in some
way responsible to somebody or something for our choice and its consequences." For Christians, that somebody is God, of course; but we are
also obligated, Bayne said, to ourselves and our neighbors. He ended
this discussion with the assertion that Christ is our exemplar in freedom.
"Most clearly — and this is perhaps the deepest truth about freedom —
He teaches us that the final end of freedom is *offering.*" Once more, as
in *The Optional God,* he points to the Cross:

The supreme moment of freedom in the Gospel is the moment of the Cross, when, "Himself the Victim and Himself the Priest," Christ offers Himself and all humanity and all the creation with Himself and in Himself to the Eternal Father, in the most final and inclusive terms this life holds. The rewriting of the creation with the Creator in this free act of offering, despite the sin which entangles and corrupts our freedom and made the Cross necessary — no, rather accepting, absorbing, redeeming that sin — that reuniting offering is the ultimate secret of our redemption "from inside."[26]

It was in the light of this understanding that Bayne discussed "workaday matters," the detailed aspects of Christian living that he defined as *the way in which we learn to bring all of our separate activities, thoughts, impulses, and decisions into one, so that we are one and whole. Thus we can offer the whole of our life to God in the supreme act of freedom.* The first practical matter he treated was the "personal religious life." We are reminded that for Bayne there was the closest possible relation between Ascetical Theology and Moral Theology, just as there was between Dogmatic Theology and Moral Theology. The Christian is the "friend of God" and the "son of God," and is obligated to pray, to fast, and to give alms. Prayer is "thinking about God, or thinking about ourselves and our neighbors in the presence of God." Fasting concerns "the whole area of the discipline of our bodies and their appetites." And almsgiving concerns "the whole field of what we call 'Christian service.' " Here are the necessary disciplines for Christian living.[27]

Bayne then considers "Sex in Marriage," "Children in the Home," "Money and Stewardship," "Vocation and Its Problems," "The Nature of the Church," "Ecumenical Churchmanship," and "The Churchman in the Church" before plunging into consideration of "The Churchman in Politics" and "The Churchman in His Community." In the last part of the book, "National and International Life," Bayne wrote on "The Churchman and the State," "The International Community," "The Structure of Liberty," and "Christian Patriotism."

In all of these particular considerations, the main theme is a governing force. Thus, for instance, he wrote in his chapter on "Sex in Marriage": "Marriage is a way of life which makes it possible for men and women, through their differences, to serve God and their neighbor and to establish a full and rich companionship for themselves and their children." Concerning money, he wrote, "Until we learn that our money either serves us or we serve it — until we get to the point of seeing that the use of our money is both the means and the greatest test of our freedom — we have not really mastered the lesson." Writing about vocation, he concluded, "Our imperfect acts, done as well as we can do them and offered to God with a humble and trusting love — this is the heart of our vocation."[28]

Bayne wrote at a time when the civil rights movement was underway. He believed that in the struggle for the rights for all people the "essential ingredient will be a willingness to entrust ourselves to God. . . . This is as true for the Negro taking his adventurous steps in a new kind of life as for the white man. The courage to endure suffering, even to offer that suffering in reparation for the long years of man's inhumanity to man, is the highest gift of faith as well as the clearest test of it."[29] In dealing with "The International Community" Bayne reiterated many of the things he had been saying all along, but he emphasized the commitment Christians have to international community, belonging as they do to "an international community far older and far more widespread than any other in human history." This internationalism involves nothing less than the entirety of mankind, for it acknowledges as Lord the One who is the Savior of the world. Bayne realized the reality of nuclear weapons dealing the "death-blow to the old idea of national sovereignty," and he underscored "the urgent necessity for a more effective organization of humanity's life and resources than the old system of absolute sovereignties could possibly give."[30]

In the epilogue, Bayne summarized the principles that should be involved in and permeate discussions and decisions of all such work-a-day matters and any others. At the heart is freedom, for "Christian living is an adventure in freedom," and freedom is a matter of choice, choice that infects everything in life. "It is through our choices that we first discover ourselves. *What we are is what we choose.*" Furthermore, Christians acknowledge that God gives us this freedom, obliges us to choose and be judged by our choices, but does not leave us there. "God so loved the world that He came inside our freedom Himself, and showed us how to use it aright." Indeed, now, our Christian living is a personal encounter and dialogue with God. Such dynamic living is characterized by "offering" — to God and to our neighbor in a myriad of ways, day by day, in the choices we make. Fundamental to this understanding is Bayne's conviction:

> God put freedom into His created universe in order that the universe could respond to His love with an answering love of its own. . . . He put into the created universe a principle of choice; and He paid a twofold price for that. First, He limited His own freedom to have everything His own way. Second, He committed Himself to having to win out of freedom what he could perfectly easily have commanded as of right.
>
> Why did He do this? . . . He did it because He is love, and because love needs an answering love for love's sake.

His last word was this: *"To live as a Christian is then to follow always the way of offering, with Him, in Him, and through Him, Jesus Christ our Lord."*[31]

The book was substantial, a work of art, with a majestic theme. It was also a work of courage, for its success or failure depended upon the author's ability to sustain that which in some parts of society is highly debatable and even ridiculous. The book witnessed to Bayne's consistency and the comprehensive nature of his human understanding and theological skill. It was widely read and used for the next twenty years. By the end of 1970, 38,660 copies had been sold, and it was still in print.[32] Furthermore, Bayne was to continue working out the implications of the basic theory for the rest of his life.

Christian Living was the basic text for the School of Worship held at the Cathedral of St. John the Divine, New York, in 1957, at which Bayne gave the opening address on "Freedom and the Free Man."[33] Also in 1952, Bayne attended and spoke at Kenyon College at a conference on "The Essentials of Freedom." This conference was devised in 1954 by Gordon Chalmers, president of Kenyon, "during a time of widespread controversy about freedom within the nation's life." Bayne's address "was by way of being a sermon — at any rate a statement embodying an Anglican theological point of view."[34] He ended with a clear and forceful assertion: "To learn how to offer one's self and one's life, in whatever vocation, to the glory of God and for the love of the brethren, this is the finest fruit and gift of freedom."[35] And in 1959, Bayne, as leader of the Diocese of Michigan Adult Conference at Cranbrook, Michigan, gave a series of talks on freedom. Preaching on John 15:1–16, he said: "The time was to come when we would see that the highest freedom of all would be that man, free and understanding, chose the service of God whose service alone is perfect freedom."[36]

There were also opportunities to deal with the "workaday matters." At Lambeth 1958 he chaired the conference committee on the Family in Contemporary Society and wrote its report. The report affirmed three things: (1) "The human family is the creation of God, as a basic unit of society." The relationships that family members have are not the only relationships, but they are the first and are therefore of consummate importance, providing "a given status and place for children as they begin their earthly course." (2) The family is regarded as a school for mature life. "The family is the God-given environment within which souls are born, to learn first the lessons of human individuality and dignity, of responsible freedom and redemptive love: the lessons which in due course must be lived out in the wider and deeper associations of humanity in Christ." (3) The family is not an end in itself. "The tie of blood is the first tie in life but not the final one. The final one is established by Holy Baptism, the fellowship of grace, of redeemed humanity, in which we are all called to take our part."[37] The committee affirmed that procreation is not the only purpose of marriage; therefore sexual intercourse is a means of expressing love. It is not "the only language of earthly love," but it is the most intimate. The committee encouraged family planning and, in a manner conducive to its chairman's teachings on freedom, emphasized that family planning ought to be the result of "thoughtful and prayerful Christian decisions." The means are largely a matter of "clinical and aesthetic choice," they said.[38] At the same time, Bayne, as a member of the General Convention Joint Commission on Holy Matrimony, was expressing his consternation at the commission's inability to reach a consensus on the revision of the marriage canons. The Joint Commission was disbanded, but Bayne was convinced that out of the turmoil there would come another commission. The problem lay in the attempt of the canons to give two schools of thought — one school committed to the indissolubility of marriage and one to pastoral concerns — equal place in the Church's discipline, or so Bayne believed.[39]

Bayne also continued speaking on and thinking about education. In the *Pi Lambda Theta Journal*, he wrote of education having as its central task that "of preparing boys and girls to take their part in the corporate experiment and adventure in loyalty" that is democracy.[40] In 1955 he spoke at the Kent School Seminar on the Christian Idea of Education, giving what he later regarded as "really a commencement address — the 'summation'... or a celebration of 'the idea of the unity of truth (which) permeated the seminar.'"[41] He said:

The fundamental thought underlying nearly everything that we would want to say about the Christian idea of education is that God is the teacher.... Therefore when we look at our earthly partnership with Him, we see certain qualities that we must have....

The first test of teaching is that it tell the truth....

The second test of teaching as the Christian looks at it is the test of wholeness....

The third test goes by the name of excellence....

Let me add two more tests.... One is that of discrimination; of being able to tell the difference between the important and unimportant things in life, true and false.

The last of all, I take it that all true teaching aims to teach mankind how to take sides.... The end of truth is not neutrality. ...The end of learning is that we may discover, in freedom and humanity, and with mature discrimination, how to take sides.[42]

In 1949 Bayne had published an article in *The Living Church* supporting John Heuss preparatory to the 1949 General Convention in San Francisco. The article applauded attention being given to adults by the

National Council's Department of Christian Education and spoke of what should be taught in the Sunday Schools of the Episcopal Church, concluding: "If a man has any right at all to give his allegiance to the Prayer Book and to the American family, it comes from the prior claim of the Church to teach the historic faith in a way fit for free men to know it and practice it."[43] In 1957–58 Bayne chaired a commission that arranged for colloquies on the Church and the universities held at the College of Preachers in Washington, D.C,. and at the Cathedral of St. John the Divine.[44]

In an address given at the 34th National Recreation Congress in 1952, Bishop Bayne considered another workaday matter — play and recreation. He spoke of the Christian doctrine of play, which he regarded as related to the Christian doctrine of work — "opposite sides of the same coin." He began with a basic theological understanding expressed in three points: (1) "man is whole and single"; (2) "his spiritual wholeness is the ultimate end of all that he does and all that he is"; and (3) "his work and his play alike derive their meaning from the fundamental quest to be a mature and full and single person." Play and work belong together; play is the partner of work. He wanted people to take play seriously and recognize the important part it had in relation to the denigration of work in modern, industrial society. If a person's "work seems trivial and unimportant, it may be within his play that he will discover something which to him will be important enough to hold his whole attention and his whole will. The less that he puts himself into his job, it may be that the more he will put himself into his play and so become a person through his hobbies and through his play."[45]

At the invitation of a local Mason, Bishop Bayne gave a talk in October 1948 on the family of nations and its dependence on the household of faith for the creation of that frame of mind, that spirit necessary for the achievement of world peace and brotherhood. He described the crisis of the time as due to the "terrible, lonely emptiness at the heart of what used to be the Great Civilization." Basing his convictions in part at least on the Europe he was able to observe while at Lambeth the previous summer, he spoke of "uncertainty as to the nature of mankind, the uncertainty as to his rights of freedom and to dignity, the uncertainty as to his very being and destiny, that deep and dark question as to which came first, man or the state." He asked, "What is a civilization?" His answer was this: "It's the way people think about their fellow men, that's what a civilization is. It is the dignity and gentleness with which men deal with one another. It is the standard of responsibility which guides men and judges men in their own consciences as to the way they're doing their business. It is the reality and the fidelity with which men cleave to ideals."[46]

In a talk on capitalism given as an after-dinner speech for the Pacific

States Association, he reminded the business men before him "that the fundamental structure of American business is built not on techniques or money or products, but it is built on people."[47] He was much concerned to understand the quality of American history and American life. At the Monday Club in Seattle, he presented a paper chiefly about Robert E. Lee, but also on Abraham Lincoln. In Lee he located the key to his Christianity and his citizenship in the sense of duty or obedience — doing his duty as he was able to see it, "with as pure motives and as great charity as God" gave him.[48] At Williamsburg, Virginia, he spoke on "Christian Responsibility of Citizenship and Leadership."[49]

On April 8, 1958, Bayne spoke during the eleventh annual seminar of the Allied Daily Newspapers, held at the University of Washington in Seattle, on "What Is the Responsibility of the Press in the Scientific Age?" The press, he said, "is the selective interpreter of a society to itself." This "selective interpreting" it does under three specific conditions:

First, it bears the *necessary discipline of the written word.* . . .

The second condition is that the Press must understand and share the living tradition of its society. . . .

Now, third, I would put down as a condition of your task *a steady understanding of man's hope.* What is important to us — what should be reported to us mortals who read your papers is the news of what has happened which bears on our present necessity and therefore on our hopes of what may be.[50]

These are but a few examples of Bayne the theologian/ethicist applying his fundamental understanding of human existence and theological truth in terms of freedom, responsibility, redemptive love, and offering in workaday matters. He viewed all in the light of the Cross, but this did not mean that his attentions were limited to an area called religion. The gospel concerns all of life, and this concern he was prepared to interpret, as accurately and as responsibly as he could with Leaven and with Light, whatever issues confronted post-Christian society.

Enter with Joy (1961); *In the Sight of the Lord* (1958)

In addition to his books on theology, largely apologetics and ethics, Stephen was engaged in thinking through his understanding of preaching in the liturgical setting. On that basis he did some teaching about preaching, and he preached widely, some of his sermons being published in the *Harper Book for Lent, 1958.* He understood that dogmatics led to living the faith and proclaiming the gospel in a world that was either indifferent or hostile. Bayne was prone to protest that preaching was not his forte. Yet he was widely known as an effective, even exemplary preacher. In February 1956 he gave the George Craig Stewart Lectures at the Seabury-Western Theological Seminary. He thought enough of them to send out mimeographed copies to the clergy of the Diocese of Olympia in Advent 1959 "as a sort of valedictory gift," and he allowed them to be printed by Seabury Press as the last four chapters in *Enter with Joy* (1961). He may have believed "that to give such talks on a foundation honoring one of our American Church's greatest preachers was an act of presumption which verged on the lunatic,"[51] but what he had to say was valued, and the talks possessed a certain wisdom that is not easily refuted with the passage of time.

In his lectures he admitted that a sermon is many things, but he chose to emphasize, as the basic definition, the sermon as conversation or dialogue. A sermon is "the personal communication of the word of God, spoken and heard within the congregation, under the common judgment and love of God, preparing the way for Christ to act. To preach is to make such a communication, and the sermon is the communication."[52] He focused upon the preacher as the priest responsible for the conduct of all worship, including the sermon.

> Because the sermon is communication, and the personal communication of the preacher in his congregation, the "spirituality" of the preacher is bound to be a prime element in the whole transaction. I say "spirituality" in distinction from such other factors as his intellectual acumen or his semantic skill or his competence at organizing his material. I do not doubt that, other things being equal, it helps a preacher to be bright and to be able to use the English language. But one of the puzzling things about preaching as you reflect on it is that those factors tend to slide into the background, and our reflection to be monopolized by another factor, namely the spirituality of the preacher. What kind of person he is, is infinitely more important than how much he knows or how well he is able to phrase what he knows.

Bayne viewed the sermon as "intensely personal," saying that "no sermon is a true communication of the Word of God which does not lead us to expect that Christ means to act in us, and that we should make straight in the desert a highway for him."[53]

The bishop *was* a preacher for whom preaching was "intensely personal," presuming that the Word of God is a lively work, affective in and for people. By his own reckoning he preached at least 150 sermons a year and by 1956 had "produced upwards of three thousand sermons." He was deeply disturbed by the neglect of preaching in the seminaries and by clergy generally. He saw the liturgical movement as a major factor in the growth of this neglect. He did not believe that the discounting of the pulpit in the modern concern for liturgy and ceremonial was deliberate: "Doubtless sometimes it is done with a bit of archeological hauteur, or a partisan sniff; but for the most part it is hardly more than a proper redressing of balance with the Church's life."[54] He was more concerned about the influence of the "Family Service" on the pulpit. Quite obviously he was annoyed by "the quite baseless assumption" that it was something new. As a child he went to church with his parents for a service that was not called a "Family Service"; "it was the congregation's service; it was designed for all who came; and the small fry, who obviously couldn't get the finer points of what went on, knew nevertheless that something great was happening and rejoiced in the companionship, in the mystery, of their elders." This is what he knew; it was not so for everyone. Furthermore, he objected to the proposition that the so-called "Family Service" must be meaningful to children, but then he doubted that any order of worship could be fully "meaningful" to adults, let alone children, and suspected that what the enthusiasts meant by "meaning" was some "neat package of diluted moralism." He concluded: "I like family services, but I don't like 'family services'; and one of the things I specially dislike about them is the practical disappearance of the sermon, in favor of a brief homily addressed (however artfully designed) to the infantry. It is the death of preaching, in many a suburban congregation, who haven't heard a mature communication of the Word of God in years, despite the bellyful of timely truisms for tots to which they have been subjected."[55]

The bishop's own preaching during these years was varied. There were sermons, sometimes two in one morning, given during Visitations for Confirmation. There were sermons for the consecration of bishops, baccalaureate sermons, meditations for clergy retreats, sermons preached at his cathedral church in Seattle, and many others. From December through March of 1947–48, he gave a weekly sermon on KJR Radio, Seattle, on a program called "God's Country." Occasionally, he was to preach to people via radio. From July through September 1959, this man, who claimed no special gifts and expertise for preaching, preached over the NBC Radio Network series, "The Art of Living."[56]

There were memorable sermons that were gems. Bayne's sermon for Thanksgiving 1957 was called "Sputnik Among the Turkeys" and was printed in the Congressional Record.[57] Here he spoke of modern fearfulness concerning the world, its too many gods, a world of surrender, of giving up the fight to make theological sense of our own science. He concluded:

> This is the 1957 face of our nostalgia. We shall bite on sputniks
> among the turkeys, like bird-shot in a duck, and be reminded of
> the other moons and the other gods. Then we shall long for the
> old days when there was just one God and one common human

condition and hope, when God sent what was His will, and we humbly gave thanks for it.

Well, my point is that, to those who will pay God (and their own minds) the respect of thoughtful reflection, Thanksgiving can be and will be a profoundly joyful feast. The gift of freedom in man's life — the perplexing, dazzling, heartbreaking, noble gift of responsible choice — this is the gift which frightens us when it seeks out the secrets of a satellite and launches it. But it is still a gift of God.[58]

There was the baccalaureate sermon preached at Annie Wright Seminary on women and men: "Women are not meant to be toys for men; and men are not meant to be bankrolls for women. They are meant to be comrades."[59] There was the Christmas sermon for 1959 on "The Tree and the Man." There he thought of the old times when men "were exactly right in their sense of the holiness of Nature, of the way God invaded Nature and made it holy." But they didn't go far enough, they stopped at trees or something else. "What was needed, for humanity, was a God who was big enough to invade all of Nature, a God who was able even to cope with human nature, to invade humanity and make it holy just as He did a tree."[60]

His sermons and meditations provided much of the content of Bayne's *In the Sight of the Lord,* the Harper Book for Lent in 1958. The publisher asked for the book, and the bishop wrote it during 1957, an extremely busy year. "It was," he recalled, "despite the pressure, a happy book to write," and he viewed it as "a fair cross-section of where he was at that point. It was well-received and has been helpful to a good many people."[61] It was subtitled "Eight Meditations for Lent" and took its readers from Ash Wednesday through Good Friday. In the preface he explained that this book was an instrument for personal devotions. Meditation, or mental prayer, he explained, "is an art of the mind and spirit which is in something of an eclipse these days." He would like to see a revival of interest in it, for it concerns two essential elements, discipline and imagination. Bayne wrote: One does not meditate simply by letting one's mind run riot through a series of unconnected thoughts and pictures; the element of discipline is an important one, which harnesses our imagination to lead us to see depths and heights which otherwise we would not see. But discipline alone is meaningless. Imagination also plays a vital part, as the instrument through which God leads us to see what He desires for us and what we are really like.[62] He enjoined people to read the chapters "as prayer and not preaching. Start then with a prayer for the light and help of the Holy Spirit. Read the Scripture passage with care.... Follow me as long as you need to; then go your own way to come to your own resolutions, without feeling you must approve

or disapprove the thoughts I have." In 1952 he wrote the meditations
for the Lenten edition of *Forward Day by Day.* "This," he said, "was
not the disaster its 1943 predecessor had been." Significantly, he began
by describing Lent as "The School for Freedom."[63]

Such was Bayne's personal spirituality that he viewed *The Book of
Common Prayer* as a "book of devotion." There were four reasons
for this: (1) "the extraordinary simplicity and objectivity of most of
the Prayer Book language"; (2) "the very act of using a book of corporate prayer itself," our filling the words and phrases of the General
Confession, for instance, "with our own personal conviction" achieving
over time "an extraordinarily deep and rich sense of the brotherhood";
(3) the ways in which the Prayer Book excites the imagination devotion-
ally; and (4) "the unique texture of the Prayer Book" serving "so well to
save us from provincial narrowness in our devotional life. By its tensions
between various ages and schools of thought, it continually stretches and
widens our spiritual experience." He recommended carrying the Prayer
Book wherever one went to dip into it and use it for private devotions.
Indeed, one might add, it was a treasure trove of materials for the kind
of meditation of which he spoke.[64]

In 1959 there was a liturgical conference at St. Paul's Church, San
Antonio, Texas. It was the second such conference, as Bayne recalled,
the first being at Madison, Wisconsin, in 1958 "under the joint aus-
pices of Grace Church and Associated Parishes." In giving his address
at San Antonio, Bayne's mind was set on reformation and renewal.
He was conscious of dubiety within Anglicanism concerning Morning
Prayer and the Eucharist. He believed that one reason, the important
reason, why some preferred the former was that the Office was more
congregational, the Sacrament too often a monologue. "God speed," he
said, "the day when we have recovered within the Eucharistic liturgy
the wholehearted congregational dialogue and participation it ought to
have; when we have brought those second cousins, the pro-Anaphora
and the choir offices, together again."[65] He also discussed the current
confusion over an understanding of the Eucharist as sacrifice, drawing on thoughts already formed and communicated in the sermon he
preached at the celebration of the tenth anniversary of Lauriston Scaife
as Bishop of Western New York.[66] The confusion was based on the
tension between the Reformation emphasis on time and the Catholic/
Orthodox emphasis on Eternity, the remembrance of the sacrifice once
for all, and the eternal fact about God, the eternal offering outside of
time itself. Both are necessary, he claimed. He put his own view this way:

> The fact is that God, in Christ, made the supreme offering for us,
> once and once only (as we count "once"). This is an event in his-
> tory, for the Incarnation is real. . . . It is also a fact about God. This

is the supreme revelation of what God is like. For both sides of the Incarnation are real. It was the Word of God who was made flesh; and what the Word did on earth is our surest knowledge of what is eternally true about God. . . .

What I am really saying is that there is an inescapable continuity, even an identity, between Calvary and the Church and the Christian within the Church; and that the Eucharist is the means of that identity, the act which establishes the bridge between Eternity and Time, and makes "identity" the right word.[67]

In *The Optional God,* Bayne considered the Eucharist in terms of sacrifice and especially in terms of that offering, divine and human, for which freedom is given and which is the end and purpose of human existence. Bayne decried the denigration of preaching, but there was no question that to him the Eucharist was the supreme act of worship. He argued there that if the Eucharist centered only on offering Christ or the memory of him, then "the Eucharist would be no more than a tragic archeology."[68] But it is so much more. It is our self-offering, "ourselves, our souls and bodies," and the work of our hands. "William Temple reminded us that the real significance of the Offertory lay not in the offering of nature itself but in the offering of nature plus freedom, nature plus work." Therefore, Bayne asserted:

The Eucharist is the Church, and it is the Kingdom, for it is the point at which the offering becomes most vivid and immediate, and where we consciously and freely join in the offering and make it our own. But Eucharist and Church alike point away from themselves. What we see and share so vividly at the altar and in the Liturgy has an inescapable compulsion about it. It will not be a right offering until all work is offered, and the nation and the school and the factory and all mankind themselves. The Eucharist is not a religious act; like the Kingdom and the Church it is continuous with all life. All life comes to its fullness in offering. The Kingdom is offering.[69]

Six

ANGLICAN EXECUTIVE OFFICER

Taking Office

On October 17, 1958, Archbishop of Canterbury Geoffrey Fisher wrote to Stephen Bayne about the possibility of his serving as secretary of the Advisory Council on Missionary Strategy and of the Consultative Body of the Lambeth Conference. The idea was not a new one to Bayne or to Fisher. At Lambeth, where the new position was created, Ambrose Reeves of Johannesburg had suggested to Fisher in a lighthearted manner that Bayne might be the one. Bayne recalled "the day you and Ambrose Reeves and I first talked about it in the tea-tent" during the Lambeth Conference.[1]

There ensued correspondence between Fisher and Bayne (and Fisher's chaplain, Michael Adie) concerning the details, especially the finances proposed for the new office and the performance of episcopal duties. Taking the position would involve a serious cut in salary, something he could not afford, with three children in college and two yet to go. Episcopal duties could be provided by arranging for Bayne to be bishop of the American Convocation of Churches in Europe.[2] With all of the difficulties, nevertheless, Bayne told Fisher that he wanted the job, although he thought Ambrose Reeves better suited to it. "I cannot shake off the challenge of this new work," he wrote. "I find myself coming back to it again and again, agreeing with all those who feel it to be of capital significance in the life of our Communion ... recalling the many times when the need of such an office was urgently clear to many of us, marveling at the limitless horizon of service and witness before our Communion if we can find the ways to fulfill the unity God has given us and join our separate strengths."[3] From the beginning, Bayne envisioned the "secretary" as no mere functionary, but as the liaison officer of the worldwide Anglican Communion, whose task was to enable greater cooperation in the Church's mission and a deeper communion with one another in the Lord.

On December 24, Archbishop Fisher wrote that he favored Reeves for the position and apologized for any disappointment he may have caused. Bayne applauded the decision and wrote: " 'Disappointing' is a word I could not honestly use, I think, about the vanishing of this possibility. Deeply as anybody would respond to a glorious task, when we are dealing with such great choices at such depth, I find myself almost clinically neutral about them — almost welcoming even a negative evidence of God's will (for so I would read the whole difficult financial business)."

On January 21, Fisher wrote to say that Reeves had declined the appointment. The Archbishop picked up negotiations where they had been left, saying that he was seeking to double the proposed stipend of £2,000 and indicating that Bayne might live at St. Augustine's College, Canterbury. Details were discussed further on February 24, with Fisher agreeing that Bayne should locate in London and stating emphatically: "I have long been aware of the fact that the Archbishop of Canterbury cannot himself as Chairman of the Conference do the kind of necessary donkey work to organize the necessary liaison which holds the Anglican Communion together. The Executive Officer I regard as the immediate personal assistant to the Archbishop of Canterbury for all this work." He added, "In a sense he will make his own job: it certainly will not mean just sitting in an office in London. It will often mean sharing personally in the outlook and interests of all the Provinces of the Anglican Communion."

On March 2, 1959 the formal invitation was made "to accept the post of Executive Officer." Two thousand pounds were to be paid by the United Kingdom, £600 by the Canadian Church, and £1,400 by the United States for the bishop to the American Convocation. The Archbishop reiterated, "you are directly Assistant to the Archbishop of Canterbury in his responsibilities towards the Anglican Communion and the Lambeth Conference in particular." On March 5, Bayne responded, indicating a positive reaction but saying that he would make a final decision by Easter. He agreed that he would be the Archbishop's assistant. He saw himself as aiding communication ("meaning a new intensity of unity among bishops and church"), carrying through on decisions made at Lambeth 1958, planning for the next Anglican Congress and the next Lambeth Conference, and "helping to develop concerted missionary plans and perhaps specific inter-Anglican projects for new areas." He believed "without weariness and without doubt in the vocation of our Communion and in the dream all of us share in some degree of what our common life and witness can be, under God."[4]

Bayne was agreeing that he would be Fisher's assistant and indicating that the job would have its own agenda in time. "I know also," he wrote, "that there will be inescapably a degree of experimentation in fitting in the various facets of this post — the missionary job, the Lambeth job, and the European Churches." On March 13, Fisher wrote to say, "You mention your own strong feeling that there ought to be a certain degree of looseness in the new post making it clear that this is not an English invention, nor merely an extension of my office. With that I fully agree. I might have been guilty of describing it as a kind of auxiliary office to me: I really never meant that." Bayne was to be responsible to the Advisory Council on Missionary Strategy for tasks performed at their request, and responsible to the Lambeth Consultative Body for assignments done at their behest (which in effect meant at the Archbishop's behest).[5]

It was then necessary to decide. Bayne had consulted the new Presiding Bishop, Arthur Lichtenberger, all along the way. He received support in accepting the appointment from John Butler, Bishops Gray, Donegan, Emrich, Higgins, Dean Rose of the General Theological Seminary, Powel Dawley, and others. Cuthbert Simpson and the former Presiding Bishop Henry Knox Sherrill were against his accepting it, the latter saying, "The Church needs you where you are."

Bayne had many misgivings.[6] In addition to the exacerbation of his financial plight, there was his aversion to administration, his uncertainty about being able to accommodate himself to the Englishness of London, and his awareness of the fact that the job in large part depended upon who occupied the See of Canterbury (he knew that Fisher would retire before long).

On April 3, 1959, Bayne wrote to Fisher accepting the appointment. The Standing Committee of the Diocese had earlier indicated their support for the acceptance. On April 16, the clergy were informed, and on April 19 a public announcement was made. It began, "At the request of the Lambeth Conference, 1958, the Metropolitans of the Anglican Communion have appointed a new officer with the title of Anglican Executive Officer."[7]

In his letter to his diocese at the time, Bayne emphasized the great need for cooperation among the churches comprising the Anglican Communion: "We need to plan a common missionary strategy; we need to keep thinking together (as we do now only at Lambeth and the Anglican Congress): we need to learn to act together more and more as a world Church rather than merely as a group of national Churches of the same tradition." He acknowledged that it was not a new bureaucracy that was needed.

We do not need new machinery, nor could our Anglican witness be given simply by multiplying secretaries and committees. What is needed is some superman who can hold all these diverse interests together, in his mind and heart, who could help each part of the whole Church to be mindful of the whole, who could excite and interest our clergy and people to see and do the common work of our household together, who would be able to dream and imagine and speak for possibilities which have never yet existed, who would have the patience and persistence to bring together the needs and hopes and insights of all our scattered brotherhood, who would be set free to think of nothing save our family as a whole, and the work our Lord has given us all to do, in this dark world.[8]

Such was his vision and his understanding as he embarked on this new adventure. It is no wonder that he closed asking for the prayers of his people.

Between April 19, 1959, and January 1, 1960, when Bayne was expected to commence his new ministry, William F. Lewis, the Missionary Bishop of Nevada, was elected Bishop-coadjutor of Olympia and began his work. Bayne continued to negotiate the details of the office of Anglican Executive Officer. In an Aide Memoire given to Bayne on September 18, 1959, after a long conference with Fisher at Lambeth, specific duties were decided, including follow-up on decisions made at Lambeth 1958. Indeed, much of the real agenda for the Executive Officer was provided by Conference resolutions, and the memorandum and other documents made this abundantly clear. There was no meeting of the Advisory Committee on Missionary Strategy save at the time of the Lambeth Conference and of the Anglican Congress. The Consultative Body (consisting chiefly of the primates of the churches composing the Anglican Communion) met only as summoned by its chairman. The Aide Memoire clearly stated that the Advisory Committee existed practically "in the Bishop as Anglican Executive Officer, and in his contacts with the missionary work of the Anglican Communion in various parts of the world."[9]

Bayne spent much time in the months before he officially began his duties in London trying to understand the position and to explain to others what he understood. He was keenly aware of his own uneasiness with the title "Anglican Executive Officer" and of the false impressions it might give to others. In *The Living Church* he suggested the alternative of "Commissary-General of the Anglican Communion," having in mind Blair and Bray, commissaries of the Bishop of London in the American Colonies. But then he realized that the title might suggest to Americans "visions of mountains of potatoes and box cars full of dried milk."[10] In *Prism* he explained that "Executive Officer" connoted, "at least in American ears, the administration of a regimented and disciplined order which, I am sure, is very far from what we sought to establish at Lambeth a year ago."[11] The Lambeth Committee on Missionary Appeal and Strategy said in 1958 that "if the responsibilities of a world-wide communion are to be grasped and its resources mobilized, fuller expression must be given to four vital principles of corporate life — coordination, cooperation, consolidation, cohesion." These terms helped define the admittedly misleading title. Bayne continued to mull over and define his title in 1962, speaking of himself "as a minister-general of the Anglican Communion — as a kind of universal suffragan to 340 diocesan bishops."[12] In time there were those who would call him "Mr. Anglican," for he became for many people the embodiment of the Anglican Communion, the "superman" of whom he had spoken.

The Anglican Communion

From the outset, Bishop Bayne's understanding of the Anglican Communion was grounded in the definition provided by Resolution 49 of the Lambeth Conference in 1930:

> The Anglican Communion is a fellowship, within the One Holy Catholic and Apostolic Church, of those duly constituted Dioceses, Provinces or Regional Churches in communion with the See of Canterbury, which have the following characteristics in common:
>
> (a) they uphold and propagate the Catholic and Apostolic faith and order as they are generally set forth in *The Book of Common Prayer* as authorized in their several Churches;
>
> (b) they are particular or national Churches, and, as such, promote within each of their territories a national expression of Christian faith, life and worship; and
>
> (c) they are bound together not by a central legislative and executive authority, but by natural loyalty sustained through the common counsel of the Bishops in conference.[13]

Bayne knew that in the 1960s this definition was dated. Prayer Book revisions underway in many churches raised questions concerning the use of *The Book of Common Prayer* as a test. Of greater importance was the establishment of full communion with non-Anglican churches since 1930. With these reservations in mind, Bayne regarded the resolution as providing the most satisfactory official definition.

At the time Bayne served as Executive Officer, there were eighteen churches in this fellowship, beginning with the mother Church, the Church of England divided into the Provinces of Canterbury and York. Since 1920 the Church in Wales had been a separate Church. The Church of Ireland, with its two provinces of Armagh and Dublin, dates its separate existence from 1870. The ancient Episcopal Church in Scotland completes the churches of the Communion in the British Isles. The oldest churches outside Britain are those of the United States and Canada, both dating their separate existences from the time of the American Revolution. There followed churches in Australia and New Zealand. In time the missionary work of the older churches produced autonomous churches in Japan and China and in India, where there was founded the Church of India, Pakistan, Burma, and Ceylon. In Africa, in the early 1960s, there were five churches of the provinces of South Africa, West Africa, Central Africa, East Africa, and Uganda, which was organized as a province in 1961. There was a separate province in the British West Indies. There were other missionary dioceses in the West Indies — Cuba, the Dominican Republic, Haiti, Puerto Rico, and the Virgin Islands — but they were all a part of the Protestant Episcopal Church in the United States at that time. This latter church also had jurisdiction over the American mission in Liberia, not yet a part of the Church of West Africa. The eighteenth church was the Archbishopric in Jerusalem, serving churches in Jerusalem, Egypt, Libya, Iran, Jordan, and the Sudan. There were other dioceses widely scattered in Argentina, Bermuda, Jesselton and Kuching in Borneo, Gibraltar, Korea, Madagascar, Mauritius, Singapore, and Malaya — all having as Metropolitan the Archbishop of Canterbury. The American Church included various missionary districts and overseas dioceses in varied states of development toward independence. The three dioceses in Brazil were, in Bayne's time, already to a degree self-governing. Three dioceses in Australia, Adelaide, Tasmania, and Willochra did not belong to any province.

There were 340 dioceses in all with about forty million church members. The majority were still citizens of the United Kingdom or of British Commonwealth nations, but there were eight million in Africa, where the most rapid growth was being experienced. All dioceses were linked by common origin, direct or indirect from the Church of England, and by Prayer Books that shared a family resemblance. English was still the common language, but the Prayer Books of the various churches were printed in 170 different languages. As Bayne stated in 1962: "The aim of the Anglican Communion is to establish, as quickly as possible, autonomous national Churches in every land. It is by 'missionary' effort that these Churches are born; but the aim is not to keep them as dependent colonies, but to lead them swiftly to the point where they are fully and strongly established in their own soil with their own leadership, managing their own affairs, and taking their full part in the worldwide life of our fellowship."[14] In this, Bayne was expressing something of what he observed to be true but also something he desired to see more fully operative. He saw missionaries and friends flowing from one Church to another "to strengthen the brotherhood everywhere in the world. This interchange," he said, "of resources and manpower and the worldwide planning of it, is a principal concern of the Advisory Council on Missionary Strategy, of which I have the honor to be the executive officer."[15]

He was also very much aware of the fact that Anglican Churches were in full communion with some non-Anglican bodies (that is, freely receiving the Holy Communion in each other's churches; bishops and clergy freely exchanged as warrant allows). Bayne explained that this does not involve organic unity or full acceptance of the teachings of each church. It does mean "that each regards the other as a fully qualified Church within the One Holy Catholic and Apostolic Church of Christ." In 1962 these churches were, for example, the Old Catholic Churches, the Polish National Church in America, and the Philippine Independent Church. Beyond that, he said:

> Anglicans are bound together closely with many other Christians in the World Council of Churches and in various national councils. Here, although we are not in full communion with each other, we have steadily deepening relationships or brotherly work and study and many aspects of common life. In many parts of the world, as in India and Nigeria for instance, intensive plans are being studied looking toward the union of an Anglican Church and others in a new and very broad national Church (as in South India). While this means, in one sense, the "disappearance" of the Anglican Communion, it also makes possible the emergence of a far more inclusive unity, for which all Christians pray.[16]

Lambeth 1930 referred to "mutual loyalty sustained through the common counsel of the Bishops in conference." This "common counsel" finds expression chiefly through the Lambeth Conference of the Bishops of the Anglican Communion. First convened in 1867 at the behest of bishops of the Canadian Church, with the support of the Church in the United States, the conference meets by invitation of the Archbishop of Canterbury. It met roughly every ten years at Lambeth Palace in London, up to Bayne's time. The Archbishop invites whom he wishes, sets the agenda, presides over meetings. It was customary for committees to meet on various themes and to make their reports, including the provision of resolutions, to the conference as a whole. As Bayne told the World Council of Churches:

> The authority of this meeting, while considerable as expressive of the common mind of the Anglican episcopate, is not coercive or synodical. Any action proposed by a Lambeth Conference can only be put into effect by each church separately. A Conference may point the way to desired action; but the essential dynamics of the Anglican Communion remain in the several churches; and the Conference retains its character as the central but informal occasion of common counsel among the bishops.[17]

There were, as Bayne entered his new work, two continuation committees of the Lambeth Conference, the "Consultative Body" and the Advisory Committee on Missionary Strategy. Both, in Bayne's view (not shared by all) had their origins in the 1878 Lambeth Conference. The Encyclical Letter in 1878 proposed that a "Committee might be constituted, such as should represent, more or less completely, the several Churches of the Anglican Communion; and to this Committee it might be entrusted to draw up, after receiving communications from the Bishops, a scheme of subjects to be discussed" at future Lambeth Conferences. Such a committee was formed in 1897, being referred to as a "consultative body." The work of this body grew through the years until in 1958, the Consultative Body, consisting chiefly of the Primates of the Anglican Communion or their deputies, was described as carrying on work left to it by the Conference, assisting the Archbishop of Canterbury in preparing for the next Conference, considering "matters referred to the Archbishop of Canterbury on which he requests its aid and to advise him," advising "on questions of faith, order, policy, or administration referred to it by any Bishop or group of Bishops, calling expert advisers at its discretion, and reserving the right to decline to entertain any particular question," dealing "with matters referred to it by the Archbishop of Canterbury or any Bishop or group of Bishops, subject to any limitation upon such references which may be imposed by the regulations of local and regional Churches," and taking "such action in the discharge of the above duties as may be appropriate, subject to the condition that with regard to churches, provinces, and dioceses of the Anglican Communion its functions are advisory only and without executive or administrative power."[18]

Bayne saw a foreshadowing of the Advisory Council on Missionary Strategy in the same Encyclical Letter of 1878, where it was suggested that a "Board of Reference" might be formed to consider "questions brought before it either by Diocesan or Missionary Bishops or by Missionary Societies." But no such body was created until in 1948 Lambeth proposed formation of an "Advisory Council on Missionary Strategy" and went on to suggest the appointment of liaison and communication officers by each national or regional church, "to promote closer co-operation and a clearer understanding between the different parts of the Anglican Communion."[19] The Council was formed, but the latter suggestion was not acted upon then. The Council began to meet, as occasion allowed, most prominently at the Anglican Congress of 1954. In 1958 it was recognized that this body, as also the Consultative Body, stood in need of a secretary, serving on a permanent, full-time basis, who would attend to the stated responsibilities between meetings of the Lambeth Conference. Lambeth 1958 provided for such an officer, and Bayne was chosen. In 1970 both of the continuing committees Bayne served were merged to form the Anglican Consultative Council.[20]

In 1963, looking back to Lambeth 1958, Bayne recognized that nine areas of special urgency were identified as responsibilities for the Advisory Council to consider: African townships, South America, the Chinese dispersion, New Guinea, the Middle East, new provinces and councils, missionary dioceses, restrictions on religious freedom, and possible conflicts with governments. Three matters were referred directly to the Council: channels of communication, exchange of materials, skills, and so forth, and polygamy. Six matters he identified as being referred indirectly: Bible study, stewardship, movement of peoples, the Anglican Congress, the *Anglican Cycle of Prayer,* and the *Pan Anglican,* a periodic publication.[21] All of these items were considered by Lambeth in 1958, and most were the subjects of resolutions. Here was an indication of the scope of work awaiting the Executive Officer.

At the same time, looking back to 1958, Bayne numbered seven areas of direct responsibility for the Lambeth Consultative Body: the wider Episcopal fellowship, the Lambeth Conference itself, the union scheme for Ceylon/North India/Pakistan, the West Asian union proposal, the Jerusalem Archbishopric, the Holy Communion Service-study looking toward revisions, and the mutual exchange of information. Areas of indirect responsibility he identified as church union negotiations, the financial crisis of St. Augustine's College, financial crisis, industrial society, divorce legislation, and marriage discipline.[22] All of these were involved in resolutions passed by the Lambeth Conference.

There was some concrete understanding of what the Executive Officer was expected to do. He was to forward the work of the two committees as best he could to deal with the matters relevant to each. The task was on the whole impossible. The committees seldom met, depending upon events such as the Anglican Congress and the Lambeth Conference itself to bring their members together. They could accomplish some things by mail. But now the chief burden fell upon the Executive Officer. He, working under and with the Archbishop of Canterbury, had to devise what of all these matters took priority and how they were to be managed.

Getting Acquainted: Seattle to London via Asia

It was necessary that at the outset Bayne gain firsthand knowledge of the Anglican Communion he was to serve. To this end, and in carrying forward the work of the two bodies, Bayne spent between a half and two-thirds of his time traveling around the world. He traveled, chiefly by air, 113,000 to 147,000 miles per year between 1960 and the fall of 1964. His travels began on New Year's Eve, 1959, with his journey from Seattle to London, a trip that serves as a sample of the kind of journeying the Executive Officer was to do almost continuously.[23]

Bishop Bayne was accompanied on this trip by Lucie and their two youngest children, Lydia and Bruce. They departed Seattle in a drizzle, were delayed in Portland by mechanical problems, and arrived to begin 1960 in Hawaii. The first lengthy stop was in Japan, where ten days were spent visiting the Nippon Sei Ko Kai, as the Japanese church was called, "from tiny parishes and schools packed to overflowing, to the great hospital of St. Luke in Tokyo, now erecting a new wing." Bayne spent time with Colonel Paul Rusch and the Kiyosato Educational Experiment Project (KEEP), and dedicated a new out-station there. While in Japan he reflected upon the gift of a nuclear reactor to St. Paul's (Rikkyo) University in Tokyo, from the Protestant Episcopal Church in the U.S.A. He noted: "Of the theological and strategical importance of this gift at this time I haven't the slightest doubt. It is a gift which bespeaks our concern for peaceful uses of the atom, our interest in higher education and in giving to the Japanese people a teaching tool of the greatest importance, and our faith in the Creating God Who teaches us all truth, for all truth is of Him." In this statement Bayne reveals something of the influence of William Pollard, the priest and physicist whom he respected. It should be noted that this was before the problem of radioactive waste was recognized as a pressing problem.

The Baynes spent a "day or two" in Taiwan and Hong Kong. In Hong Kong, Bishop Hall took Stephen Bayne through the resettlement areas in Kowloon. What he saw deeply affected him. There were great new blocks of buildings, eight stories or more high, teeming with humanity, mostly Chinese refugees. Before, they lived in the streets or in packing boxes; now they had about 64 square feet for five American dollars a month, a substantial but manageable sum for people who earned about a dollar a day. But to qualify for such a room (eight feet by sixteen) a family had to consist of ten people. If the family were smaller, they might have a smaller room or share sixty-four square feet with another family. Bayne recognized this as a work of great merit by the government. "Yet it was hard to sleep easily, back at my hotel that night.... Sixty-four square feet for the pathetic little bundles of family heirlooms, for love and whatever individuality and decency there might be — sixty-four feet for the tired sleep which gives the only moments of peace and hope for these thousands of people." He concluded: "The Gospel, if it is real at all, must make sense to a humanity which needs sleep. Does this sound ridiculous? All the highflown theology in the world must sometime be tested by what difference it makes to the universal necessities of mankind. What had Christ to say to people who need room to sleep and dream?" Bayne was intensely appreciative, after this experience, of what the Church in Hong Kong was doing under

Bishop Hall's leadership in providing to these refugees schools for their children, rooms where they could meet, hostels where young men and women could come, and places "where they can meet the Lord who loves them and Who stayed awake while we slept."

There followed five days in the Philippines, visiting churches and institutions. Bayne met with some forty bishops of the Philippine Independent Church, listening to them and talking about mutual concerns. Three days were spent in Djakarta, Indonesia, where Bayne celebrated the Holy Communion "for a congregation nominally English, but including almost every variety of Anglican in the world today." This group was ministered to by a priest with the amazing title "Vicar of Java with Sumatra." Bayne noted that there was only one priest "there to bear witness for our whole Anglican family among the more than eighty million people of Indonesia."

From Djakarta Bayne went to Kuching in Sarawak, where during five days he met with the Southeast Asia Council. This, he reported,

> is a new development in our Anglican life. It brings together the Churches from Seoul to Rangoon; bishops, priests and laymen from Korea, Hong Kong, the Philippines, Borneo, Singapore and Rangoon, European and Asian, all sharing the enormous, aching problems of the new countries and societies of Southeast Asia.
>
> We discussed every aspect of our Church's life and mission and of the people we serve. And, in a richly symbolic act, we consecrated a new assistant bishop for Borneo, James Wong, a Chinese of Australian citizenship. Bishop Wong began life in China and then, as a businessman and part-time parson, he served the Church in many parts of Asia.

A day was spent in Singapore, visiting St. Peter's Hall, a theological college supported by the American Church. There Bayne found an American priest teaching with a Norwegian-born priest of the Church of England. "The latter's earlier ministry as a Lutheran missionary in China now bears extraordinary fruit in theological leadership for many of our clergy in Southeast Asia."

During three days in Calcutta, Bayne "began to learn what the Anglican Communion really looks like, and received orientation about the present stage of the negotiations for Christian unity in North India." Two days were then spent in Jerusalem and a day in Beirut, Lebanon, where he encountered the very difficult mission of the Anglican Communion to the Arab world.

Then came Rome, where his brother Ned lived and served as a warden of St. Paul's, the American Church there. Stephen was now with one of the congregations for which he was responsible as bishop and rejoiced to be with his own, using the Prayer Book (American 1928) that he loved best. On February 15, 1960, the Baynes arrived in London.

Being the Anglican Executive Officer

Upon arriving in London, the Baynes took up temporary residence at Lambeth Palace. The bishop had been negotiating from the spring of 1959 the settlement of issues such as permanent office space, staff, and living quarters for the Executive Officer and his family. He had made little or no headway on these matters by the time of his arrival in February, and some months were to pass before 21 Chester Street in London was secured as both home and office. Bayne expressed exasperation at the slowness with which the officials of the Church of England moved in making a final decision and securing a leasehold. As to staff, he relied heavily on Mrs. Nigel Irvine, his Administrative Assistant whom he brought to London from the United States. She oversaw the rest of the staff, helped organize Bayne's schedule, supplied him with background materials, and served as his representative in meetings and in other business during his frequent absences from London. Bayne was to feel the pinch of being shorthanded and underfinanced. Some essentials were covered in the beginning out of funds put at the bishop's disposal by friends at home, funds that might have been used to ease his own financial burdens.[24]

In the first year as Executive Officer, Bayne traveled 130,000 miles, including the long trip from Seattle to London via the Far East. He subsequently made four trips to North America: to Canada for a meeting with the committee there arranging for the 1963 Anglican Congress, and to the United States for meetings of the National Council of the Protestant Episcopal Church, of which he was still a member. Two journeys were made to South Africa and about a dozen to Europe and elsewhere. His trips to Europe were chiefly concerned with his duties as bishop in charge of the seven American (Episcopal) Churches there and of Episcopalians in the United States Armed Forces in Europe. Such travels involved official visits to churches in Canada, Japan, Scotland, South Africa, the United States, and to the Philippine Independent Church. In this travel he recognized "the heart of the Executive Officer's work." "The occasion may be," he said, "a meeting or conference or lecture or whatever, but what happens is orientation and the interpretation of one part of our companionship to another."[25]

Planning for the Anglican Congress in 1963 and the corollary meetings of the Consultative Body and the Advisory Council was begun in that first year, as were the studies requested by Lambeth, studies that would form the basis for decisions in 1963. Bayne had the American Church make a preliminary survey of the situation in South America and reported that major area studies were underway. The South East Asia Council undertook, with funding from the churches in England and the United States, responsibility for a study of its territory. He proposed to the Overseas Council of the Church Assembly of the Church of England a study of the Church in Africa "with a view to assembling and interpreting the vast accumulation of data already in the possession of our churches and missionary societies, to prepare suitable proposals for the future." He was concerned that the churches in the areas being studied be involved in these studies, for the aim was to achieve "the most responsible planning and partnership on the part of the churches concerned." This was a major challenge, given the missionary history of the areas, the dependence upon "sending churches," the lack of encouragement given local churches to plan for themselves, and the fact that the studies, of necessity, were funded and thus to a large degree controlled by the older, more established churches of the "first world."[26]

Of all the specific matters referred by Lambeth 1958 to the continuing committees, Bayne gave priority to the North India, Pakistan, Ceylon unity proposals. In 1960 a study was published by S.P.C.K., edited by Bayne. This contained an introduction "written in Nice, in the summer of 1960." The book contained reports, documents, memoranda intended to assist all parties to the negotiations. At the conclusion, he explained that as editor, the Executive Officer was carrying out one of his chief duties, that of communication. Knowing that many serious questions were being raised concerning the negotiations and that the Anglicans involved wanted to consult their fellows in the Anglican Communion, Bayne sought "to make accessible, as widely as possible, the fundamental documents involved, and to seek to win from all in our household the informed and concerned counsel it would be in all our hearts to give."[27]

Also important for communication was the establishment of *Anglican World,* a publication intended to take the place of *Pan-Anglican.* Bayne was involved in this and in arranging for an adjustment in the financial support of St. Augustine's College, Canterbury, an inter-Anglican responsibility. This he was doing as a second inter-Anglican study center was being established at St. George's College in Jerusalem.[28]

Reflecting on what next steps needed to be taken, Bayne spoke (1) of the need for greater recognition of the purpose and character of the office he held. He felt most keenly the United Kingdom's lack of understanding and said: "It is disconcerting to feel that of all our churches I am the least at home in England (in the sense of meeting any broad understanding of my job, and the inter-Anglican character of my ministry and of our churches' life.)" (2) There needed to be a routine routing of appeals for financial and personnel aid through his office, not for decision making, but for the sake of communication and cooperation.

There needed to be (3) "vastly more consultation" than then existed on matters in general. There was (4) an "urgent need to develop planning facilities and organs, even in our smallest churches." And (5) "there is a clear need for all of us to make a frontal attack on provincial and national narrowness." The aim in all was unity, as Bayne understood it: "The point is that the Church is the one body in the world which is bigger than any human differences; the point is that we have a duty to placard before the world the reconciliation God has worked in us through Jesus Christ."[29]

The year 1961 was marked by the retirement of Archbishop Fisher and the choice of Michael Ramsey to be the one hundredth Archbishop of Canterbury. This was of critical importance to Bayne and will be discussed at length later in the next chapter. It is sufficient to emphasize its importance here. The Executive Officer was in many ways an assistant to the Archbishop, and it was necessary that they be able to work together amicably. Bayne was able to work with Ramsey but did not find in him the kind of encouragement and support that he had found in Fisher.

During 1961 Bayne traveled 122,000 miles. Seven of these trips were made to the United States to attend meetings of the National Council of the Episcopal Church, the General Convention in Detroit, and meetings of the newly formed Strategic Advisory Committee, the Episcopal Church's central planning body of which he was an *ex-officio* member.[30] Other journeys included official visits to churches in Japan, India, South East Asia, Taiwan, and Uganda. The latter in April he considered exceptional, for it involved the launching of a new province, that of Uganda and Rwanda-Burundi. "In a most moving ceremony in the Cathedral in Kampala, the responsible care of the life of its nearly two million members was entrusted to the new church, until then a congress of missionary dioceses."[31] Bayne also traveled in England, addressing diocesan conferences in Birmingham, Canterbury, Hereford, Manchester, Sheffield, Worcester, and York, as well as preaching or speaking in Chelmsford, Exeter, Guildford, Liverpool, and London.

The bishop also took upon himself other engagements, such as clergy conferences in Delaware and Virginia, lecture series in Texas and Michigan, and preaching assignments in Boston, in Detroit at General Convention, and in Philadelphia at a meeting of the Overseas Mission Society. He accepted assignments on radio and television, chiefly with the BBC, taking his turn at a devotional program called "Lift Up Your Hearts," but also participating in such secular programs as "Meeting Point" and "Brains Trust." The latter was a game show on which he was reported to be the "wittiest and the brightest" of the "brains." Along with such luminaries as Lord Boothby, Bernard Williams, Margharita Laski, John Wain, J. Bronowski, and Kenneth Younger, Bayne confronted such questions as: "Even assuming that an agreement on the abolition of nuclear weapons can be achieved, the threat remains. How will the consciousness of this threat influence coming generations?" and "On the synthesis of religious and scientific concepts of man, do the members of the Brains Trust believe such a synthesis will ever be achieved?" Bayne would have been delighted to tackle the question "Should reference to the devil be eliminated from the new Anglican Catechism?" and "My God is black; what colour is yours?"[32] In addition, the bishop continued meeting his responsibilities in Europe as Bishop-in-Charge of seven American churches and as Ordinary to Episcopalians in the Armed Forces in Europe.

Bayne was able to report that during 1961 the Overseas Council of the Church of England agreed to conduct a survey of the needs of the Anglican Churches in Africa. The Protestant Episcopal Church in the U.S.A. was sponsoring a study, being conducted by the Bureau of Applied Social Research of Columbia University, of South American needs. Other studies were underway. A proposed African liturgy prepared by the Archbishop of Uganda after consultation with five other African churches was being circulated among other primates and metropolitans and was the focal point for the liturgical study suggested by Lambeth. The study of family life in differing societies was being aided by preliminary studies conducted in Canada, England, and the United States.[33]

The Executive Officer continued to work on communications. *Anglican World* was being published six times a year and its circulation was slowly growing. He initiated a bulletin called *Exchange,* dealing with missionary affairs. The word *exchange* was derived from Lambeth and signified "the deployment of all our resources, wherever they may be within our Communion, to meet our tasks most effectively."[34] It was, he believed, the heart of his task, a task hardly touched to date.

"Yet," he said, "there are most encouraging stirrings everywhere in our Communion — chiefly in the form of volunteers and suggestions, often coupled with an increasing knowledge of corresponding needs." He identified a fundamental truth about the Anglican Communion: "There is no church which has not something to give and something to receive."[35] He reported with satisfaction the continuing development of the South East Asia Council, now with its own liaison and field officer, and the development of other regional councils in the South Pacific, including the dioceses of Polynesia, Melanesia, New Guinea, and Carpentaria, and the American jurisdiction in Samoa and in the Caribbean, "where the bishops of the American missionary dioceses have launched a regional council of their own," which he hoped would in time include the dioceses of the Province of the West Indies.

Plans for the Anglican Congress were progressing, the *Anglican Cycle of Prayer* was in use, St. Augustine's College was a continuing worry, still seriously underfinanced, St. George's College, Jerusalem, was taking shape. On the ecumenical front, the great event was the Third Assembly of the World Council of Churches at New Delhi. In connection with that event a meeting was held that "provided opportunity for discussion among a score of representatives of Anglican Churches and of the churches of the wider [Episcopal] fellowship."[36] In addition, Bayne presided at a "consultation on Inter-Communion, called by the World Council of Churches at Bossey" in Switzerland.

In the midst of all this, Bayne was led to ponder "confessionalism" — an idea seemingly of great importance in ecumenical circles. It was a somewhat opaque term to him, it being used "to describe not only churches of a common doctrinal allegiance, but also international structures of church federation, and the like, which are often structures of considerable collective power and durability." Most commonly at the time it was a catchword "to describe inter-regional and international ecclesiastical organizations, based on some common statement of doctrine or faith which differentiates the group in question from other Christian people."[37] He did not like it and thought it was inappropriate when applied to the Anglican Communion. He judged confessionalism to be divisive. The Anglican Communion he viewed as "fellowship of regional and national churches, which hold no particular, private doctrinal statement of our own, which look back to no founder save Our Lord, which have no particular theological school or bias of our own, which define as little as possible (within the universal historic definitions of the Catholic Church), in order to be free to offer our societies the full and unchained faith of the universal church in its most liberal and inclusive form."[38] Here was an issue that was to remain alive for him for years to come.

During 1962, the year of the Cuba missile crisis and the Second Vatican Council, Bayne traveled 147,000 miles, including official visits to the Anglican churches in Australia (the first synod of that united church under a new constitution), Canada, Central Africa, Ireland, Jerusalem, and Japan. In February he was able to be in the Philippines for the formal inauguration of the concordat between the Episcopal Church in the U.S.A. and the Philippine Independent Church. In June he was in Lisbon for the consecration of Luis Pereira as the second bishop of the Lusitanian Church. Another visit was paid to the Ecumenical Patriarch of the Orthodox Church. Bayne continued traveling on the continent of Europe, in fulfillment of his duties there as bishop.[39]

In the United Kingdom he preached at the universities of Birmingham, Cambridge, Oxford, and St. Andrew's. He led a clergy conference for the diocese of St. David's and lectured or addressed the St. Andrew's Summer School for Clergy and diocesan groups in Llandaff, Norwich, Salisbury, and Southwark. In addition, he preached a missionary ser-

mon in Coventry Cathedral, dedicated a new tower in the Washington
family's ancestral Church, ordained an American priest, Charles Tait,
at Plymouth, and had "the great honor of a Sunday in Sandringham
Church." In the United States he attended meetings of the National
Council and the Strategic Advisory Committee, and gave the Bohlen
Lectures in Philadelphia and the Pitt Lectures at the Berkeley Divinity School. He visited the Diocese of Honolulu on the occasion of
their centennial celebration and during the summer moderated a gathering of theologians and scientists at the Seattle World's Fair. The latter
eventuated in the book *Space Age Christianity*.[40]

Bayne especially noted the beginning of the Second Vatican Council
and the immediate improvement of Anglican-Roman Catholic relations, especially in the United States on the local level. There were
signs of renewed interest in Anglican-Orthodox conversations in England and North America. Concern over union negotiations in Ceylon,
North India, and Pakistan continued. Negotiations in Nigeria among the
Presbyterians, the Methodists, and the Anglicans seemed to have "progressed with warmth and promptness." Anglicans and Methodists in
England were engaged in dialogue. In 1962 the Consultation on Church
Union began with the invitation of the United Presbyterian Church to
the Protestant Episcopal Church to engage in discussions looking forward to unity. By the end of the year, COCU, as it was familiarly
known, included "almost every tradition in American life from the congregational to the Old Catholic." Bayne was appointed a delegate to
the Consultation. He noted that "there is hardly an Anglican province
which has not evidenced a new stirring of concern for Church Union."
Keeping up with these ecumenical developments and assisting with them
as best he could was becoming a major part of his job.[41]

The Canadians were chiefly responsible for organizing the Anglican
Congress for the summer of 1963, which now promised to bring together a thousand bishops, priests, and lay people representing nearly
350 dioceses. Bayne found himself having to defend the holding of the
Congress, a "confessional" gathering rather than an ecumenical one,
against the objections of those who viewed it as detrimental to the flour-
ishing ecumenical movement. Bayne's response was that the Anglican
Communion "is an expression of Christian unity" and that the leadership of the Congress was dedicated to church unity. "I have no doubt
myself that the Congress will be a positive ecumenical event of very considerable magnitude."[42] Bayne's specific responsibilities were twofold:
the meetings of the Consultative Body and the Advisory Council, for
which he was preparing, and for consultations on general education
and theological education preceding the Congress, as well as consultations on Church unity negotiations and liturgical revision following the
Congress. Missionary executives were to meet in advance of the two

councils. His attentions were focused on preparations for all of these meetings as he worked through 1962, looking forward to the summer of 1963.

The development of the regional councils proceeded slowly, the most notable of 1962 being the adoption of a Constitution for the Council of the Church of South East Asia. "This action," Bayne commented, "marked another step forward in the exploration of what is for our Communion a new form of regional, interprovincial association." Regional councils were meeting basic needs. "One is that of the highest degree of local initiative and responsibility consistent with the wider unity of the Church. A second need is that for a deeper level of common life among Anglican churches of different backgrounds, sharing a given area of the world. The third is that for every positive step we can take toward a fully-united Christian body" in every region.[43]

In addition to *Anglican World* and *Exchange* there was now *Compasrose*, a periodic newsletter to bishops. These publications were the main instruments, other than the Executive Officer himself, for the improvement of communications in the Anglican Communion. Bayne also noted his monthly columns in *Church Times* and *The Living Church,* and the "modest and tentative 'treaty' between the Seabury Press and SPCK," two major publishing houses. He expressed concern for communications in "depth," of knowledge of one another, requiring "the most personal of relationships — communication in prayer, in individual acquaintance and friendship, in the exploration of one another's ideas, in common enterprises shared, in common judgment accepted." Here was the greatest challenge, especially considering the obstacles to the accomplishment of such communication.[44]

Bayne gave much thought to missionary strategy during 1962 and identified as major elements in such strategy the development of responsible, corporate planning in localities and regions, "steady consultation and shared planning by all our churches, 'sending' and 'receiving' alike, 'new' and 'old' alike," the "co-ordination . . . of the unused and unawakened resources, and the development of them where they are needed," and, finally, "decision in consultation about priorities, so that our obedience to mission represents the best offering we can make, in terms of our own strength, our ecumenical responsibilities, and the needs of the world."[45] These were the elements needed to strengthen the Anglican Communion and its missionary endeavors. Some progress could be noted in all areas, but such progress was minimal and feeble in the face of what was needed.

The year 1963 was the year of the Anglican Congress in Toronto. It was also the year of the assassination of President Kennedy. Bayne was on his way from New York to London at the time. He was taken by helicopter from Heathrow Airport to the BBC headquarters for an

interview. He was then the best known American resident in London, a
media figure, and was naturally called upon to interpret the events to
the English public. On November 24, he preached a sermon at Christ
Church, Oxford, repeated the next day at St. Peter's Church, Eaton
Square, London. The sermon, "following the death of John F. Kennedy,"
referred to "the passions and suspicions and violence" that run high in
modern society. "All the long inheritance of bitterness and guilt is there
to be accepted and borne by everyone. You cannot secede from humanity. There is one humanity, and glory and shame are alike woven into it,
and every man is part of it." He felt the burden of those days.[46]

Because of the time spent in Canada in the summer of 1963, that
year Bayne traveled but 113,000 miles. Several visits were made to the
Anglican Church of Canada, apart from the Congress, and official visits were made to the Church of Ireland and the Church of Wales. In
February he attended a meeting of the Joint Council of the Philippine
Independent-Philippine Episcopal Church and in May paid another visit
to the Ecumenical Patriarch. Twelve trips were made to Europe in connection with his "responsibilities as Bishop in charge of the American
churches and ordinary of the Episcopal military personnel in Europe."
His duties as a member of the American House of Bishops and of the
National Council necessitated six trans-Atlantic trips. In Britain he paid
two visits to St. Augustine's College, preached at missionary services in
the dioceses of Leicester and St. Alban's, addressed the clergy in Ely
and at the Clergy School in the Diocese of Blackburn. He was also
a visitor at King's College, London, and Christ Church, Oxford, and
preached at St. Paul's, London, Southwark Cathedral, Gray's Inn, Sand-
hurst, and in several parish churches. He led an American congregation
in the celebration of the American Thanksgiving Day at St. Nicholas
Cole Abbey.[47]

In January the fruits of all the labors spent on studying the needs of
the church in South America were garnered at the Consultation on the
Anglican Communion and Latin America held in Cuernavaca, Mexico.
Representatives of the Anglican Church of Canada, the Church of England, the Protestant Episcopal Church, U.S.A., and the Church of the
Province of the West Indies participated under the chairmanship of the
Archbishop of York. The gathering demonstrated a remarkable degree
of mutual consultation and planning and a new grasp on the nature of
the Anglican Communion's role in Latin America. The role "is not to
be understood merely as a chaplaincy to foreigners, but as 'obedience
to Christ's command to preach the Gospel,' whose 'primary objective is
the development of Latin American churches, expressive of the genius
of their own countries and of the unity of the Anglican Communion.' "
The report of this consultation was to be a major agenda item at the
meeting of the Advisory Council in July.[48]

During 1963 Bayne was engaged in planning for the conference of the "Wider Episcopal Fellowship" scheduled for April 1964 in Canterbury. Eight churches were now included: the Old Catholic churches (including the Polish National Catholic Church in the United States), the Churches of Finland, South India, and Sweden, the Lusitanian and Spanish Reformed Episcopal Churches, the Philippine Independent Church, and the Mar Thoma Syrian Church. There were misgivings about the increasing emphasis upon this fellowship and its concern for the historic episcopate, a concern especially expressed by those Anglicans committed to the larger ecumenical movement. Bayne found himself having to defend the upcoming conference.[49] Other ecumenical developments, in Ceylon, India, and Pakistan, in West Africa, in Canada and Australia required the attention of the Executive Officer. Once more circumstances prompted him to think about it all. Prominent in his thinking was a shift in his position vis-à-vis confessionalism. He wrote:

It is no secret that I am entirely content with our freedom from a confessional theology; we hold no other standard than the confession of the whole Church of Christ. But this nobility, as it sometimes is, can lead us to a dangerous illusion, that no confession is called for from Christians. The problem with what the younger churchmen call "confessionalism" is not that Christians confess before God; it is what they confess. The utter irrelevance to our time of so many medieval and postmedieval distinctions hardly deserves mention. What should our confession be, in the face of racial strife, of a cold and triumphant secularism, of the increasingly irrational and ungoverned use of power? It may be that a new confessionalism — one that may chafe tender Anglican shoulders — is required for this age and unity.[50]

He was to give this matter further and deeper thought.

The year 1963 was chiefly important in the Anglican Communion for the Congress in Toronto, the events preceding and following it, and above all for the idea and program called M.R.I. (Mutual Responsibility and Interdependence), during what Bayne called "The Canadian Summer." This was the high point and the culmination of Bayne's tenure as the first Executive Officer of the Anglican Communion.

Seven

BAYNE'S GROWING TRIUMPHS

The Canadian Summer

July and August of 1963 were two of the busiest months in Bayne's life, as they were for many others as well. The fourth World Conference on Faith and Order was held at Montreal in July. Bayne was a delegate to it and had agreed to lead one of its services of worship, but illness prevented him from attending.[1] There were meetings on the edges of the main events, a "group life laboratory" in Cambridge, Massachusetts, for some thirty bishops from around the world, and consultations on the Church and education held at Cranbrook, Michigan. As noted earlier, there were conferences on ecumenical and liturgical concerns immediately after the Toronto Congress, as well as a gathering of representatives of the laity of the churches. Before Toronto, the center of attention was on five gatherings at Huron College, London, Ontario: a conference of the heads of Anglican theological schools and colleges, a conference of the five archbishops of the African churches, a meeting of missionary executives, and meetings of the Advisory Council and the Consultative Body. Bayne considered the conference of missionary executives to be the most important of them all. For a week, some fifty representatives of missionary societies and boards, and churches, "spent long hours in surprisingly swift-moving discussion of the mission of the Church in all of its aspects. From this group," Bayne reported, "came the germ of the proposal, later adopted by the Lambeth Consultative Body, for 'Mutual Responsibility and Interdependence in the Body of Christ.'" Indeed, in the discussion on the first day of the meeting Bayne spoke of Church responsibility, of the need for planning and the setting of priorities, of planning as being mutual: "No one is independent. We must find ways in which this mutual planning can be developed. Each Church has something to teach the others." Mutuality became a dominant concept, expressed by Bayne repeatedly. "No church ought to send anyone," he said, "without asking in depth what it wants and needs in return. Then the element of mutuality comes into existence." He also placed emphasis upon spirituality in mission: "We must look at the questions of financial inability against the background of spiritual inability."[2]

The Advisory Council on Missionary Strategy met at Huron College, August 5–8, under the chairmanship of the Archbishop of Canterbury. It was an impressive assembly of primates, metropolitans, provincial presidents, representatives of extraprovincial dioceses, and staff advisers, including Eric Trapp of the (SPG), Noel Davey of the (SPCK), David Paton of the Council for Ecumenical Cooperation, and John V. Taylor and M. A. C. Warren of the Church Missionary Society (CMS). Bayne served as secretary. In the first session, the Executive Officer reported that the missionary executives "had been led to a new understanding of brotherly, mutual relationship."[3] Out of this had come a draft paper called "Mutual Responsibility for Mission." The discussion of this paper by the Advisory Council revolved around two poles: "One was a question of a financial goal, whether it should be mentioned or not and whether, if it were, the figure given in the draft paper was adequate. The other issue was that of the nature of what was envisioned: Was it a new 'appeal,' or was it a new level of relationship? His Grace the Chairman summed up this preliminary division by saying that, in the main, what was proposed was a new process."[4]

It is true that the draft paper, introduced by the Archbishop of East Africa and twice redrafted by the missionary executives, was concerned in a major way with specific programs of mutual assistance, including raising $15 million immediately to meet numerous special needs, ranging from the training of clergy to the building of new mission churches and the provision of adequate literature. This sum was to be over and above present overseas commitments. The report said: "This is an immediate necessity, not a final goal. It will not meet the great capital needs of our churches at work on every continent. We do not now know even the scope of such fundamental needs. But we do know the immediate emergency needs of the explosive frontiers of the Church; and we know our own need to move forward in brotherhood in mission."[5]

At the beginning of the second session, the chairman appointed a committee to prepare a new draft of the "Mutual Responsibility" paper. That committee was composed of the Archbishop of East Africa, the Bishops of Accra and Brandon, the Reverend Dr. Moore, the executive of the Strategic Advisory Committee of the American Episcopal Church, and the Reverend John V. Taylor of the CMS. At the final session, on August 8, the new draft was presented. Capital funds had earlier disappeared. The principal emphasis now lay on mutuality. The new draft dropped the word *mission* from the title "and what was proposed was nothing less than a new form of the Anglican Communion." After much discussion and the addition to the drafting committee of the Archbishop of York and the Bishop of Singapore and Malaya, the Council voted to adopt the proposal of "Mutual Responsibility" — as further amended in the light of discussion — "as a fundamental statement of policy" of the Council, and that this be reported to the Congress and the statement transmitted to the churches of the Anglican Communion for "appropriate action."[6]

There were other matters dealt with by the Council, including a resolution from the African archbishops, the studies of Latin America and the South Pacific with recommendations, the Church and education, regional officers, the Wider Episcopal Fellowship, and much else, but the evolving mutuality policy statement was dominant in the thinking of the Council members and engendered an excitement that grew as time passed. There should be mentioned a working paper on the structure of the Advisory Council prepared by Bayne that strongly supported the continuance of the council but set forth numerous proposals for its strengthening.[7]

The Lambeth Consultative Body met August 8–10 chaired by the Archbishop of Canterbury, with primates and metropolitans present and the Executive Officer serving as secretary; it was on the whole a smaller gathering. There was a lengthy discussion of the Lambeth Conference with the conviction expressed that it meet next in 1968 and that the meeting place be shifted from London to Canterbury, partially in order to accommodate the growing number of bishops. The agenda for the conference was also discussed but not finally set. The Wider Episcopal Fellowship received attention, as did the Nigerian union scheme, regional councils, St. Augustine's College, Canterbury, along with other matters. There was considerable discussion of the Executive Officer of the Anglican Communion. Bayne proposed and the Body agreed to the need for a larger staff, specifically for an additional assistant.

It was clear that, although it did not appear on the Body's agenda until the last item on the final day, the Mutual Responsibility proposal was uppermost in the minds of the bishops. Bayne himself was trying to think through the implications of the new policy for his office. Speaking as "one more bishop," he acknowledged being impressed by the size of the Mutual Responsibility proposals and the speed with which they had taken form. "They were," he said, "the outgrowth of two weeks of meeting in some depth, by representatives of all provinces; they had sprung spontaneously from the free discussions of churches at every stage of life; they would be explosive and searching in the life of each church, if taken seriously — so much as to amount to a spiritual revolution." The speed with which they took form necessitated "a willingness to improvise as one went along and a recognition that at any given time both our structures and our financial support would very likely be inadequate to the actual needs of the moment."[8]

He therefore did not make all of the suggestions concerning his office that he might have made. There was need to rethink things. It was agreed that the Consultative Body should meet April 17 and 18, 1964, at Canterbury following the conference of the Wider Episcopal Fellowship. It was also agreed that "Mutual Responsibility" should be presented to the Anglican Congress, that the Archbishop of Canterbury make the presentation, and that the Executive Officer and others be included "perhaps as a 'panel' — to assist in interpreting the proposals and underscoring their significance."[9]

The Anglican Congress met in Toronto from August 13–23, ten full days of fellowship, worship, and study. Representatives of all eighteen churches of the Anglican Communion — bishops, priests, and laity — assembled at 3 P.M. on Tuesday, August 13, in the Canadian Room of the Royal York Hotel for the official opening and reassembled at the Maple Leaf Gardens that evening for a service attended by 16,000 people, including a choir of 1,000. The primates and metropolitans sat beside the altar at one end of the arena, while the Archbishops of Canterbury and Rupert's Land (the host primate) sat on thrones in front of the altar. It was a majestic service with two sermons, preached by the two archbishops. A. M. Ramsey said: "Towards the world we renew our mission. It will be more than ever a mission of involvement.... Towards one another as Anglicans our unity will be one of giving and receiving. We must plan our mission together and use our resources in the service of our single task.... Towards other churches we work for unity in truth and holiness. That work is one of giving and receiving, and we only give if we are humble to receive."[10]

The sessions of the Congress were devoted to major addresses and panel discussions on (1) The Church's Mission to the World (on the religious frontier, on the political frontier, and on the cultural frontier) and (2) The Challenge of the Frontiers (training for action, organizing for action, and the vocation of the Anglican Communion). Inserted between these two parts was the presentation of the "Mutual Responsibility and Interdependence in the Body of Christ" document (MRI). This occurred on the morning of Saturday, August 17. The document, which had been circulated the day before, was presented by the Archbishop of York, F. D. Coggan, and was supported by statements from the Archbishop of Canterbury; David Goto, the Bishop of Tokyo; John W. Sadiq, the Bishop of Nagpur, India; Richard R. Roseveare, the Bishop of Accra, Ghana; and Bishop Bayne.

The document asserted at the outset as self-evident, that the full communion in Christ which has been the traditional tie of the Anglican communion of churches has now "taken on a totally new dimension. It is now irrelevant to talk of 'giving' and 'receiving' churches. The keynotes of our time are equality, interdependence, mutual responsibility." It then referred to three "central tasks at the heart of our faith" that "command us in this":

The Church's mission is response to the living God who in his love creates, reveals, judges, redeems, fulfills. It is he who moves through our history to teach and to save, who calls us to receive his love, to learn, to obey and follow.

Our unity in Christ, expressed in our full communion, is the most profound bond among us, in all our political and racial and cultural diversity.

The time has fully come when this unity and interdependence must find a completely new level of expression and corporate obedience.[11]

The churches were then summoned to study the needs and resources of the Communion, and in the meantime to increase their financial support to meet the most pressing needs, providing at least $15 million over the next five years. They were asked to make a parallel commitment in manpower, to extend the process of mutual consultation, to reconsider the commitment of the churches to missions, and to cease from making distinctions between "older" and "younger," "sending" and "receiving" churches. A program was proposed involving immediate increase of money and manpower for the study in and by each Church of its obedience to mission and of the structure, theology of mission, and priorities existent. A Church would study (1) ways to receive as well as to give, (2) ways to "test and evaluate every activity in its life by the test of mission and of service to others, in our following after Christ," and (3) ways to develop "every possible channel for communication with its companions in the Anglican Communion — indeed in the Church of Christ as a whole." The document ended by saying:

We are aware that such a program as we propose, if it is seen in its true size and accepted, will mean the death of much that is familiar about our churches now. It will mean radical change in our priorities — even leading us to share with others at least as much as we spend on ourselves. It means the death of old isolations and inherited attitudes. It means a willingness to forgo many desirable things, in every church.

In substance, what we are really asking is the rebirth of the Anglican Communion, which means the death of many old things but — infinitely more — the birth of entirely new relationships. We regard this as the essential task before the churches of the Anglican Communion now.[12]

The reactions were mixed. One American exclaimed, "I came to Toronto expecting a series of great meetings; I am going home with a

burning sense of mission." One group stated: "We endorse the finding of the document...that a new approach to this challenge [that of
the world situation] is immediately urgent, and we commend the whole
subject to the prayer and consideration of every part of the church."
But there was confusion concerning the document and its presentation
and some strong negative reaction. Bayne summarized this, saying that it
was interpreted by some "as (a) an arbitrary dictate from higher authority, (b) a proposal for greater confessional cohesion, and (c) a disguised
appeal for funds for missions overseas."[13]

Bayne was to spend considerable time dispelling these misunderstandings. He carefully explained the genesis of the document, demonstrating
how it had emerged through revision after revision out of the consultations of many during the two weeks preceding the Congress. He denied
that he was its author, although it was impossible to deny that the general tone and key concepts such as "mutuality" and "interdependence"
had direct relationship to much that he had been saying and doing in
the past three years. Bayne regarded the document as ecumenical rather
than confessional. On one occasion he said that "the central drive of the
proposal is to set churches free from any coercion by others, whether
exercised in financial or cultural or institutional or any other terms. And
this is a major ecumenical necessity, for unity must be sought locally
and regionally."[14]

In his own remarks after the presentation of the document at Toronto, Bayne denied that MRI was a program to raise funds for overseas
missions, although it did call for the raising of funds. "This is not an appeal for funds," he said. "This is not a drive for a new central fund.
The incidental mention at a point or two of an immediate need for a 30
percent increase in the money now in the tissues of our interchurch relationships has nothing to do with the future.... This is a way in which
we can begin to share at a level which will permit decent and mature
partnership in important things, and that is all it is. Nor is it an appeal.
As long as I live I will never appeal for money for the mission of God
in this world. This is a degradation of God and of ourselves, which has
pauperized us in every way over the centuries."[15]

In the following months Bayne was to explain, interpret, and elaborate upon the document. In the United States, those concerned to launch
a new program to advance the missions of the church in urban and industrial life were concerned that MRI would divert attention from their
program. "Why should there be a collision here?" Bayne asked. "Should
not the response to the challenge of the urban mission be understood
from the start as a major obedience to Mutual Responsibility?" He felt
the same way about Anglican-Methodist relations and the Paul Report
on Manpower in the Church of England then commanding attention
alongside MRI. He wrote: "These instances illustrate three central prin-

ciples of Mutual Responsibility. First, we begin our response to the proposal where we are, as we are. Second, the obedience to mission each church shows by understanding and facing its own tasks in greater depth and more radical freedom is an essential expression of mutuality and interdependence. Third, the problems of each church are of concern to every other church."[16]

Three months after Toronto, Bayne was able to report that the churches had received the document and were beginning to act on it. Canada was the first to receive it officially. A cathedral in England contacted him asking for suggestions as to how they might bring some priests from the "younger" churches to join their fellowship and assist them to see what they should be doing in their community. In the United States the clergy of four urban churches "met and prayed, and thought, and then agreed that the first frontier of 'Mutual Responsibility' for them was a pooling of the combined strength of their congregations in a united ministry to the inner city." There was an immediate increase in giving in the Canadian Church, and the bishops of that church agreed to give an additional 5 percent of their salaries, above their present giving, to lead the way. One bishop reported that all plans for development in his diocese had been halted in order that their goals and resources might be reexamined in the light of MRI. Bayne found the most dramatic response to be that of the five African Churches. "Through their archbishops, the nearly fifty dioceses in Africa have prepared and sent me for circulation proposals for more than a hundred projects towards which our increased strength should flow."[17]

A major occupation for Bayne during the remainder of his tenure was the preparation of regional directories of projects growing out of MRI. Another was the request that there be a study of the needs of the churches of the Anglican Communion as initiated by the projects list from the churches in Africa. Six regional directories had been issued by September 1964. Those directories were circulated, and nine churches or councils responded. The Canadian and New Zealand churches proved to be most active and Bayne was pleased to note that five of the so-called younger, or receiving, churches had undertaken specific projects. Of the 580 projects in the directories, roughly a quarter were due for final approval, 19 had been completed and 93 were underway toward completion. Bayne was aware that the beginning efforts were imperfect; he specified four areas of concern: (1) "*Design* — the actual, practical forming of a plan," (2) "*Decisiveness* — especially in determining priority," (3) "*Wholeness* — of seeing a society whole, of seeing the Church as a whole, of seeing the available resources as a whole," and (4) "*Mutuality*, both within a church and across the world. . . . The point of projects, surely, is to provide ways in which one church can share what it is and has with another, in common obedience to Christ." All of these matters needed attention, and to his mind, especially the fourth. He expressed his fear: "If 'Mutual Responsibility' were to become simply a swapping of men or money, it would be of little significance. It is in working together in common enterprises that we shall give and receive, perhaps without being very self-conscious about it. The more the element of mutual involvement is stressed, the greater blessing will projects bring to all of us concerned."[18]

The Lambeth Consultative Body met April 17–20, 1964, at St. Augustine's College, Canterbury. The Archbishop of Canterbury presided, and Stephen Bayne served as secretary for the last time. There was a thorough discussion of the Wider Episcopal Fellowship, which had just met. Anglican-Roman Catholic relations were considered, and the ecumenical implications of MRI were discussed in the light of questions asked by other churches, particularly concerning the development of regional offices and directories. There was attention given to problems concerning St. Augustine's College, the Church of England in South Africa, the Nigerian scheme of church union, and other similar negotiations. Bayne presented a report on a conference of Anglican publishers and a report on the *Anglican World*. The suggestion of an Anglican Diocesan Information Digest was considered and the possibility of a Church Information Conference. These were some of the items on the agenda for which Bayne had responsibility. Toward the end of the meeting, Lambeth 1968 was discussed, and the matter of a successor to Bayne was considered. A list of bishops was compiled, and the Archbishop of Canterbury was requested to choose one of three to succeed Bayne on October 31, 1964. It was also agreed "that the title 'Anglican Liaison Officer' was preferred to the current title; that it was important not to seem to alter the terms of the office in appointing a new officer; and that therefore it would be convenient that the newly appointed Officer should himself make the change in title after his appointment."[19] The choice fell on Ralph Dean, the Bishop of Cariboo, in Canada.

Bishop for Americans in Europe

Partially as a means to supply the Anglican Executive Officer with an adequate salary, the Presiding Bishop of the Episcopal Church in the U.S.A. appointed Stephen Bayne Bishop-in-Charge of the Convocation of American Churches in Europe, a position Bayne was to occupy to the end of 1968. At the request of Henry Louttit, the Bishop of South Florida and chairman of the Armed Services Committee of the Episcopal Church, Presiding Bishop Arthur Lichtenberger also appointed Bayne on November 22, 1960, "as Bishop to the people of our church in the Armed Forces in the European theatre."[20] Both of these positions were considered to be part-time, but taken together they constituted a considerable responsibility and taxed Bayne's energies, energies already taxed by his position as Anglican Executive Officer. Yet he welcomed the appointments, in large part because they provided him with a "diocese" and a church home in which to function as a bishop, in addition to being an episcopal bureaucrat.

The Convocation consisted of seven congregations, with fifteen clergy and about 2,300 baptized members.[21] There were the Church of the Holy Trinity, "the American Cathedral in Paris"; the Church of the Holy Spirit in Nice, France; St. Christopher's Church in Frankfurt, West Germany; the American Church of the Ascension in Munich; St. James' Church, Florence, Italy; St. Paul's Church, Rome; and the American Church in Geneva, Switzerland. In addition to "settled" members, there was always "a considerable floating population of tourists, students, and the like, many of whom are ministered to by the seven congregations as well as by the many more chaplaincies under the Bishop of Fulham (northern Europe) or in the Diocese of Gibraltar (the Mediterranean basin)," so Bayne reported in 1964.[22]

There was also a large American military population in Europe, chiefly in West Germany. Bayne estimated twenty-five to thirty thousand Episcopalians, military personnel and dependents, ministered to by the American congregations in the seven churches of the Convocation or in some eighty other places where an effort was made to maintain regular services and to provide pastoral care. Bayne wrote that "this side of our Church's life is presently in the hands of another fifteen military chaplains, five or six nonparochial civilian priests, and some one hundred and thirty lay Readers, civilian and military. While the bishop in charge does not have technical jurisdiction over the military personnel, he is in effect their bishop and ordinary in many ways, and functions as such as far as time allows."[23]

These appointments necessitated regular visits by the bishop to confirm and to superintend. In March and April 1963, while fulfilling his arduous duties as Anglican Executive Officer prior to the Toronto Congress, Bayne was to be found in Paris, Poitiers, Verdun, Bad Kreuznach, Frankfurt, Wiesbaden, Mannheim, and Paris again.[24] In March 1960, newly on the job, Bayne had reported:

> I have had most happy visits to four of our congregations since we got to Europe: Rome on February 14th, with the joy of celebrating and preaching with a good congregation despite the rain; Frankfurt for a two-day visit, with 53 confirmations..., followed by still more at Kitzingen; Munich for another two days and still more confirmations; and then Paris, on Shrove Tuesday and Ash Wednesday, for dinner with our man there and for the Holy Communion with which Lent began.[25]

In July 1961, Bayne wrote to Canon F. A. McDonald, the bishop's colleague working with military personnel:

We are luxuriating on our canal boat; but before I forget it, I'd better report on the Baumholder — Bad Kreuznach trips. It was excellent, and Col. Chappelle was kindness itself. I confirmed 8 at Baumholder (including two small Chappelles) and then celebrated and preached at Baumholder and Bad Kreuznach Sunday morning July 15th and had lunch with the congregation. They elected a Bishop's Committee (after I had talked about the usefulness of such things and how informal they were).[26]

There were meetings of the Council of Advice of the Convocation to arrange and attend, annual meetings of the Convocation, and clergy conferences at Berchtesgaden. The first Annual Meeting of the Convocation under Bayne was held in Munich. The Convocation began with Evensong, the clergy sitting in the choir ("scarf and hood, please"). The next morning after Communion and breakfast, there was a retreat, or "quiet morning," with business after lunch. That evening there was the Bishop's dinner. Another business meeting was held the next day before adjournment at noon.[27] It was a small affair, more like a board meeting than a Diocesan Convention. The conferences at Berchtesgaden were a highlight for the year and involved guest speakers, such as Bishop Emrich of Michigan, Bishop Corrigan of Colorado, and Bishop Louttit of South Florida.

Bayne was concerned for budgets, for replacement of clergy, on one occasion a very difficult and trying matter,[28] and for establishing regulations, such as those governing lay readers and the admission to Communion of those not confirmed. He produced a regular newsletter, provided pastoral care for clergy and their families, and dealt as lawful ordinary with marriage cases, some in connection with military personnel. He exercised great care in dealing with marriage cases, ruling in some instances that he lacked jurisdiction, granting petitions for remarriage in the church of divorced persons in some cases, and denying permission in others.

In his newsletter, Bayne kept his people informed concerning his itinerary, events of note in the Convocation, major events in the Anglican Communion, and new books worthy of attention. His pastoral care for clergy is illustrated by letters of advice, such as one to a harried priest to whom he wrote advising that he set aside at least one full morning a week for study and, if possible, an hour a day. "It's not too much when you consider all that must come out of you, somehow. I manage it even at my great age and decrepit condition. Don't take any back talk about this."[29]

From the outset Bayne was disturbed by the composition of the seven churches. They had at one time been composed of retired people, students, and those engaged in business or commerce. As such they had steady, dependable congregations. Following the Second World War they were more and more dominated by military personnel and their families. The number of tourists greatly increased, and the population of retired persons declined. Bayne remarked that they seemed to have become "chapels of ease," or worse, "Episcopalian Clubs." They were more sect-type than church-type, which may have meant, Bayne admitted, that they were more conducive to existence in a post-Christian world. But Anglicanism, he was convinced, could abide neither "chapels of ease" nor "Episcopalian Clubs." The parish church may have been under assault, but he for one believed that it was essential.[30] Furthermore, there was something un-Christian in withdrawal into exclusive enclaves.

The Mission of Anglicanism

Bayne was able to describe Anglicanism in terms of the Anglican Communion readily enough, but Anglicanism as a concept was a different matter. What is Anglicanism? Bayne found it much easier to discuss Anglicans than Anglicanism. There were Anglicans of various nationalities all owning membership in one of the churches of the Anglican Communion. He notes: "Their general Anglicanism is only a deduction from their particular Australianism or Latin Americanism, and really quite secondary to it." There were and are certain unities. The lesser unities, such as cultural habits, language, and "general Tudor ambience," were gone. There were other unities, such as Bible, sacraments, creed, and ministry, but they were not distinctive. There was *The Book of Common Prayer,* or perhaps one should say there *were* Prayer Books, "still sufficiently alike so that one knows where one is in a general sort of way." The Prayer Book was certainly considered a point of unity in the 1930 definition of the Anglican Communion. That Communion was there described as consisting of churches that upheld and propagated the Catholic and Apostolic faith and order "as they are generally set forth in *The Book of Common Prayer* as authorized in their several churches." But with the occurrence of revisions that statement is not altogether appropriate.[31]

In an address given in Londonderry in 1963, Bayne pursued this point further:

> It is perhaps not too difficult to describe the governing elements in Prayer Book *worship*. But one may well wonder whether the essential gifts of the Prayer Book — its most important elements — are those merely of worship. The Prayer Book is, for all of us Christians of the Anglican Communion, far more than merely a

directory of worship. It is our teacher; it is the guardian of our traditions; it is the broad and noble guide to our belief and our life. And as revised Prayer Books proliferate, and as the forms of our worship change, in increasing adaptation to the needs and the conditions of each of our societies, we begin to grow aware that it is not nearly as easy to define the Prayer Book as we once thought it was.[32]

Having concluded that the lesser unities had passed away and the greater unities were not as clear or certain or exclusively Anglican as was once the case, Bayne still argued that there was something that could be called Anglican, "pure and general Anglican." But it was elusive. He thought of it "as a certain constellation of attitudes, habits of mind, tempers of spirit, values, which can be discerned in great Christians who happen to be Anglicans, and which can be identified as characteristic of Anglican hopes and ideals."[33] This "something" cannot be located in the Thirty-Nine Articles, "it cannot be expressed in sectarian or denominational theology." Where administrative or organizational matters were concerned, he had long held that the only unity was full communion.

The spirit that was Anglican was such that it was encountered, as Bayne encountered it while growing up, in that which was. He found Anglicanism as he learned

> to take bishops seriously but not superstitiously, to receive with a certain gentle scepticism the fierce totalitarianisms in Christianity, to distrust detailed formulations of how God was bound to work, to value deeds — including sacramental deeds — rather than mere words, to understand that history was continuous and I a momentary part of it, to believe that no human wisdom was infallible, to expect that roaring lion of Holy Scripture to tear apart any human pretension, and to know that Christianity was for grown-up people who were expected by God to stand on their own feet.[34]

These were the things Bayne learned, quite unconsciously, without identifying them with anything distinctively "Anglican." Such a configuration — "the patterning of poised and responsible freedom, of respect for history, of gentleness toward others and a refusal of the sectarian mind, of responsible following of the Incarnate Lord into the turmoil and confused values of the secular world" — was for him "probably as close as one could come to the characteristic spirit of the Prayer Book and of the people of the Prayer Book."[35]

The spirit of Anglicanism was born in the midst of the historical events of sixteenth-century England. It involved accommodation and compromise. Its birth was certainly not noble. Nor were those things that compose the Anglican configuration sought for themselves. The concern was for the Church and the gospel and the saving means of grace. The spirit was enfleshed in liturgies, constitutions, books, laws, and institutions, all of which were and are to be judged in terms of their fidelity to the central spirit. "But the commanding question is not, 'is this Anglican?' but 'is this right?' The Anglicanism will take care of itself, if the things are true, and needn't be worried about."[36]

There were for Bayne three lessons in all of this. "First, the miracle itself — that what began as a particular response to a particular historical situation in a particular country among people with particular gifts should turn out to be exportable and universal."[37] Bayne wrote this in the summer of 1963 after almost four years as Executive Officer, having observed Anglican life in diverse nations and cultures, all sharing in what Bayne described as the Anglican spirit or constellation of attitudes. "Second, the word 'Anglican' is both an accurate tribute to history and also a seductive and perilous ambiguity." He was convinced that "Englishness" was a detriment, not an asset — a thing of the past, irrelevant to the future. "Third, the Anglican tradition was not an end in itself." He had spoken earlier of the Anglican vocation to lose itself (thus dying as a separate entity) in the greater unity of the Church. This was what he saw happening in the Wider Episcopal Fellowship and in the disappearance of dioceses in India into the South Indian Church.

In struggling to define Anglicanism, Bayne was influenced in part by his aversion to "churchiness," "a sort of ecclesiastical equivalent to what used to be known, in more opulent times, as 'housemaid's knee.'" Churchiness was defined for him by the XVIIIth Article of Religion: "They also are to be had accursed that presume to say that every man shall be saved by the Law or Sect which he professeth.... For Holy Scripture doth set out unto us only the Name of Jesus Christ whereby men must be saved." He was also influenced by his aversion to internal divisions, another sign of sectarianism. So much energy is dissipated "in keeping the Church from being captured or at least seriously bamboozled by the 'other side of the house' ('Catholic,' or 'Evangelical,' or 'Liberal,' or whatever one happens not to be)."[38] He did not view "parties" and differences of opinion as wrong. He wrote in *Church Times*:

> I am a child of the "Catholic" side of the house, I suppose, nourished in the great tradition of Bishop Hobart, taught from youth a vigorous sense of the sacramental and institutional, historic life of the Church. I did not know it then, but I know it now, that such a "Catholic" sense was the result of a virile and often pugnacious witness of a minority school of thought — that had it not been for men willing to be different and often divisive, few of the treasures

of a steady, healthy sacramental life which are now so freely found in all our churches would have been even suspected.

Quite equally, I know that the kind of healthy sacramental life which was taught me would be impossible to maintain were it not for the persistent reminders of the supremacy of Holy Scripture and the primary necessity of personal devotion and faith, which came from the other side of the house. Any sacramental life will degenerate into magic without the constant, purifying witness to the Almighty God who alone can save. Any historic institutional Church will degenerate into a superstitious club or worse if it is not continually leavened by its independent minds who remember that God is "able of these stones to raise up children unto Abraham" (to say nothing of bishops, priests, deacons, executive officers, etc.).[39]

Bayne was convinced that the strength of the Catholic position was due to the vigor with which it was taught and the vigor with which it was questioned by those in other positions. Indeed, the dialogues that occurred among differing parties were healthful and life giving. No one "knows all the truth or understands even what he knows; it is only by dialogue and confrontation that we grasp even what we have, let alone what someone else has." Yet this healthful condition can and does all too often degenerate into harmful, "petty suspicion and quarrelsome egotism." This happens because of "three seeds of death": (1) "we forget that the Church is Christ's and not ours"; (2) "we forget that the Church exists, in Russell Barry's phrase, 'mainly for the sake of those who don't belong to it' "; (3) "we forget that all truth is of God, as far as it is true at all, and that truth is mainly learned, grasped, held, used, in intercourse with other truth." He concluded:

My own infantile, positive, Anglican rule of life in these matters is simply this: to meet every argument about Churchmanship by going back to the Bible and starting there (which is the only cure I know for possessiveness); to ask of every refinement of this or that partisan point what difference it would make in the conversion of Mr. Khrushchev (or reasonable facsimile thereof); and to keep reminding myself that it isn't only Anglicanism which is supposed to include both Catholic and Protestant streams within itself, nor our Anglican Churches individually, nor our parishes. It is we ourselves, as single, believing Christians. Each of us has got to be both, in one soul. We cannot take refuge in a closed mind or a closed system — not if we are going to be true to the truth. This makes it somewhat uncomfortable to be an Anglican, at least a good one. But I don't know that being any kind of a Christian is supposed to be painless.[40]

The consequence of such thinking for the mission of Anglicanism was clear. That mission is fundamentally no different from any other Church's mission. "It is to preach the Gospel and bear witness for Christ, in our way, in every place, that He may be seen and heard and His life implanted in every society we can penetrate." This is how he understood Anglican "strategy." "It is not a strategy of establishing little Anglican churches in congenial corners of the world. It is not a strategy of providing chaplaincies for the status quo."[41] In another place he said that mission "is not simply making more Episcopalians.... Mission is obedience."[42]

In a speech before the Hong Kong Diocesan Association in 1962, he declared: "The mission is God's and not ours. The Church is God's and not ours. God is standing knee-deep in Hong Kong working, creating, loving, judging, guiding, teaching, feeding, moving in the hearts and wills of people.... He does not have to wait for Anglican missionaries. ... The privilege that is given to Christian people is to respond in obedience to the God who is already at work, and who calls us in Christ's dear, wonderful words, calls us to *follow*."[43]

Bayne preferred to think of ecumenical relationships in relation to mission. Thus he insisted that the primary concern for Anglicans was to work out their own unity in terms of their sense of mission, which was their sense of mutual responsibility and interdependence. He was made uneasy when the concern of the churches was more for unity than for mission — more for people thinking alike than for people acting together in the common cause of God's mission. He was especially pleased by the assertion of the Orthodox theologian Nikos Nissiotis at New Delhi in 1962 that "the Church does not move towards unity through the comparison of conceptions of unity, but lives out of the union between God and man realized in the communion of the Church as union of men in the Son of Man. We are not here to create unity but to recapture it in its vast universal dimensions." Bayne commented that he was pleased in part because this statement "spoke so profoundly to our deepest Anglican thoughts about unity."[44]

There were times when Bayne was disturbed and annoyed by the accusations of some that he was not committed to ecumenism. He insisted that the achievement of unity in Anglicanism was an ecumenical venture, contributing to the larger ecumenical movement. He also recognized that he was a newcomer and had much to learn.[45] It is questionable whether or not Bayne ever felt entirely at ease in ecumenical gatherings called to work on unity. Participation in the Faith and Order Movement where large theological issues were discussed was something he relished and understood. As an Anglican he was suspicious of bureaucracies and felt that full communion and the kind of unity that comes with worship, especially the Eucharist, was superior to the bureaucratic unity that so many seemed to be pursuing.

Continuing Concerns

During his tenure as Executive Officer, Bayne continued thinking and talking about issues that concerned him. Through the work he did at Lambeth 1958, he continued his defense of the family. Recognizing that the family was under assault, he spoke out at a mass meeting sponsored by the Mothers' Union. "The only hope," he is reported as saying, "is to lead people to discover the unchanging theology of family life, to lead them to discover the essential holiness of the family, because the family is the essence of God's creation."[46] In an article for the *Church of England Newspaper,* Bayne argued that in the light of the reexamination of family life in all societies, the Church faced three tasks: (1) a realistic identity of the enemies of the family (he emphasized poverty); (2) being theological in its thinking and in its defense of the family (as was Lambeth in asserting that the family is "the God-given environment within which souls are born"); (3) not forgetting "that the life of a family is something chosen by us as well as willed by God." Concerning this last task he said, "A family does not merely happen, it is ordered by God in creation, but it must needs be fulfilled by the devoted and determined wills of the fathers and mothers and children of every generation."[47]

All of this led to thoughts about responsible family planning. In responding to a statement of Roman Catholic bishops in 1960, Bayne pointed to Lambeth 1958 and then indicated four factors to be taken into account in any discussion of family planning and public policy: (1) "there are not many families and not any societies within which some degree of family planning is not practiced"; (2) "the problems of family planning are inseparable from all other problems which the world faces"; (3) " 'overpopulation' is created by precisely the same humane use of scientific knowledge which is at stake in all the discussions of family planning"; and (4) "the question of the right of any governmental or public agency to spread or endorse methods of family planning which are morally abhorrent to sections of the population ... is a practical decision, from which there is no escape."[48]

In 1960 Bayne spoke formally on three separate occasions on the subject of education. On April 29 he was given an honorary Doctor of Letters degree by Kenyon College and spoke on the revolution of the present day, for which education is preparation. He had in mind a non-Christian in Calcutta who told him that what the East needs is not "your denominations," but rather a new sense of social dignity, a new appreciation of the worth of human beings, a more humanitarian spirit, a new sense of community, greater tolerance for human limitations. Bayne identified all of these things with the Christian faith (and thus with Western civilization as he preferred to view it) and what it had given and was capable of giving to the world. He was careful to say that the outcome of the revolution in the world was not for the West to determine. "Our part is the simpler part and the more humble one: it is that of giving to the revolution the things it needs and seeks and wants — the size of a man, the glory of hope, the depth of life, the wonder of uncompromising truth."[49]

From November 3–5, 1960, some five hundred representatives of church and church-related schools in the United States met. Bayne presented three addresses to them intended to introduce three themes: curriculum, religion and worship, and school relationships. In his first address he asserted that Europe (the West, the Christian West, the biblical civilization in the West) "is the one existing whole in contemporary history. It is from this that all of the present revolution springs." He then described the revolution of his day: "The revolt, the upsurge, the universal convulsion in Asia and Africa, the convulsion of racialism, of the new nationalism — all of this is a revolt from something, against something. It also is historical; it is not a theoretical revolt. It is a revolt against 'Europe,' against that vast, many-faceted, deep historical phenomenon, that historical hope called the West."[50]

Later in his address he spoke of the vastness of the revolution taking place, "putting to an end once and for all the rule of the white West." But at the same time those in revolt crave the values of the Christian West. They hunger for plenty, for dignity, for a place in the world, and many of them are emerging from tribalism to modern industrialism, "leapfrogging a thousand years into the middle of the 1960s."[51] Bayne's concern was that modern education should lead people into a deep encounter with Western civilization and its values, not hold on to the past as it was remembered, but enter into the revolution of our times, "aggressively concerned with what hasn't yet existed." He was concerned that schools were often viewed as holding operations for the immediate past. He was also fearful that society was ignoring the revolution or was attempting to do so, "more and more concerned with how we are doing; more and more narcissistic."[52]

Bayne argued for a more vigorous teaching of history, language, and literature. He emphasized the necessity of teaching theology. Why? In discussing this he revealed that he was profoundly troubled by the threat of communism, "a heresy of the West, which is presenting itself as a viable alternative, indeed the only viable way of revolution, for the next generation." In this claim there was an immense spiritual and theological challenge to the Christian West. He viewed communism as "a challenge to all the great biblical ideas as to the size of a man and the 'dignity' of a man. It is a challenge to all that we have inherited from our fathers about the immortality of the human spirit and the decisive character of human responsible freedom." He was convinced that the study of theology was of the utmost importance, "from the very beginning of a child's education."[53]

In another address, Bayne spoke of the setting in which education took place — the learning community. He defined community chiefly in terms of relationships: "The community is a place where duties are perceived and accepted and where room is made for different people in their different needs and situations." A community is inclusive, not exclusive, when it is understood according to the root sense of the word *community*. Bayne and others were disturbed by the number of Episcopal private schools being founded to provide alternatives to the racially integrated public schools.[54]

Worship "must hold the central place in the school," Bayne argued in another address, "both as a test and as an expression of the school's life, and the fulfillment of its vocation as one of the Church's schools."[55] Worship was uppermost in his mind during his years as Executive Officer, as it had been before and was to be subsequently. In a sermon preached at the University Church of St. Mary the Virgin, Oxford, Bayne spoke eloquently of worship as an end in itself. "The basic motive for worship," he said, "is that God exists, man worships, and our worship is the inescapable response of the creation to its creator — first man alone, and God alone." He spoke of worship in terms of awe and wonder and of the "withering of the sense of wonder" in the twentieth century. He did not recommend attempting to recapture the sense of wonder, but rather urged an upgrading of "our awareness of what it is to be, to exist." In the end, the Christian arrives at the conviction "that our existence is an act of love born out of love, and that what lies behind the veil is the goodness of God. And here our worship becomes for the first time deeply and truly Christian."[56]

There follows his response, beyond the initial response of awe and thanksgiving: "Worship is always more than merely a passive acknowledgment of the fact of God and our dependence upon Him. Worship always unavoidably leads us through the acts, the thoughts, the words, the prayers, to life which grows out of this acceptance of our creatureliness. The biblical drama sees this response in terms of Christ, in the act of God who himself reaches across the void into our humanity and makes the perfect response ... to the love that was in creation at the outset."[57] That response is sacrifice, self-offering. Bayne said:

> Because we are free, because we are real mortals, the only response we can make is true of wills obedient and disobedient. The only response we can make is by offering to him what we have, imperfect though it be, offering it to him in obedience. This is why, because we learn this about ourselves, that our eyes turn to Christ and we recognize in him the truth about ourselves. In this sublime

self-offering, in this perfect obedience, in this complete and whole response to God, this is God's idea of what it is to be a man.[58]

In the pursuit of self-offering, Bayne regarded the Eucharist as pre-eminent. In it and through it we share in Christ's offering and are enabled to offer ourselves. "He offered himself once, and yet because offering is the truth about life, the work of God will not be done until the offering is fulfilled in the heart of every living human soul."[59] In offering, then, we have the source of worship. In this sermon, given in the place where Thomas Cranmer was tried and John Henry Newman showed a world beyond this world to a generation of Oxford undergraduates, Stephen Bayne preached one of his most effective and intellectually as well as spiritually challenging sermons.

There followed the publication of two rather slight books. In 1961 there came *Enter With Joy,* containing two sets of lectures: the Stewart Lectures on preaching, originally given at Seabury-Western Seminary in February 1956; and the Easter Lectures on worship given at Kenyon College in April 1960. Bayne rightly felt that the book was of some value. It received some positive reviews and was used as a text at the College of Preachers and at some seminaries. But he thought it contained little "fresh thought" and "what was good in it was skimpy."[60] The second book, *Mindful of the Love,* was published in 1962 and was composed of addresses given as the McMath Lectures in April 1961 in Detroit. It too was considered by Bayne to be inadequate. He wrote the addresses for thoughtful but not theologically trained men and women. As a result the product was sometimes thin. He regretted not having the time to re-write it and had to be satisfied with the addition of Chapter IV. Nevertheless, years later, he acknowledged that *Mindful of the Love* was dear to him for a number of reasons: "First, it is about the Eucharist. Second, its title is drawn from a hymn much loved by him and by his parents. Third, it has a measure of leaven in it coming from the experience of the Executive Officer. It is too short. There should have been more adequate consideration of the Eucharist as celebration, for example, of its social implications, of its relationship to other forms of worship, and so on."[61]

In both books there is a clear and steady emphasis on offering, involving remembrance of God's acts in Christ, culminating in his sacrifice, his self-offering, and our participation in that offering, our offerings conjoined to his and thus acceptable. In *Enter With Joy* he wrote: "Worship is a supreme moment of offering. It is not the only such, nor necessarily the most decisive; but our worship is always a steady, unwavering point of offering."[62] In *Mindful of the Love* the Eucharist was considered chiefly in terms of remembering, sacrificing, offering, giving thanks, and sharing in the Holy Communion. Remembering, focused on God's mighty acts, and chiefly on the Cross, is a way of opening up to God and claiming God's remembrance. God "meets us in our remembrance, in His gracious presence and activity." Sacrifice is presented as the principle of life, "the principle that life must be released to serve its true Lord and master." In the Eucharist the sacrifice once for all is remembered. It is unrepeatable, but it is also an eternal fact, and because it is "basically a fact about God . . . it is also an eternally continuing act of God." It follows that our sacrifice, that is our living out the basic principle of life, "is made only through Him and in Him, and that it is our oneness with Him in all things, even in death, which supremely matters."[63]

Leaving London

There is evidence to show that as well as being challenging and to a degree fulfilling, Bayne's time as Anglican Executive Officer was not altogether satisfactory. At the outset he felt frustrated, writing to Charles Ross of Seattle in July 1960 about his feeling of being overburdened, in a new job with a new staff and work piling up before him. "We have had the wearying vexation of living out of suitcases since New Year's Eve. We are still doing so, but the end is in sight. After a long house hunt we finally located a good London City house not far from Victoria Station — 21 Chester Street, S.W. I and Lucie hope to be in it by September."[64] In August 1960 he wrote to Howard Shefelmann saying, "I don't for a moment regret what God has asked me to do; yet it is a singularly lonely and depleting task by contrast with the glorious years in Seattle."[65] In September 1961 Bayne wrote from Detroit to the Reverend Glyn Jones in the U.S.A.F. hospital in South Ruislip, Middlesex, England. Jones, who was suffering from tuberculosis, had written of his concern for the burdens Bayne was bearing, "perhaps beyond the capacity of your body to bear," and Bayne replied:

> You are very thoughtful to worry about me. I don't defend my present life; it is senseless in one way and I know it. But after more than fifty years of living and thinking a lot about these things, I keep coming back to the memory of the woman with the alabaster cruse of perfume, who broke it and poured out all she had. I'm not being romantic when I say this; I think any man has only one life to live, and it ought not be wasted; but there are moments when we really have to shoot the works. And I think this stage in my life is one of those moments.
>
> I hope it will not be so for long, for I grow daily more depleted and less able to give what I want to give. But I am just at the point now when I can see the job beginning to take form. I only pray

that another year will see the form established, so that then I can begin to look to take parts of it.

I hope this isn't egotistical. I don't feel egotistical about the job at all. I didn't want it; I never wanted anything more than the wonderful glory and privilege of being the father to my little family in Olympia. But I honestly don't know any other way to tackle this job, so new and so fathomless, than to press to the limit of my strength.[66]

Bayne's commitment to be Anglican Executive Officer was made after lengthy personal negotiations with Geoffrey Fisher and largely with an assumption that Fisher would remain Archbishop of Canterbury until the new office had been established. But it was during Bayne's first year that Fisher announced his plans to retire.[67] On January 13, 1961, Bayne met with Mr. Stephens, the Prime Minister's Secretary for Patronage. Bayne was pleased to be consulted on the choice of the next archbishop, a move he interpreted as a recognition on the part of the government of the critical role the Archbishop of Canterbury played in the Anglican Communion. In that interview, it was apparent that Michael Ramsey, Archbishop of York, would be named. Stephens asked Bayne if he knew of "any commanding reason against it." Bayne remarked that he "would be a problem, and his appointment would please the wrong people (i.e., the party extremists) and discourage the central body of the Church. There would also be difficulties in public relations, entertainment, etc. On the other hand he delegates well, dislikes fussy administration, and would be likely to encourage me to get my work done. I would have to spend much time sweeping up after him, I feared." In the end, with all his qualms, Bayne agreed on the choice of Ramsey: "When in doubt, I always bet on greatness."[68]

The degree of confidence that prevailed between Fisher and Bayne was not to be attained with Ramsey. In time, the archbishop made clear his preference for an Englishman as Executive Officer, his desire to restrict the authority of the same, and his feeling that Bayne should vacate the office at the end of his five-year term. Such at least was Bayne's understanding. He was aware of conflict, and the notes he made after his meetings with Ramsey indicate something of this. But a letter dated January 11, 1962, is more revealing than the notes. In this letter Bayne protested against the possibility that he should "report" to anyone but the Primates of the Anglican Communion and chiefly to the Archbishop of Canterbury. There had been some suggestion that he should report to John Satterthwaite in respect to the Wider Episcopal Fellowship. It would seem that a committee of the Church of England was attempting to deal in an authoritative way with something Lambeth had delegated to an inter-Anglican agency. The letter was also somewhat directive, and

Bayne recognized the fact, saying: "Well, please forgive me for seeming to tell you how to run the Anglican Communion! I really don't mean to." He ended his letter expressing appreciation for their meeting. "I pray for many more of them, for I have felt profoundly out-of-touch with you and what you expected or wanted from me. So if I have responded with improper frankness, please lay it to the account of a strange and demanding and isolated job."[69]

In October 1962 Bayne wrote to Donald Coggan, Archbishop of York, of the loneliness he felt in the office he held and of his need to have the support of friends such as Coggan and Robert Stopford, then Bishop of London. Coggan then set about arranging "Save Bayne" meetings, which were convened in March, June, and November of 1963.[70] This did much to alleviate the loneliness.

Nevertheless, beginning in the fall of 1962, the possibility of leaving London was much on Bayne's mind. He wrote to Geoffrey Fisher for advice, telling him of the suggestion he had received that he should succeed John B. Bentley as Director of the Overseas Department of the Episcopal Church's Executive Council. Fisher responded, on November 27, saying that he would not object to the move, but hoped that the successor to Bentley would not be needed for at least a year after the Toronto Congress, in order that Bayne might be able to follow up the decisions made there. He wanted Bayne to consider other options before settling on Bentley's job, however, wondering if some American diocese might elect Bayne as its bishop. "For myself," said Fisher, "what I should really like to see you doing ... is to be Archbishop in one of the Provinces of the Anglican Communion; or even if there were a vacancy, Archbishop in Jerusalem, where you would in fact have this new seminary under your control."[71]

In March of 1963 Bayne was writing again to Donald Coggan, who had hoped that Bayne would stay in office until 1970, "to see us through the next Lambeth." Toward that end, and given the burden of the job, he had suggested adequate holidays; serious consideration as to Bayne's continuing as Bishop-in-Charge of the American Convocation of Churches; some regular, but light episcopal work in England; and the appointment of two assistants "of some status." On March 18 Bayne wrote to report that he had talked with Ramsey and had come away with the feeling that the Archbishop was opposed to his continuing beyond 1964, speaking of the danger of Bayne's becoming rootless, convinced that the emphasis must be on particular churches, not the Anglican Communion, and that the next Executive Officer must be an Englishman to involve more deeply the Church of England. All of this Bayne absorbed along with the knowledge that Arthur Lichtenberger, the Presiding Bishop, was very ill and needed Bayne in the Overseas Department. "I am grateful for his [Ramsey's] frankness," wrote Bayne,

"and reassured that there is no element of personal discontent in his decision. And I do not disagree (even if I could!) I am glad, selfishly, to
feel that it is apparently not due to any failure on my part, which had
been very much in my thoughts, as you know."[72] Coggan responded
on March 26, saying he found it difficult to agree with Ramsey's arguments as Bayne presented them. "I hope you will come to no hurried
decision — too much hangs on that. ... I hope to see the opportunity
to talk with Michael. Perhaps I shall be able to unburden some of my
anxiety."[73]

Negotiations now began in earnest with Lichtenberger and the Executive Council. In May of 1963 Bayne and Ramsey talked again about
the former's future and in particular about the Overseas Department
of the Episcopal Church. In August, at the time of the Anglican Congress, Bayne wrote again to Coggan justifying his move, reiterating the
earlier arguments, but now speaking of personal factors: "Lucie's own
disrupted and lonely life, our financial worries which increase each year,
the rootlessness of my life in England."[74] There is little doubt that such
personal factors weighed heavily on Bayne's mind. Lucie had not been
well and was not happy. Bayne continued to borrow money to cover his
expenses. He loved to entertain, generously and well, but did not have
the income to do as he wished. He enjoyed belonging to the Athenaeum
Club on Pall Mall, but must have had some qualms over the expense
of that, justified, of course, by his office and responsibilities. He took
speaking engagements in part to cover his financial needs and could always justify doing so in spite of the price he had to pay in physical
and psychological depletion. His family was scattered. There were still,
as there had been for years, the expenses involved in educating his children. He had difficulties with English reserve and lack of comradeship —
with notable exceptions. From the English point of view he was, in this,
sometimes overly sensitive.

The die was cast. Bayne accepted Lichtenberger's invitation and knew
that he had Ramsey's support. Indeed, at their meeting on September 30,
1963, Ramsey told Bayne that he positively favored the move and believed that Bayne might be chosen Presiding Bishop. If chosen, Ramsey
had said, Bayne would be under the strongest compulsion to accept. The
official announcement was made on October 11, 1963. Sturgis Lee Riddle wrote from Paris: "Your surprising announcement has reached us. I
don't quite know what to make of it, as yet. Does it mean that Bishop
Lichtenberger plans to stay on as P.B. after the Convention of '64, or
what? ... Certainly you would make the best possible head for the Overseas Department, but what about the top job?"[75] Sherman Johnson
wrote: "I have been meaning to write to you and congratulate you, but
mainly ourselves and the whole Church on your appointment as head
of the Overseas Department. ... You cannot fail to realize that, even be-

fore this appointment was announced, many were thinking of you as our next Presiding Bishop. You won't want to comment on this... but this kind of talk is just an indication of the confidence everyone feels."[76]

Letters poured in from every part of the Anglican Communion recounting all of Bayne's achievements and expressing regret at his leaving his post in London. Archbishop Lesser of New Zealand wrote, "I just tremble to think of the poor man who is compelled to replace you! With what trepidation he must face the colossal tasks awaiting him, knowing how meticulously you have attended to multifarious pieces of work and kept them all moving smoothly."[77] Archbishop Brown of Uganda wrote: "It is exceedingly difficult to see how anyone else will be able to do your job with the same grace and acceptance that you have shown. No matter how long your memoranda, we have always read them through, largely because of the unexpected snatches of humour which you use to enliven even your heaviest paragraphs."[78] Noting the announcement of his resignation, the *Christian Century* editorialized: "His eminence in the Christian world is attested by the frequency with which his name is mentioned in influential circles when the question arises as to who will succeed soon-to-retire W. A. Visser t'Hooft to the general secretaryship of the World Council of Churches."[79] Fred McDonald wrote, expressing relief that Bayne would continue as Bishop-in-Charge of the American Convocation of Churches in Europe. He paid Bayne high tribute: "Let us be honest, you have given more true sense of a common church life to our convocation than has ever been known before here, and fractiousness in almost non-existent."[80]

At a meeting of the Church Assembly of the Church of England, a resolution of gratitude was drafted and unanimously approved. On that occasion Archbishop Ramsey said: "I share personally in the great debt felt widely throughout the Anglican Communion for the labours of Bishop Bayne in the last five years, and to his personal comradeship I myself owe very much. By his work and especially by his arduous journeys, Bishop Bayne has done much to help the different parts of our Anglican Communion to know one another far better, and also to know far better the meaning of our unity and mission throughout the world, both as Anglicans and in our service together with other churches in Christendom."[81]

Sometime later in answering a letter from Bayne, Michael Ramsey wrote: "You remember that some months ago we talked about this 'Bentley' possibility, and I came down on the side of the idea, feeling already that the true continuance of your work of these last years was going to lie in our church's response to it. During Toronto, when the new vision was coming to the fore so creatively and spontaneously I was having many thoughts about you, and was asking myself whether what was happening ought to alter the advice I had given to you or your plans.

Eight

A NATIONAL LEADER IN A TIME OF TURMOIL

General Convention at St. Louis

In the fall of 1964 Bayne returned to New York to begin the task to which he had been assigned by Arthur Lichtenberger. By that time, the situation had changed drastically. Due to ill health, Lichtenberger had resigned and a new Presiding Bishop, John Hines of Texas, had been elected. Hines's closest rival in the election had been Stephen Bayne, who now served under Hines as Vice President of the National Council of the Episcopal Church and Director of the Overseas Department.

Bayne had attempted to turn down his nomination as Presiding Bishop, but had been persuaded by Lichtenberger not to do so.[1] Having accepted appointment to the Overseas Department, Bayne felt reluctant to be a candidate. Nevertheless, many felt that with his experience as Anglican Executive Officer he was the logical choice and if nominated would surely win. At the convention, MRI was endorsed by the Episcopal Church, and Bayne spoke at the Joint Session of the House of Bishops and the House of Deputies on Mutual Responsibility.[2] Bayne also addressed a large throng gathered on October 15 for a Service of Renewal and Dedication.

Then came the election. It took place at an executive session of the House of Bishops at the Cathedral in St. Louis, with no press and no observers present. The procedures began with Holy Communion, after which the voting started. Three persons were nominated: Bishop Emrich of Michigan, Bishop Hines of Texas, and Bishop Bayne. There were two additional nominations from the floor. Bishop Bentley nominated Bishop Wright of East Carolina, who had been chairman of the Overseas Department for six years and had presented the MRI document to the convention; Bishop Scaife nominated Bishop Louttit of South Florida. On the first ballot Bayne was clearly ahead with 43 votes as opposed to

34 for Hines, 32 for Emrich, 30 for Louttit, and 14 for Wright. Bayne,
Hines, and Emrich all gained on the second ballot, whereas Louttit and
Wright lost support. By the third ballot, Louttit and Wright had with-
drawn, and Bayne had 56 votes to 51 for Hines and 46 for Emrich. With
the fourth ballot, Emrich's support began to fade, and by the fifth, Hines
had 73 votes to Bayne's 71, with 78 needed to elect. On the sixth and
final ballot, Bayne had 70 votes to Hines's 83.[3]

Afterward Stephen Bayne reflected on what had happened. Why did
he lose when so many thought he would surely win? He wrote in a private memorandum: "I think there isn't any question — immodest as it
sounds — but that I would have been elected, except for one thing, that
I was already slated for the Overseas Department and had accepted it.
I doubt if more than a handful of the overseas bishops voted for me,
on the ground that they knew me and welcomed my appointment and
feared what might happen otherwise." Bayne rejoiced in the election of
John Hines and thought that those southern conservatives who switched
from Louttit to Hines were in for a rude shock. He was pleased that the
bishops had chosen an able administrator (he did not regard himself as
such) and a man "of the utmost integrity and power in our House." He
went on in his personal reflections to say:

> We both began our ministries in St. Louis 30 years ago (he mar-
> ried a St. Louis girl), and we have worked together for so long on
> so many things that there could not be a happier boss for me to
> have. We don't agree on many things liturgical and ecclesiastical,
> but we are at one in what we feel and hope for the Church's mis-
> sion everywhere. If he wants me as Overseas Director, I could not
> possibly imagine a happier situation. And I am glad now . . . that
> I let my name go forward, for it aided our House in coming to a
> clear mind, and it will give this Church a very strong team at a
> time when we need it more than ever.

Such was Bayne's understanding. Many were sorely disappointed and
wrote to console him. Bayne himself was disappointed, but resigned. He
wrote to Bishop Crittenden after the election, saying, "I am sure that
it was right for me to let my name stand, and you were the one who
principally encouraged me in this. Because I did, we were able to reach
a firm and unquestionable decision, which could give all of us secure
guidelines for the future. I see that now, although at the beginning I
guess I was thinking too egotistically, and only about what I would like
to do myself."[4]

The fact is that John Hines was elected and wanted Stephen Bayne by
his side. And so Bayne returned from London in November 1964 to be
the Director of the Overseas Department of the Episcopal Church.

Director of the Overseas Department

Stephen Bayne began his new work in a time of rapid change and manifest discontent. Addressing the Synod of the Fourth Province of the Episcopal Church, he spoke specifically of discontent in the Church, discontent among the clergy "who feel that they are not doing what ought to be done or what needs to be done," and discontent among the laity "who feel that the timeless patterns of worship and prayer are simply ridiculous in this twentieth century."[5] He could feel the foundations shaking. The civil rights movement in 1964 was still gathering momentum. There was still discrimination, and as long as race prejudice prevailed there would be injustice and violence. Nuclear and environmental crises were now identified but were found to be virtually unmanageable. A war was developing in Southeast Asia. The Near East was ready to explode. A president had been slain as he passed down an American city street. Women were expressing their deep discontent at being treated as second-class citizens.

The problems of the age, as he viewed them, were related to the erosion of faith and commitment in the sacred society identified with the body of the Incarnate Word. To the clergy and laity at Sewanee he cried out: "I say to you with the utmost seriousness that the only thing the Church exists for is to obey; and to obey means to join our Lord in his offering, offering all that is and all that happens."[6] If the people of God were to lose confidence, where then would be hope? If God were dead, as Gabriel Vahanian announced in 1961 and the Episcopalian Paul Van Buren seemed to confirm in 1963, what would be the use of gathering on Sundays for worship?

It was in the context of this concern that Bayne began his work as an administrator at Episcopal Church headquarters. The Overseas Department that he managed was by 1966 the "planning unit of the Church with respect to the church overseas, the primary channel of communications to and from the church overseas, the primary resource for interpretation, and the principal organizer of relationships." Planning involved everyone in the department and some key persons overseas, such as a planning officer in the Caribbean and regional officers in those parts of the world where the Episcopal Church was especially involved. There was a division for personnel management. There were 300 Americans ministering overseas "in some 46 dioceses under 42 different flags."[7]

In 1966 the department was responsible for "about 125 projects totaling about $2,000,000, supported by voluntary gifts over and above quotas from some 84 dioceses of our Church. In addition, Companion Diocese relationships involved about 45 dioceses."[8] The department was responsible for some eighty exchange clergy and laity from over-

seas — providing financial, educational, and pastoral support. There was
a heavy emphasis on communications. Bayne himself began two newsletters: "Letters to all the Bishops" and "Dear Nephews." In addition,
the department Bayne headed was concerned for the spiritual welfare
of Americans overseas — Bayne himself continuing his responsibilities as
Bishop-in-Charge of the American Convocation of Churches in Europe.
Corporate planning was being refined to assure that the resources of the
Church were being expended wisely in assisting overseas jurisdictions
through projects and through companion diocese relationships.

There were problems to be faced. The Home Department of the
Executive Council proposed in 1966 that all domestic missionary districts should be converted into dioceses. Some believed this sort of thing
should happen with American overseas jurisdictions. In a memorandum
on the subject, Bayne argued that the domestic and overseas situations
were not comparable. With the exception of special cases such as those
of Hawaii and Alaska, the aim was not the creation of American de-
pendencies — dioceses or provinces. The aim "is that of planting and
nourishing indigenous churches, helping to guide and support them as
they grow, preparing them for autonomous life, and at the appropriate time, releasing them into their own responsible provincial freedom."
To put it bluntly: "Our job is to put ourselves out of business, with
respect to our overseas jurisdictions." This was the policy, and this
was a point of real tension in the Church, where some people still regarded missionary work as concerning "them" not us, and being "ours"
not theirs.[9]

Another concern was that those composing the Overseas Department
staff were moving "into a positive and aggressive role, step by step."
Bayne welcomed this, but he advised caution, for it was happening at the
same time that people — through MRI — were being encouraged to take
individual initiative and make voluntary responses to the appeals they
received. "There is a real tension and polarity here, as anyone can see,"
Bayne observed. "If the unity of our Church's obedience to mission is to
be maintained, then there is an inescapable degree of corporate, central
action which is essential. Yet this must be continually reconciled with
the need to develop the voluntary sector of response to the maximum
possible extent." In this Bayne emphasized an issue of great importance,
one he grappled with as Anglican Executive Officer, "how to presume
an essential unity in action without throttling responsible individual initiative," or, to put it another way, how to preserve the creative tension
and a just relationship between unity and diversity, a major and precious treasure of Anglicanism. The marriage between the two was not
an easy one, necessitating constant alertness and attention as well as
"pretty constant fidelity on the part of everybody involved."[10]

Much of Bayne's attention went to the promotion of MRI. His immediate responsibility was to the development of the program in the Episcopal Church after its endorsement by General Convention in 1964. A directory of projects was prepared after much consultation, investigation in the field, and by correspondence and careful evaluation. There was the necessity of helping dioceses make choices and, as time progressed, make decisions in relationship to involvement in companion relationships with dioceses overseas.

The first directory was issued early in 1965 and contained 250 projects.[11] By September, 85 of those had been undertaken with a total cost of $550,000, far short of the target in that initial year of $1 million. In September 1965 a second directory was issued containing 320 projects with a goal for 1966 of $2 million and for 1967 of $3 million. In introducing the second directory, Bayne offered four considerations: (1) the need to respect the initiative and judgment of the planning Church, which meant fidelity to the projects as listed, (2) the need to welcome "the willingness of our companions overseas to share their daily needs and ask for our partnership," (3) the need to be concerned for the lack of any clear ecumenical dimension in the projects themselves, and (4) the need to be concerned that only two of our constituent overseas dioceses (Taiwan and the Philippines) "are represented in regional directories."[12] The production of such a directory necessitated close cooperation with those preparing directories for other churches and regional councils. Bayne was much involved in this and also in advising and counseling those outside the United States.

Bayne was involved in education for MRI. He gave the Kellogg Lectures at the Episcopal Theological School in Cambridge, Massachusetts, and addresses at the Finger Lakes Conference, which were the basis for *Mission Is Response,* a "slim book...published at the urging of the MRI Commission who were hard at work developing a study program to support PECUSA's response to the MRI challenge."[13]

He championed the concept of "companion dioceses," seeing it as a forceful expression of MRI, leading a conference in 1968 at Roslyn, Virginia, of those involved in it.[14] Again he found it necessary to prevent misunderstanding, writing to Bishop Warnecke of Bethlehem: The aim of companionship is not to provide a financial pipeline. "Its sole purpose is outlined in its title — to provide a way in which two dioceses can discover each other and their common obedience in the Body of Christ." Bayne acknowledged the natural tendency for there to be financial undertakings in the development of the companionship. "But," he said, "our policy is to soft-pedal this as much as possible."[15]

Bayne also wrote articles for various church publications explaining and defending MRI.[16] In May of 1966 the *Church Times* of London published an editorial suggesting that MRI was in trouble, not having met its financial goal of a five-year emergency increase in giving (of approximately a third) to support overseas churches of the Anglican Communion, a failure due, so the *Church Times* said, to a lack of administrative authority.[17] In a lengthy letter to the editor, Bayne suggested that the Anglican conscience was able to accept the failure (with notable exceptions) to meet the five-year goal "and also to carry out the fundamental reconstruction of Church life which is summarized as MRI." He did not regard the failure as due to a lack of administrative authority, for no amount of authority "can change the hearts and minds of people or lead them to a more generous obedience to mission." He then wrote:

> It is not "MRI" which is in trouble. It is Christians who are in trouble — Christians in young Churches overseas who need the support and comradeship of their brothers, Christians at home who need to share more deeply and at greater cost in the single mission of our Lord, Christians at home and overseas who need to give and to receive in ever greater mutuality and humility. We do not care enough. This is the simple truth; and it should not be obscured by irrelevant editorial jargon about central authority.[18]

Here Bayne was seeking to preserve recognition of the necessary tension in Anglicanism between "central authority" and individual response, and to acknowledge that at root what mattered was the commitment of the people of God — such commitment as cannot be coerced.

In his letter, Bayne then faulted the *Church Times* for its constant misinterpretation of MRI as a "financial programme," "a child of the Toronto Anglican Congress," and "a scheme of Christian charity." The editors replied with a leader in the same issue, accusing Bayne of being "betrayed by apparent emotion into making...wild allegations." But they pleaded that they "intended no criticism of Bishop Bayne, whom indeed we did not mention." The editor, the Reverend Roger L. Roberts, wrote a letter expressing personal good will, and Bayne responded with thanks.[19] Douglas Webster wrote to Bayne: "This is just a short note to say how deeply I agree with your letter in today's *Church Times*, and how bewildered I am at the extraordinary leader they have written about it." Bayne answered Webster saying that the editor wrote "to say that he was sorry that I had felt that the original article [editorial] made some personal reference to myself. How stupid can a man be! I don't propose to carry on the debate with the CT, you may be sure. I have said what needed to be said; and I am content. But how annoying that fantastic operation can be, when they get in one of their stuffy moods."[20]

MRI was of personal concern to Bayne. Misinterpretation of it hurt, as did any attack upon it, however well-meaning. The MRI principles were all important to Bayne. Finances were secondary and after the principles were fully in operation would take care of themselves. But it was not to be as Bayne prayed and hoped. In 1973 at Dublin in Ireland, the Anglican Consultative Council reported that MRI had "been too largely identified with the Directory of Projects, and this in turn has led to a 'shopping list' mentality." In an attempt to recover the original vision of Toronto, the ACC initiated a program called "Partners in Mission," which concentrated on priorities, not money, and involved consultations in which churches, with the assistance of partners from different parts of the world, engaged in self-examination, planning, and the fixing of priorities.[21] Although there was no denying the failures, there was also no denying the fact that many people, including Church leaders, caught the vision of MRI and would not surrender it to its enemies.

If Bayne had expected an easier life in New York than he had had in London, that was not to be. In a "Dear Nephew" letter of July 1967 he told of traveling 101,000 miles in the first six months of the year, and he was writing his letter on the second trip away from New York since the end of June. "I can't complain," he said, "except that in the 21st year of our episcopate I ain't as young as I used to be; and it is depressing to come home to so many unanswered letters."[22] While doing his job, he had to contend with efforts to have him move: to be president of Hobart and William Smith Colleges; rector of the Church of the Advent, Boston; bishop of California, or Long Island, or Spokane — all in 1966 and all declined.[23] He was to be found one day in São Paulo, Brazil, for a consultation on the Anglican Communion and South America; a follow-up to that at Cuernavaca in 1963; another day at Kampala; then at Mukono, consulting with leaders of the new Province in Uganda; in London for a meeting at SPCK; in Jerusalem for a conference on "Projects"; in Nice and in Rome to fulfill duties as Bishop-in-Charge; and in New York for endless meetings and for mountainous piles of correspondence. In the midst of all, between 1964 and 1968 there was the agonizing Pike affair, which engaged Bayne's attention and taxed his diplomatic skills.

Dogma and the Pike Affair

On his arrival from London, Bayne gave a series of sermons at Trinity Church, Wall Street, on Dogma and Reality. At the outset he disclaimed any attempt to provide "some kind of response to Bishop Pike, or to Bishop Robinson." J. A. T. Robinson's *Honest to God* (1963) had already aroused considerable debate, especially in England, and James Pike's *A Time for Christian Candor* (1964) was the cause of considerable consternation among conservative Christians for its seeming dismissal of the traditional doctrine of the Trinity, as well as doctrines of the Incarnation and Virgin Birth. Bayne was, as he described himself, "a conventional catholic Christian."[24] He relied upon the dogma of the creeds, which was the dogma of the Church as a whole, then and through the ages. He knew that human words were inadequate to express the great truths toward which they pointed, but with all their imperfections they managed to do that for which they existed — to guarantee the Church's unity. They have not always succeeded in doing that. "The great doctrinal statements of the Christian faith" have on occasion been divisive. But, he argued, "when they did become divisive, more often than not it was because those great statements were being used for wrong motives, or because they were being made to say more than they really said." He then put it another way. The great doctrines "were intended, and they still are intended, for one purpose — to guarantee the continuance of the worshiping, intercessing community of Christians; to guarantee its unity, to make it possible for people of different minds to live and pray and work and die together."[25]

Bayne, however, had no use for doctrine, belief, or faith that deteriorates into "conformity or credulity." When that happens, the Church is sick indeed. "The Christian faith is not a test that people must pass or fail. The Christian faith is not a policeman to keep wrong-thinking people out. The Church is not a collection of people who think alike. Intellectual conformity is not a virtue. . . . Nor is credulity a virtue."[26] Diversity within community — this describes Anglicanism; it also describes the Christian Church, where faith and understanding are concerned. And thus dogma, the great doctrines authoritatively taught, is necessary. However, words are inadequate, break, crumble, fall apart under the burden of the mystery they convey. In faith — in the great catholic creeds — they convey the mystery as they crumble, and crumbling into nothingness serve to reveal that which is trustworthy, that for which one can give one's life with confidence.

It was in this spirit that Bayne observed and participated in the events beginning with charges made in July 1965 against Bishop Pike by certain clergy of the Diocese of Arizona. The charges, chiefly that Pike repudiated the doctrines of the Virgin Birth, the Incarnation, and the Trinity, were presented to the House of Bishops meeting at East Glacier, Montana, September 7–9, 1965.[27] The Theological Committee of the House considered the charges and reported that the Bishop of California was not on trial and defended his right to engage in theological inquiry. The report, read by Bishop Emrich of Michigan, stated that "language changes; the concepts which are the furniture of men's minds change; the Faith given in the mighty acts of God does not change. Nor do we doubt that many an allegation of heterodoxy against any of us, or our clergy, is in fact a covert attack on legitimate Christian social concern and action."[28] Bishop Pike responded to the report, after its approval by the House, thanking his brother bishops and saying: "I must be faithful to the task to which I believe God has called me — that of seeking to distinguish the earthen vessels from the Treasure, and in the hope of setting forth, with integrity and dedication, more contemporary carriers of the Christian faith." He bemoaned the tendency on the part of mass media to distort his statements, and he reaffirmed his "loyalty to the Doctrine, Discipline, and Worship of the Episcopal Church."[29]

The Pike affair might have ended at East Glacier, Montana, had it not been for the disturbed conscience of Henry Louttit, Bishop of South Florida, who, in September 1966, made a formal presentment against Bishop Pike, accusing him of heresy (specifically: "Holding and teaching publicly and advisedly, doctrines contrary to that held by this Church"). Bishop Louttit wrote the presentment for a committee that he created called the Committee of Bishops to Defend the Faith. In an appendix, five charges were made, citing offenses and quoting grounds chiefly from Bishop Pike's writings. The presentment was considered at the meeting of the House of Bishops in Wheeling, West Virginia, October 23–27, 1966. The majority of the bishops decided against a heresy trial. "This 'heresy trial' would be widely viewed as a 'throw-back' to centuries when the law, in Church and State, sought to repress and penalize unacceptable opinions.... We believe that our Church is quite capable of carrying the strains of free inquiry and of responsible, and even irresponsible, attempts to restate great articles of faith in ways that would speak in positive and kindling terms to men in our own time."[30]

Nevertheless, they felt it necessary to censure "the time and manner of much that Bishop Pike has said as being irresponsible and highly disturbing within the communion and fellowship of the Church." The outcome was not pleasing to Pike, who requested a formal investigation (i.e., a heresy trial), or to the minority, which pointed to the Toronto Congress where new frontiers in mission were explored.

> We happily agreed that there are frontiers of political and social and technological and theological thought and action confronting Christ's Church; and that our mission is to pierce them. Few of us have done so, in large part because of the risk involved and because of the danger of the task. Bishop Pike has faced, often hurriedly, the demands, intellectual and theological, of our time in history, and we commend him for doing so. If he has to be a casualty of the Christian mission in our day we regret that this is so.[31]

Bishop Bayne, according to the information he provided to William Stringfellow and Anthony Towne, voted against the presentment and for the censure, and thus he stood with the majority of the bishops. In part to satisfy Bishop Pike, but more to deal with issues dividing the Church as a result of the Pike affair, John Hines as Presiding Bishop appointed a committee, chaired by Bishop Bayne, including Bishops

Jones of West Texas and Barrett of Rochester, Louis Cassels of UPI, George Shipman of the University of Washington, David Sills of the International Encyclopedia of Social Science, Theodore Ferris, Rector of Trinity Church, Boston, John MacQuarrie of Union Seminary, A. T. Mollegen of Virginia Theological Seminary, Charles Price of Harvard, and one non-Episcopalian, Paul Minear of Yale Divinity School. This was to be an advisory committee, intended to report to the Presiding Bishop, who was then to determine what use would be made of their findings.

The committee was asked to consider a wide range of issues: (1) the present theological situation, (2) the "scope of legitimate openness in our Church for theological reformation," (3) the "permissible breadth and variety of modes and manners of statement in our time," (4) the matter of "Anglican comprehensiveness" and its limits, (5) the "issue as to what extent problems, doubts, and new or radical positions should be shared with the laity," (6) the "scope of freedom in the Church in all these matters, modes of official judgments with special attention to the place of the ecclesiastical equivalent of 'due process' in the decision-making procedures," (7) the "nature of 'heresy' in the light of the increasingly complex relationships and interactions between 'Faith' and scientific knowledge," and (8) the "role of responsible bodies such as the House of Bishops in interpreting a wise and effective stance under the umbrella 'Defenders of the Faith,' and including an appraisal of the possible world wide effect of presently provided canonical procedures with reference to a trial for heresy."[32]

Bishop Pike was pleased regarding Bishop Hines's creation of the committee and the charge to it, a "creative — indeed historic — step which gives a comprehensive opportunity to move toward a consensus regarding the issues of which the draft heresy presentment and the House of Bishops censure have made me for the time being a focus." He was willing to have his request for investigation by canonical means be shelved while the committee did its work.[33] The committee had little time, having to aim at presenting its results to the General Convention meeting in Seattle the fall of 1967. An organizing meeting was held in February at which it was determined to invite a representative group of consultants to deal with these issues, the issues that were to provide the framework of the report:

1. What obligations does the Church have for encouraging theological inquiry and social criticism? What procedures should it provide to fulfill those obligations?

2. What obligations should be assumed by those who participate in theological inquiry and social criticism?

3. What is heresy? How should the Church define, detect and deal with it?[34]

Those consultants whose papers were printed with the report were J. V. Langmead Casserley, John Knox, Eric Mascall, Paul Moore, Jr., John Courtney Murray, J. A. T. Robinson, Theodora Sorg, Albert Stuart, Arthur Vogel, and James Pike.

When the report was finished in August, the *New York Times* proclaimed in a headline: "Episcopal Body Assails Idea of Heresy."[35] The report termed the concept of heresy "anachronistic" and called for a revision of canon law to make heresy trials almost impossible. The committee said, "Any risks the Church may run by fostering a climate of genuine freedom are minor compared to the dangers it surely will encounter from any attempts at suppression, censorship or thought control." The committee stopped short of calling for a complete eradication of heresy trials. It was doubtful that the General Convention could be brought to agree to a complete ban. Bishop Pike himself, appearing before the committee in April, argued that the committee should not propose a complete ban because the Church, he believed, must retain the ultimate means to protect itself. The committee thus stated: "The Church may feel it must maintain a last-resort power to deal juridically with bishops or priests who publicly engage in persistent and flagrant contradiction of its essential witness."[36]

Where was that essential witness to be located? Reflecting on the criticism of some people that the report "does not seem explicitly to affirm the faith of the Church as expressed in the Bible and the creeds," Bayne suggested that the critics read John Knox's statement "which the committee made its own at the outset of the report." That statement expressed Bayne's view, defining the Church not in terms of particular officers or instruments such as Bible or creeds, "but the whole body of those united in Christ" — in other words, organically rather than sociologically or politically. Bayne furthermore emphasized the report's discussion of the Prayer Book "and our characteristic Anglican *lex orandi.*" The center of Christian life in the Anglican Communion is in common worship, according to *The Book of Common Prayer.*[37] "When Episcopalians," the report says, "are questioned about the supposed orthodoxy or heterodoxy of one of their members, their most likely response is to ask whether or not he wishes — sincerely and responsibly — to join them in celebration of God's being and goodness in the prayers and worship of the Prayer Book. Assuming his integrity, they would not be likely to press the question beyond that point."[38] Here was the one critical test, and here in a fresh way, a way pursued by many theologians and other church leaders since, the center of authority was being defined in terms of the Church as an organic community of those worshiping God together rather than in terms of Scripture, Tradition, and Reason, or the Lambeth Quadrilateral, or any other such statement.

The report was on the whole well received. Pike regarded it as "a breath of fresh air." The temper and position of the report was affirmed by the House of Bishops, and its recommendations concerning changes in the canon laws were adopted. The report itself was further commended to the Church for study. In a "Dear Brother Bishops" letter, Bayne commented: "According to which paper you read, this is the report by which (a committee) (the 815 hierarchy) (led) (hornswoggled) the Church into a (new climate of freedom) (rejection of all Catholic faith) and was (endorsed) (forced through) (with virtual unanimity) (against the heroic resistance of one true bishop) in order to (strengthen legitimate debate) (please Bishop Pike)."[39] There was dissatisfaction, but it was limited.

The committee's work was done and it was disbanded, but there appeared at the end of its report a recommendation that "a standing commission on the teaching of the Church" be formed. An attempt was made to do just that in 1969, at the instigation of John Hines and with Bayne actively guiding the preliminaries, but the attempt to form something comparable to the Doctrine Commission of the Church of England and to produce something like *Doctrine in the Church of England* was frustrated when the proposal of an Advisory Council on the Church's Teaching was defeated by the Special Convention meeting at Notre Dame in 1969.

Seattle 1967 — the Special Program

By 1967, as the Episcopal Church made preparations for its triennial General Convention at Seattle, it was clear that the American people were in the midst of a major national crisis. Writing in the *Church Times,* Stephen Bayne referred to civil disturbances growing in magnitude and violence in the American cities. Earlier, in London, Bayne had been challenged by English friends to explain the civil rights disturbances, mostly in the South and mostly concerned with issues of discrimination and segregation. At that earlier time he had predicted that there was more to come, that the basic issues would not be reached until the civil rights stage had been passed, and that the center of attention would shift from southern to northern cities.

> Now the events of our turbulent summer are validating that prediction. Newark and Detroit are but two of more than 40 northern cities which have seen violent disturbances in these steamy months. And of the many lessons that those disturbances teach, some are of

commanding clarity and importance. Significant as the civil rights movement was, the greatest strains on underprivileged people are those imposed by their shameful housing, the poverty which robs them of the gifts of the rich economy they see trumpeted on television, the lack of education which closes employment opportunities to them, and running through all those, the despairing fear that it will never be any different, that the American dream will never come true for them.[40]

Bayne sensed the urgency of the day. The patience of the poor, so many of whom were Blacks, was running out, and violent eruptions between the Black subcommunity and the larger community were the result. To correct the situation, money on an unprecedented scale would be needed and every available human resource. The situation was exacerbated by the highly controversial and divisive Vietnam War. "The comfortable, sectarian, club psychology of American Christianity" was no longer valid, and the spiritual resources for dealing with the crisis were thin at best. Many despaired of the Church's being able to do anything meaningful or effective. Some grasped at any opportunity for effecting social change without regard to theological basics. Some resorted to action as the solution. There was a widespread disregard for history. Caught in confusion and uncertainty, the Church spoke without "the self-confidence and power God means it to have." Bayne reported that a friend of his "said the other day, when we were worrying together about the difficulties the General Convention will face, that if our eyes can be turned away from ourselves, to the unsuspected, now appalling breakdown of American society, the Church may in fact rise to its calling." Bayne agreed. "There is no reason why this should not happen; but it will not happen without pain and cost."[41]

At Seattle the Church sought to rise to its calling. In August, Bishop Hines had toured the Bedford-Stuyvesant area of New York and the slums of Detroit, spending a day in each, walking, asking questions, listening, and all the while being more and more deeply affected. He spoke, only a day or two after, to an emergency session of the Urban Coalition, and his speech there marked the first development of the speech he was to give at the opening service at Seattle. As Stephen Bayne said, Hines "put squarely before the Church a proposal for a ghetto program in which the Church would devote itself or part of its energies and resources to trying in whatever seemed possible, trying to help ghetto people stand on their own feet. He put it in very dramatic terms. One of the terms which was heard was, there were to be no strings attached to grants which were to be made under the program. I think that disturbed a lot of people until they began to understand the necessity of this." Bayne had learned long ago that if you wanted to empower someone —

say a missionary Church — to act for itself, you must put the power in its hands. Such was the General Convention's Special Program, "a program of providing funds in the form of small grants and in providing the advice of skilled counselors to community groups."[42] Hines met with an enthusiastic response, including the provision of very large sums of money not in the budget (he asked for $3 million out of a yearly budget of $12 million), part from Convention Funds and part from the Women's United Thank Offering.

The Convention set forth three goals: to empower the poor, to combat racism in the Church, and to "encourage the use of political and economic power to attain justice and self-determination for all men."[43] There were four criteria for grants made as a part of the program: (1) The people in the ghettos should "set, pursue, and achieve their own goals" with Episcopal Church money enabling this process. (2) There was to be understanding and use of normal procedures for granting funds to community organizations, including fiscal responsibility, competence and training, evaluation, etc. (3) "Episcopal enabling money for community organization should be 'under the control of those who are largely both black and poor.'" (4) There should be a policy of "working mutuality and interdependence with other Churches and with secular agencies." Two agencies noted were "Urban America" and the "Inter-religious Foundation for Community Organization (IFCO), both ecumenical in nature. After Seattle, a Screening and Review Committee was established with a small staff, with membership drawn from the Executive Council of the Church and from certain ghetto-related organizations. After some dispute it was agreed that grants made by the committee must be approved by the bishop of the diocese in the area affected. If the bishop objected, grants could be made only by the Executive Council.

The crisis program had serious consequences for the budget of the Episcopal Church and for the budget of the Overseas Department in particular. After Seattle Bayne wrote a "Dear Nephews" letter:

Let this bring greetings from the abysmal post-Seattle confusion in these parts. And I mean confusion. For one thing, we are having to go through yet one more round of budget adjustment ("adjustment," as usual, means a downward drift; it is reminiscent of the wartime phrase "rectification of lines," which always turned out to be a euphemism for getting licked). For another thing, we are in the thick of improvising the new structure which the Executive Council must have to administer the crisis program. So our days are not dull.[44]

The First Vice President — Reorganization and Crisis

Stephen Bayne was in the midst of all of this. In 1968 he relinquished the Overseas Department to Bishop Brooke Mosley and became First Vice President of the Executive Council and Deputy for Program. At the same time, he ceased to be Bishop-in-Charge of the American Convocation of Churches in Europe. As Deputy for Program, Bayne exercised a critical role in the re-organized Executive Council.

In 1969, looking back, Bayne reflected on the new structure, a structure designed to better enable the executive branch of the Church to administer the Special Program. A study was made leading to proposals adopted by the Council at meetings in February and May of 1968. It should be noted that this structure was regarded as temporary and was made possible by the suspension through September 1970 of the Council's By-Laws. Bayne reported:

> With the suspension of the Council's departmental structure, the way was opened to establish new and corporate planning and administrative procedures. The program and related staff members were grouped in four "Sections," that word being used to make clear that the Staff as a whole was the basic unit. Coherence and identity within each Section is given by the main common elements in the programs as grouped: i.e., "Professional Leadership Development" or "Experimental and Specialized Services."[45]

The section for overseas was, because of the nature of the Overseas Department's work, somewhat different, but even here some of its functions were deployed to other sections. The directors of the five sections — Overseas Relations, Service to Dioceses, Professional Leadership Development, Experimental and Specialized Services, and General Convention Special Program — together with the Presiding Bishop and the Deputy for Program constituted the "Staff Program Group" chaired by the Presiding Bishop. The group was charged with two chief responsibilities: (1) "To assure, and achieve, necessary central planning on behalf of the Executive Council" and (2) "To function for staff program activities as the central point of decision, coordination, and integration, of the General Church Program." These persons, with the Treasurer of the Executive Council and the Director of Communications, who sometimes sat with the Staff Group as advisers, and with the Vice President for Administration and the personnel officer, constituted the "Management Group, responsible for the policies and procedures governing the internal management of the Center and the Staff." Bayne commented: "Thus the reorganization of the staff has moved toward a group-style of decision making, a more flexible deployment of the staff, and a steadily growing use of intersectional teams for planning and program service."[46]

There were problems in the reorganization; both losses and gains could be identified by Bayne in 1969:

The losses seem to be mainly in two areas: the disappearance of familiar lines of communication both within the Council and with the Church at large, and the weakening of the continuing relationship of Council members and staff which the old departmental structure provided. The gains are perhaps most clearly seen in the flexibility and coordination which is made possible, chiefly through the group-style of decision making, although there is yet much to be learned and established, even after a year of experience.[47]

There also was developing considerable strain between the dioceses and the Executive Council and the Church Center Staff. Not everyone was in step with the changes that were happening. Some suspected that the reorganization was done to further strengthen the Church Center's crisis program (actually General Convention's crisis program). Bayne viewed what was happening in terms of MRI, writing shortly after the Seattle Convention that the Episcopal Church and its overseas companions were being taught a lesson in interdependence: "Because of the new crisis program, everything else that our Church is doing must be reevaluated. Many familiar programs will disappear; most of the rest will be leveled off to a plateau, in order to provide the resources needed for the emergency program in the cities."[48] There were to be those who would suffer for the sake of this program, including overseas jurisdictions, service agencies of long standing, and dioceses dependent upon national church resources.

During 1968 Bishop Bayne made visitations to the dioceses to explain what was happening and to listen to what people were saying. He was pleased by the growing support for the Special Program and by the growing interest in experimentation, but he was disturbed by the misunderstanding still evident and by the widening theological cleavage in the Church — "the divided mind about our social responsibilities and the like." He recognized that the Church was increasingly polarized, for instance, as between "activists" and "passivists." But he went on to say: "I have the feeling that none of these polarities and divisions is new in the life of the Church; most of them can actually be traced in the New Testament. I doubt if the Church has ever lived by consensus or compromise; it has always had to make decisions within the tension between great polarities." How has it been able to do this? By lifting the differences and resulting conflicts

to the theological level, where differences of opinion and differences of emphasis and differences of technique can find a new unity in a common obedience, which overrides the differences among individuals. The trouble with us is that we have failed to present the theological setting and foundation for the decisions we have made. The General Convention Special Program is a case in point. Whatever social or political justification this might have is really irrelevant; the Church has only one obedience, which is to mission; and it was in the profound surge of obedience at Seattle that this program was undertaken. If it has lost that theological setting, the Church is lost; and we shall have nothing left to us but misunderstanding and suspicion and lack of confidence — precisely the qualities which appear so often in the reports of visitors to dioceses.[49]

Bayne was deeply pained by the lack of theological understanding and commitment on the part of so many, both opponents and exponents of the Special Program.

Indeed, it was at this point that Bayne was feeling more and more ill at ease. He believed that the Church was moving in the right direction, generally, but often for wrong or inadequate reasons. In one letter he spoke of himself as being a "New York traditionalist ... and like any traditionalist, I am suspicious of quick and radical discontinuities with the past. I don't believe that near-violent change by itself, in institutions and Church services and forms of ministry and the like, necessarily produces changed people or changed society." Furthermore, he was disturbed by

> what seems to me the excessive concentration of that whole movement on social change, at the expense of a continuing concentration on the building up of the personal and individual discipleship which has been the treasure at the heart of the Christian faith. I don't mean that it's one against the other. I think it's a very false distinction to set personal and individual needs over against those of our whole society and nation. We are what our brothers are; and we are hopelessly involved in the total life of our society; and I agree that you can't deal with one side alone. But I have honestly to say that I think, at the moment, the young leadership of the Church is far more interested in the social aspect than they are in the other, and I'm sorry for this.[50]

Nevertheless, Bayne expressed his "enormous faith in the integrity of our Church, and its leadership, even where I don't feel comfortable with this and that decision or movement." As Deputy for Program, Bayne was responsible, with the Presiding Bishop and the Executive Council, for the Church's total program, including the Special Program. He had, or felt he had, responsibility for explaining and defending grants made to controversial persons and causes, including grants for the "Huey Newton film" and the Malcolm X University. In some instances grants were made over the strong opposition of diocesan bishops. In some quarters of the Church it was believed that the Special Program was supporting the growth of violence in American society and seemingly endorsing Marxist activists. Resistance stiffened. Some people left the Church in protest. Many more decreased or withheld their financial contributions.

In February of 1969, Bayne wrote to Ivol Curtis, Bishop of Olympia, to explain the situation.[51] The shortfall in the budget of a little over 3 percent was not large and was accommodated in the 1969 budget by cutting back in "household expenses" without damage to the Church's programs and by holding staff down to 273 persons, 64 lower than the top limit set in 1964. The signs were, however, disturbing in terms of the cessation of the year-by-year increase in income in the parish churches. There could be many explanations for the decrease, as in dissatisfaction with the Church or in distrust of government. Bayne was not prepared to nail the blame to any one cause. He was convinced that the situation would continue to worsen, expressed his dissatisfaction with quotas, and informed Bishop Curtis that the Executive Council was exploring ways of (1) "achieving full support of the General Church Program from the jurisdictions...(2) enlarging the voluntary sector through extra budgetary giving...and (3) enlisting designated support from non-ecclesiastical sources (as foundations)." Furthermore, there was to be a study made of "program-priorities, especially with regard to grants" and "an evaluation of the projects funded through the General Convention Special Program." He denied that the last was caused by suspicion of the Special Program and argued that the Special Program evaluation was not concerned with fiscal responsibility only. He maintained: "It is rather missionary responsibility. Contrary to what many have said, the GCSP is not sociological meddling; it is an attempt to be obedient to mission on perhaps the farthest-out frontier our Church has ever touched. It must be evaluated against that mission."

The challenge was to recognize in the Special Program the mission of the whole Church, admittedly a difficult matter. Bayne saw the challenge as a theological one and pointed to three tools: (1) Education for the realization of a "deeper, wider common understanding of the Christian's mission in our world." (2) "Achievement of unified planning across the board, so that parish, diocese, and national church were all working toward the same goals, and knew they were, and knew what the goals were." And (3) the most difficult to imagine, actually "a whole group of instruments by which we can recover a lost sense of the greatness of what Christian mission is about." Bayne wrote that the budget difficulties confronting the Church signaled the end of an era "of cheap and easy popularity." The process of disengagement of Church and American culture, both complicated and painful, had begun. This time of adjustment "will be seen by most of us in terms of unfamiliar demands of Christian moral standards, of new forms of ministry, of unprecedented (for us) emphasis on evangelism, on stewardship, on discipline." And he decried the tendency to set in opposition "changing individuals" and "changing society" with the assertion that one is the business of the Church and the other not.[52]

In an address to the Advisory Committee for Work with the Deaf, Bayne acknowledged mistakes in the Special Program but concluded: "I think the score is pretty good."[53] Then something happened to further heighten the tensions in the Church.

The Black Manifesto and the Notre Dame Convention

On April 25–27, 1969, in Detroit, the Interreligious Foundation for Community Organization with which the Episcopal Church had been affiliated held a conference on Black economic development. James Forman of the Student Non-Violent Coordinating Committee was there and presented a manifesto that after much debate was adopted by a 187–63 vote. Forman, with others, went to the Episcopal Church Center on May 1 and asked to see Bishop Hines.[54] Because the Presiding Bishop was not there, they asked to see Bishop Bayne. Bayne asked Bishop Mosley to accompany him, and they spent the better part of three hours mostly listening to Forman. Forman next went to the National Council of Churches General Board, Riverside Church, the Lutheran Church of America, the headquarters of the Roman Catholic Archdiocese of New York, and a Presbyterian agency. On May 13 he returned to the Church Center to speak with Bishop Hines and took with him a letter demanding over and beyond whatever was committed to the Special Program, a contribution of $60 million to the Interreligious Foundation for Community Organization to be used for the implementation of the Black Economic Development Conference. The letter, signed by Forman as Chairman of the United Black Appeal, also called upon the Episcopal Church "to donate each year sixty percent of the profits of all its assets, including real estate and stock holdings, etc.," as reparations (the Manifesto required $500 million, reckoned at "$15 a nigger," as Forman put it) for the centuries in which black people in America have been forced to live "as colonized people inside the United States, victimized by the most vicious, racist system in the world," to quote the Manifesto itself. Third, Forman called for "a complete listing of all assets of the Episcopal Churches in all dioceses."[55]

Bayne summarized his reaction in a letter to his brother Ned.

> We are having a pretty difficult time here, as you know. While I am sure that Mr. Forman is playing an astute political game, in

the power vacuum at the heart of the black community, he has certainly found a vivid way with which to confront the churches with the superficiality of their own priorities and the lethargy of their own leadership. I welcome that side of the maneuver, if somehow the Church doesn't approach the confrontation feeling that we must somehow respond directly to the Manifesto. The Manifesto is typical political rhetoric, and I think is of little significance — indeed it speaks for itself. But the needs of the people, and the people themselves concerned, are what is really at stake. And how easy it would be for the Church, in some hasty action, to give the impression that we really don't care about those things at all, but only our own peaceful procedures.

I hope John Hines can lead us in a real quickening of conscience, and without anger and further division. But I've never known either the Church or the City to be as polarized as we are now, and I take it New York is not alone in this. My days and nights are not easy ones.[56]

Bayne's days and nights were spent dealing with what should or should not be done. If the Church Center were occupied, what should or should not be done. If the diocesan offices were occupied and church services and diocesan conventions disrupted, what should or should not be done. He was busy with conference calls, meetings, the writing of long explanatory letters to bishops and to the Executive Council, to alarmed priests and angry laity. Countless hours were spent dealing with the confrontation at the National Council of Churches. The NCC staff was divided, largely on the basis of Forman's occupation of NCC offices. Bayne was concerned that NCC might be unable to make a response to the Manifesto acceptable to the churches on the one hand and the black caucuses on the other. "Some of my friends tell me that it will mean the end of the NCC — at least in its present form — and I more and more come to that mind myself."[57]

In May it was decided that the Church needed to act in consort and it was therefore suggested that there be held a Special Convention. The bishops were polled, and a sufficient number responded positively for there to be one.[58] It was decided to hold it at South Bend, Indiana, on the campus of Notre Dame University in August. That unique gathering of Christians was marked by confrontation and reconciliation. The Black clergy and lay delegates identified themselves with the Manifesto and demanded that the Convention make a positive response to it. Rather than see the Black delegates walk out, the Convention authorized a special fund of $200,000 for the Black clergy to dispense to what was now the Black Economic Development Corporation. It was reported in the press that the Convention had thereby accepted "the concept of reparations." In a letter to the *New York Times,* John Coburn as President of the House of Deputies and John Hines as Chairman of the House of Bishops, denied this.[59] The grant that was made was in keeping with the action of General Convention in 1967 in establishing the Special Program. The significance of the grant and of other actions reflected, they said, "the determination of the Episcopal Church — to the eradication of racial injustice in our land and in our Church. The focus was upon present and future attitudes and actions rather than upon the acknowledgment of a right to compensation for injuries in the past."[60]

Stephen Bayne's own comment was that the "convention at South Bend was a very confusing event.... To many of the members, the open and harsh confrontation was shocking. It would have been very easy to have run away from the encounter altogether. But they didn't; they dealt with it the best way they knew how; and at the end of the Convention, despite all the tensions, there was a greater feeling of brotherhood and unity than I personally have ever seen at a General Convention."[61]

Fundamentally, as he saw it, the truth in the Manifesto had been affirmed without affirming the Manifesto itself, and that truth was embodied in the Special Program, which also provided a response. The nature of the truth was expressed by Bayne in a baccalaureate sermon he preached at Trinity College, Hartford. With reference to the Black Manifesto, he said: "It could well have been that another Manifesto and another word would have confronted the churches and synagogues. The slogan is not the point. Let it be what it is; the situation would be no different. The eyes of the poor and the justly aggrieved of this world would still be turned in penetrating contemplation on men and women of faith, and on their churches and synagogues, to see if they mean what they say.... Is our behavior to be that of responsible people who act like the stewards of the mysteries of God?"[62]

Bayne, in a letter to his friend Joe Emrich, Bishop of Michigan, spoke of his own failing and of his understanding of the polarizing activities of Blacks:

I am guilty of "racism" — at least to the extent that, unconsciously, I have thought of the Negro as a permanent appendage on a basically white society, to whom I had obligations, as to an unfortunate relative; I don't think that consciously I have ever agreed to this, but I am sure that my easy acceptance of the white role in society which I play is in fact "racist," and in fact is now seen as such by my black companions. And if they are to find their way into an integrated society, in which they are treated with the dignity you and I would want them to have, I am quite prepared to believe they must go through a time of intense polarization — a time of the rejection of integration — until they feel they in fact have power to take a meaningful place in our society.[63]

There were many who did not have such an understanding. At the Convention in South Bend, Oscar Carr was given a standing ovation for a speech in which he told the delegates of his doubt that they, at that time, possessed the expertise needed in the Church to stage "verbalized value judgments into well-functioning programs." He added: "I believe that a climate of trust develops when participants sense they are not being manipulated toward some unknown destination and that communication — the *sine qua non* of any society — is the key to developing that society." One friend of Bayne's wrote saying: "We are shocked at the church handing out money to the black people, and we want not one cent of our money to be used in this way. This may sound very unchristian, but we are so tired of hearing the black people put all the blame on the whites."[64]

In fact, Bayne found himself in the middle of opposing forces. He defended the Special Program, and especially its theological foundations, against those who opposed it. But he had difficulty with some of the people most zealously promoting that program. He abstained from voting on the Alianza grant because he would not vote on any grant disapproved by the bishop involved, but, as rumor had it, he was not altogether opposed to the grant, which was for the support of a Hispanic organization in New Mexico.[65] He wrote to the bishops of Province Eight expressing his dissatisfaction with a resolution on "Crisis in American Life" passed by members of the Executive Council in May 1970. He was offended by the statement that "there is continuing oppression of black and brown people in America" but did not deny "the fact of continuing 'racism' in our Church and society." He decried the vapidity in the "call" for an end to the Vietnam War. "I am certainly one of those who believes that a withdrawal of all our forces from Southeast Asia is a necessity, if our republic is to survive. But to 'call for an end to the war' is like 'enter, rest, pray' on a church sign or 'the time has come for the Church to speak out against evil' in a sermon."[66]

The reduction in the Council's income from the dioceses required cutting back on the Church Center's staff and program. The reduction in staff was especially painful, involving resistance on the part of staff members and a movement toward collective bargaining, pitting the Management Group against the rest at 815 Second Avenue.[67] By March the staff reductions had been completed. The St. Louis Convention had set a ceiling of 337 employees for the Church Center. The authorized level was 271 at the beginning of 1970; the count was now 215.[68]

Bayne recognized the crisis. The Seattle Convention authorized a quota total from the dioceses of $14.7 million for 1970, but the dioceses were able to pledge only $11.4 million, $1.3 million less than the dioceses paid in 1969. In another "Dear Ivol" letter, Bayne discussed where the work of the Council was hurt. He wrote: "I would suggest that our work is hurt most sharply in three areas — our capacity to support ongoing commitments, overseas and at home; our capacity to maintain experimentation and development work; and our capacity to support some of our less-glamorous but still important ministries to handicapped children, et al." Specifically, Bayne was deeply hurt by the "closing-out of the Latin American desk." It was a crushing blow to both Bayne and Mosley. Bayne commented: "If we could see some end in sight to these years of sharpening tension and distrust, we could bear almost any temporary calamities. But what is bewildering to me is to see no doors to open, no way to restore the sense of united obedience I think we once had." He said to Bishop Gooden: "I do not despair, really; if I mourn my own incapacities, I do not imagine that there is not leadership in the Church which God will use to cleanse and heal and restore. I pray it may be given us swiftly."[69]

To Ivol Curtis he said, recognizing the specific matters involved, "The Special Convention in South Bend and its attendant confusion, the Alianza grant, et al.":

> To me, the most disturbing element is our inability across the board to come to grips with our history theologically, and find the new and deeper level of obedience in mission which we lack.... The task, the theological understanding of mission, remains our Church's central task, I should think. You will know how greatly I had hoped for the establishment of the "theological process" which a group of us proposed to the South Bend meeting. Such a process is an absolute necessity, in my view — I know I can't propose it again, but I hope more persuasive people can and will, for until systematic dialogue can be sustained so that the Church can find the degree of unity in mission and service we don't have and desperately need, we are simply not being true to our nature as His Body. End of Sermon.[70]

The defeat at South Bend of the proposal for an Advisory Council on the Church's Teaching was strongly felt by Bayne. He wrote to Massey Shepherd and A. T. Mollegen asking for "some understanding of where we went wrong."[71] The proposal in 1969, he told John Krumm, "was swallowed up by dragons." In a sense, he was to regard the action as a rejection of theological process as necessary to the Church's meeting the challenges it faced. Some saw the danger of the creation of "a vested interest" and preferred the use of ad hoc groups of theologians called together to deal with a specific issue. But Bayne was concerned "for a *process,* which seemed ... to require some continuity in the monitoring group. I heard again," Bayne said, "that there was doubt as to the possibility of communication across some of the main theological cleavages; but here again the experience of our small group had led us to a good deal of confidence in the possibility of just such communication."[72] Bayne most likely saw himself, in his waning years, working to create such a process and contributing to the theological reflection on the issues in a group that might fairly be regarded as representing the Church.

Bayne's influence is discernible in the report made to the South Bend Special Convention, a report that recommended the establishment of an advisory council, the production of a series of issue-oriented books, and regional assemblies "for consideration of the Church's teaching in the moral and theological issues we face." These recommendations were being made to counter the increasing loss of certainty in the Church as to the integrity of its teaching. In making the recommendations, the report said:

> We aim...at something more fundamental than the patching of rents in our corporate life or the plastering of cracks in traditional structures and statements. The processes of theological exploration, teaching, learning, dialogue in our church are not adequate to the requirements of our history. Neither our clergy nor laity are prepared for the actual choices which have to be made, even by failure to make them. Christian discipleship and comradely obedience to mission, which are intended by God to be joyful and fulfilling privileges for churchmen, are more and more cloudy, unhappy and divisive. It is unbearable that the birthright of the baptized be denied them because of the inability of the church to provide the tools for mature and renewed engagement in the one Lord's single being and mission.[73]

The rejection of the proposals was a major defeat for a man whose understanding of history and of the issues in the present crisis was rooted in theological understanding. What went wrong? Bayne was convinced that much of the difficulty at "815" was related to the haste with which the reorganization had taken place and to the difficulty of bringing people along as the decisions were made. He was aware that much of the turmoil in the Church was related to decisions made in 1967 and after, to deal with the crisis in American society, decisions not made in such ways as to explain on theological as well as sociological grounds the reasons for the action taken. He had to face the possibility that the failure of the proposal for an advisory council on the Church's teaching was due to a failure of understanding and thus of communication and teaching. The frustration he knew was almost unbearable and he had to consider to what extent he himself was involved in the tragic result and would be responsible for the tragic consequences.

Church Unity and Liturgical Renewal

Stephen Bayne was engaged in a life that was in some ways just as demanding as that he had led as Anglican Executive Officer. He was, as usual, much in demand on the preaching, lecturing circuits. In the years from 1967 to 1970 he gave a baccalaureate sermon at Stanford University in California; in one week he spoke at the convention of the Diocese of Texas, spent three days in East Carolina and Southern Virginia, and spoke at the convention in the Virgin Islands; he addressed an ecumenical gathering at St. Anne's Roman Catholic Church, Garden City, New York; he preached at St. James's Church, New York, and gave a series of Lenten sermons at St. Bartholomew's Church, New York; he gave an address on preaching at the Northern Baptist Seminary in Oak Brook, Illinois; he spoke at an anniversary celebration at St. John's, Northampton, Massachusetts, and at another at St. Barnabas' Church, Bambridge Island, Washington; he spoke at St. Mary's School, Peekskill, New York; and he preached at the Church of the Epiphany, Washington, D.C., and at Grace Church, Brooklyn Heights, New York.[74]

On April 5, 1968, Stephen Bayne preached on Martin Luther King Jr., whose violent death he mourned along with the nation. "His death is a tragic one," he said. "His going creates a problem for the black community, for he was central in their struggle for self-determination and he was in their eyes a symbol of all that was right and true and strong." But his death was also "a problem for the white community because for that part of our life he stood for the hope that somehow there could be an end in peace and justice to the tragic division of our country." Bayne saw in Dr. King a lesson: "The only way in which you can break the long chain of wrong is by breaking it. There is no way to come to some easy solution to the hurt, injustice, cruelty," he said. "The only way to break that chain is by *breaking* it."[75]

On June 9, 1968, after the assassination of Robert F. Kennedy, Bayne preached: "We mourn, not because he was a saint . . . we mourn because he was us — impulsive, eager, strong, foolish, brave. We mourn not because of the hurt to him as much as for the hurt of ourselves, to our pride." Bayne bemoaned the fact that we inhabit a world that spawns men who kill, "men demented, enraged, deluded." This is "a world that can bear a people tender enough to be shocked and ashamed at violence; and it is a world capable of bearing a people who can work violence and even ignore the fact that they are working violence." This is the setting, he believed, in which we are called to minister.[76]

Bayne was involved with the development of stewardship in the

Church,[77] he was active in the work of the Advisory Committee on
Christian Marriage,[78] he was watching the development of the movement to ordain women and preparing for the vital role he was to play
in the 1970s,[79] and he was concerned for the course of liturgical revision, the movement that was to eventuate in a new Prayer Book in 1979
and a new hymnal in 1982. In an article in *St. Luke's Journal of Theology* he gave his assessment of the trial liturgy of 1967, noting four
areas of discomfort. Two were of little account, the Peace and the lack
of a priestly blessing. Two were of great importance: the prayer of Intercession and the Penitential Order prescribed for use on five days during
the year. He commented on each and then at the end noted the main issue — that the liturgy should proclaim the death of Christ and the death
in life and life in death of every Christian. He understood and shared
the contemporary "wish to escape from the gloom of the Reformation
and post-reformation Eucharistic devotion." But, he said that although
"a wedding garment is called for ... the man who is to wear the garment
is coming to a banquet which he has no right to share." And he concluded, "The communicant who is able to take his place in the offering
of the Eucharistic sacrifice is simply not worthy of this, if it is in fact
the reenactment by our Lord, in and among us, of His offering which
I take it to be."[80]

In May 1970 Bayne expressed his basic agreement with the Standing
Liturgical Commission's work on Baptism and Confirmation in Prayer
Book Studies 18, but he was concerned "that the response of faith and
commitment to the Act of God in Baptism not be lost." He explained:

> Confirmation of boys and girls now offers an opportunity for ex-
> pressing this response, imperfectly and with all the reservations
> expressed by the commission. Theoretically I agree with the com-
> mission's points ... as to the recurring moments of commitment
> in the life of the Christian and the parish. In fact, however, such
> continuing, corporate commitment presupposes a change in the
> "life-style" of the Episcopal Church considerably more radical
> than the proposed rite. I do not know the answer: I do not there-
> fore prefer to stay where we are: I only think that the adoption
> of such a rite should be accompanied by a massive movement for
> conversion of the Church's people to new emphasis on corporate
> and individual witness.[81]

Stephen Bayne continued to be involved in the ecumenical movement,
in Faith and Order discussions, and in the Consultation on Church
Union (COCU) in the United States as a delegate of the Episcopal
Church. Bayne was often impatient with the COCU process. In 1969
he wrote to Ned from Atlanta:

I'm here for the annual meeting of the Consultation on Church Union; it's not one of our more exciting meetings, I must say. A commission is in the middle of preparing a plan for a united church, and I think it would have been better to wait a year until they had finished, but we are so institutionalized after 9 years that an annual meeting becomes a must: and the result is nit-picking and second-guessing on a large scale. More and more I get the feeling that this kind of ecclesiastical diplomacy is the least exciting and original kind of ecumenics. We are all old, and too well-known to each other.[82]

Bayne's special interest was with the discussions of worship. In 1966 he considered where COCU was with regard to Baptism, the Lord's Supper, and Worship in general — three frontiers.[83] There was wide agreement among the participating churches concerning Baptism, but the frontier "between those who hold to so-called' 'believer's Baptism' and those who accept the Baptism of infants" was yet to be faced. The problems on the frontier of the Eucharist were more numerous and troublesome, although in some ways less fundamental than those concerning Baptism, and include "the question of a universally accepted ministry" and differences "in devotional habits, ritual and ceremony, frequency of observance, and the like." The problems on the third frontier, that of worship in general, he found most vexing, in part because here there should be the greatest agreement. "At one pole," he wrote, "is the Episcopal Church, with its profound loyalty to the ordered worship of *The Book of Common Prayer*. From that pole, the practice of the companion Churches in the Consultation moves through greater degrees of individual and congregational liberty of worship to the point of the entirely spontaneous and unstructured." Here was a formidable challenge in working toward a united Church. To Bayne's mind "there could be no sensible or possible thought of a united Church with a single, uniform order of worship." And for this reason, as well as others, Bayne argued against viewing union in terms of a single organizational identity, with a single order of worship. Rather, he preferred to advance union through full communion: "We are concerned to be able to break the bread of life together, to be able to go into any house of worship and feel at home, to join with every Christian, whatever his background and tradition, in joyfully and thankfully accepting what the one God had done for the one humanity."[84]

Stephen Bayne identified worship as central to unity of any kind in the Christian context, whether it was unity in COCU, on the global scale, or in the congregation, the Episcopal Church, the Anglican Communion, or society at large. "I believe it is in worship," Bayne said, "that we men and women can discover our unities most clearly and sharply.

All our separatenesses — cultures, words, traditions — can be brought together and offered in the great free acts of worship, and in the common offering we can discover one another, and the unities God has given us."[85] He was therefore frustrated by the avoidance in COCU of discussions of worship and by the apparent concentration on bureaucratic issues.

Leaving the Church Center

On December 9, 1969, Stephen Bayne announced to the Executive Council that he had asked the Presiding Bishop to accept his resignation as First Vice President and Deputy for Program effective June 30, 1970, and that his resignation had been accepted. He reported that as long ago as the past summer, Sam Wylie, the Dean of the General Theological Seminary, had invited him to return to the seminary where he had been a student and where he began his ordained ministry more than thirty-seven years earlier, and he had accepted. He would "teach a little, as an interpreter of missions," serve as a "link between the Church that is and that which was," write, take part in continuing education, and in general "be a kind of spiritual handyman." He regarded this as an ideal way to spend his time until he retired in 1973.[86]

Bayne acknowledged that this was not a sufficient basis on which to leave the Council. But his retirement was nearing. He did not have many years to go, and "the Council needs other and younger gifts and a flexibility and imagination a man like me does not have if we are to move as far and as fast and as freely as our history calls us to do." He was admittedly battered and weary. He was under attack, so it seemed, from every side. A scurrilous accusation by Lester Kinsolving had appeared in *Washington Daily News,* saying that Bayne had garnered power to himself and was "now virtually eclipsing Presiding Bishop John Hines." The article said that Bayne had appointed favorites to key positions, had embarrassed the Church in his treatment of Dave Beck, was involved in the questionable means used to censure Bishop Pike, and had taken a $5,000 salary increase at a time when the Church was hard-pressed to meet its financial obligations and overseas missionaries received "salaries running as low as $3,408."[87] That Bayne was angered and hurt by this is indicated by the "comments" he prepared, pointing out the factual errors in Kinsolving's article. But he agreed that it was necessary to refrain from entering into debate and recognized, as a seminary classmate said, that "no man who has achieved high position can escape opprobrium." It was left for friends such as Anson Phelps Stokes, Jr., to speak up in Bayne's defense.[88]

Bayne was also aware that he was sounding at times more and more negative concerning the ways in which the Council met the challenges of the day. Most seriously, he now had to face the reality that his health was failing. A lifelong cigarette smoker, he was now afflicted with emphysema. The progress of the disease was intermittent. There were plateaus, and there was hope that he would have some time left upon retirement; but the persistent cough and the shortness of breath indicated the necessity of curtailing some of his activities.

John Leffler, whom Bayne brought to Seattle to be Dean of St. Mark's Cathedral, wrote to Bayne on first hearing of his resignation to say that he hoped that health was not the chief reason for the resignation, "but if it is an important factor, may this move enable you to live and serve a bit longer." Bayne really could not talk about his health, except in a veiled way, and so he wrote to his old friend, "It wasn't my health which directed the choice, thank the Lord, although the pressure and constant heartache under which all of us here must work takes a heavy toll."[89] In June, a young lady, his namesake Stephanie, who had been present at dinner with Bayne in Seattle, wrote: "Here is a booklet [on smoking] I got for you. Please use it. I noticed at dinner in Seattle you didn't smoke much. Do that all the time. Love you." The bishop responded, "I was glad to have the booklet about smoking and I have been trying very hard to do what it says. Some days I feel better than others, I'm afraid. It is *so* hard to break an old habit. I wish I hadn't started it so many years ago. I hope you won't."[90]

In his report to the Council he spoke of misunderstandings:

> I will be told that I am only getting out of the kitchen, and perhaps this is so. Some will say that my leaving is an admission of failure, because of staff problems. It is not; it would be splendid if our problems could be blamed on one man or on twenty, but they cannot; and I will take only my share of whatever blame there may be. Some will suppose that John Hines and I have had a falling-out. This is not the case. Very few things in my life have moved me more and warmed my heart more than his wanting me by his side, and his inflexible support and trust.[91]

In a letter to John Hines, with which Bayne conveyed a copy of his report to the Council, he spoke his mind, knowing that the Presiding Bishop did not want him to resign.

> I know your feelings, and I am very deeply torn, because of duty as I saw it, but more because of love. I don't think it was accidental that you and I were brought together when and as we were. But I can't shake off the deepening feeling that this is what I should do *now*. It isn't just to clear the way for a new chapter in the Council's life. . . . It is rather that I want to see what time and gifts I have in ways that I think will be more productive for the mission and use of me than what I can do here.

I do know and respect the strength of your own feelings, and I don't deal with that lightly. Yet over the last weekend I came to the point of recognizing that I wanted to say what I have drafted. I hope you will let me say it without feeling that I am running away from my duty or spending these next three years foolishly. I honestly don't feel I am doing that, and I pray you won't feel so. I can never thank you enough for the years we have had.[92]

He signed himself, "Affectionately and most deeply yours."

After the Council meeting, Bayne wrote to his old friend Tom Fraser, Bishop of North Carolina. Bayne was conscious of the misinterpretations people would make and were indeed making of his resignation. He wanted to stress that the resignation was not due to a rift between John Hines and himself. It may have seemed to some that Hines was stuck with Bayne after the 1964 Convention, Bayne having been appointed Director of the Overseas Department before that, but he denied that. "Certainly he has given me every possible sign of trust and support," Bayne said. "He has put up with a lot of short-comings and let me take a lot of chances; and I know he did not think the decision [to resign] was wise even though he stands completely behind me." Bayne added that it was his judgment that Hines would be better helped "by a younger, different deputy than I — somebody who could improvise more readily than I and who could tackle problems we have to face with more ingenuity."[93]

Bayne further explained that the invitation to go to General preceded "the current ferment — either our internal problems here or the drizzle of post-South Bend disapproval under which we huddle." He denied that his resignation had anything to do with the Alianza grant. "I hear that in some Western sectors it is alleged that I resigned in anger because the grant was made." He reminded Bishop Fraser that he abstained from voting on that grant simply because he "followed the personal rule of not voting on any grant disapproved by the bishop."[94]

In a positive sense, Bayne admitted that he was leaving to do something he wanted to do, had long dreamed of doing. He told the Executive Council: "It will be said that this is a return to the womb of Mother Church. Greatly as I revere my alma mater, the General Seminary, I would not identify the Church's maternal functions quite that closely; and no seminary in the world these days has quite that amniotic atmosphere. I want to go, and I think I should go because I truly think I can be more useful there than here, and do a better job, and be more supportive of our mission.[95]

To Brent and Ethel Orcutt he wrote saying that he was leaving "the very exacting administrative post I now have, to return to GTS." It was a returning not only to a beloved, familiar place, but to a career that was aborted when he first went to St. Louis. As he told his friends, he was returning "to teach again, and write, and try to be a helpful interpreter to the young men preparing there for the ministry. In a way it will be a return to my first ministry. When I was ordained, in 1932, my heart was much set on a life of teaching theology, and I did in fact spend the next two years preparing for that. But it was not to be so, and my ministry was in very different places. Now, at long last...!"[96]

As had been the case on other occasions Bayne had consulted numerous people and anguished over the decision for some time.[97] But at last the die was cast. He rather fancied being a "Mr. Chips with credibility," as Wylie put it. He was comforted by the fact that Roger Blanchard would be his successor at "815" and that John Hines was feeling better about his resignation. There was the personal side, of which he wrote in a letter to Archbishop Coggan. "I keep thinking how wonderful it will be to have time to read again, and write, and think some connected thoughts. These last breathless years have held very little opportunity for reflection; and with three years to go before I can retire, I'd like to begin to distill some sense out of what I have been doing."[98] He could not then foresee that he was to be as busy as ever, in the midst of the fray, hampered only by worsening health.

Nine

THE LAST YEARS

Return to General Theological Seminary: The Teacher

On July 1, 1970, Stephen Bayne became Professor of Christian Mission and Ascetical Theology at the General Theological Seminary, and he and his wife moved into an apartment at Chelsea Square. In the summer, the *Pan Anglican* published an article in which Bayne wrote of the Episcopal Church as entering into a period of decline in terms of numbers and of financial support for the Church's national program. He also wrote of signs of vitality. The seminaries were full, "the Church had identified itself with the nation's poor and powerless," and liturgical experimentation and new focuses of ministry were exciting interest. He suggested that the " '70s must be a decade of searching examination and costly decisions" especially in terms of sexuality, secularity, worship, and discipline.[1] "The contraceptive explosion — 'the Pill' " was forcing society to develop a new sexual ethic based on choice rather than fear. This would raise all sorts of basic questions for Christians and force the Church to question its position on abortion, on homosexuality, on monogamous marriage, and on the place of men and women in society. He believed it imperative that the Anglican Communion consider the question of ordaining women in this broad context. To do less was to "run the risk of trivializing the issue."[2]

Bayne longed to see the Church take steps to reestablish a fruitful partnership between the sacred and the secular. He emphasized "partnership," recognizing that when the emphasis is placed on one or the other damage is done. When otherworldliness is stressed we have a cruel pietism, when the secular is stressed we engage in "an exercise of hopelessness." In the partnership there would be found "the opportunity to capture the glorious, sacramental liberation of the Gospels."[3]

There were twin dangers to be faced where worship was concerned. One was to deal with it as "instrumental to something else"; the other was to deal with it as unrelated to anything else. Both dangers were apparent, he believed, in current liturgical experimentation. "We may try to use worship to achieve some goal of our own, social or personal.

Or we may try to preserve some imagined ideal of worship to which we flee for various forms of succor. Either way we are doomed to lose the gift we most deeply need — the time and place for the bringing of ourselves and our tasks and our freedom, deliberately and thoughtfully, before Him Who knows us and gave Himself for us." Thus he warned against guarding the Prayer Book because of what it has meant in the past. But he also warned against tinkering with worship, bedecking it "with exotic innovations," "for then it ceases to be much more than a mirror of our own condition."[4]

Finally, there was discipline, "the kind of obedience which issues from a high sense of freedom." He recognized the fact that discipline was a word suggestive of authoritarianism in 1970, and authoritarianism understood as coercive power was suspect. Nevertheless he argued for the need to consider the place of discipline — and authority — in the Christian life as one of the great, pressing needs of the Church in the '70s.[5]

In an address given in November at North Presbyterian Church in Geneva, New York, Bayne spoke again of frontiers and of directions into the '70s. He reported what he said in the *Pan Anglican* on sexuality, but added two other modern issues concerning mission and the theological/philosophical challenge of the times. During the development of the General Convention's Special Program, the question was raised as to whether or not the Church should use "missionary money" to fund militant Black groups, assisting them in changing their communities. Bayne admitted, sorrowfully, that there were some in the Church who believed that the money should not be so used and that the Church should not take sides on social and political issues. But these are people who confess to loving the Lord who "above all others taught of the living and determined will of God to change the form of human society so that the mighty would be put down from their seat and the humble and meek would be exalted." God, Bayne asserted, "is not disturbed by militancy, nor by empowerment of the powerless, nor by taking sides."[6]

Bayne spoke also of the remorseless widening of the abyss between the life of faith and the secular mind, building on what he had said in the *Pan Anglican* about the sacred and the secular. This widening he viewed as due to the skepticism in the secular mind of the possibility not only of making theological statements about reality but also of making any basic philosophical statement. Behind the skepticism was the erosion of common assumptions and the disappearance of a common language. The problem was thus not for the Church alone but for all society. The Church's part in the crisis, Bayne believed, was "to press the dialogue with the non-Church world," working with everyone concerned "to establish common assumptions and understand each other's presuppositions and find the new language we need to talk about them."[7]

In the fall of 1970 Bayne taught a course on Christian Mission. He admitted that getting back to classroom teaching was exhilarating and challenging.[8] In the second semester he gave one course in Christian Ethics and one in Ascetical Theology. The ethics course he viewed as "a quick introduction, first to some of the main traditions and directions in Christian ethical thought, then to some of the main tools we use, finally to some of the most urgent problem areas in our society."[9] The course on Ascetical Theology was concerned with particular areas or activities "in the life of most priests," such as prayer, public worship, preaching as prayer, the discipline of time and of thought, routine, sickness and dying, obedience and mission, vicariousness, and so on.[10] Bayne viewed himself then as teacher, and he was that in the classroom at General; but he was continuing what had always been a teaching ministry for him: in articles, such as that in *Pan Anglican,* in addresses such as that given at North Presbyterian Church, and in sermons and sermon series. He continued to conduct preaching/teaching missions, such as one on "The Church in a Changing Society: A Fair Hearing" at Grace Church, Brooklyn Heights, where he spoke on creation and the divine initiative, responsible freedom, the credibility of Christianity, forgiveness and mutuality, and commitment: "the statement of a person's life and values."[11] There was an address on William Porcher DuBose, given at the 1970 DuBose Symposium in Charleston, South Carolina.[12] There was a lecture on "History and Hope" given at Huron College in November, in which Bayne contended: "The theology which can speak to our times must be a theology rooted in history and rooted in hope, presenting man as ever choosing a new tomorrow, presenting God (in the phrase of one theologian) as 'the presence of the future.'"[13] There were addresses given as the Fifth Annual Gray M. Blandy Lectures: "Things Done in the Way and the Breaking of Bread" in October 1971, essays in Christian apologetics in relation to pastoral ministry.[14]

One of his most impressive ventures as a teacher and prophet is found in *The Anglican* in an article called "The Crisis of Spirituality in the Church." It was first presented as an address on "The Condition of Spirituality in the Church" at the Trinity Institute in December 1970. The article dealt with three crises: (1) the Prayer Book crisis, (2) the faith crisis, and (3) the identity crisis. It concluded with four proposals: (1) that the "Bible must again be a familiar, used, major element in spirituality," (2) that "we must all, clergy and laity, learn all over again how to pray," (3) that "the teaching of theology must emphasize encounter with divine personal reality," and (4) that we must have a future orientation and hope.[15] Bayne was at his rhetorical best in this article. For instance, he recognized the great contribution *The Book of Common Prayer* made to the development of Anglican spirituality, but he also recognized the damage done when too much was made of the Prayer Book. He pointed to the way in which it bred a churchgoing spirituality too frail to survive the truth of life, a spirituality too formal, with little silence and little allowance for spontaneity. He said that "the spirituality established by the Prayer Book all too often became a spirituality limited to the Prayer Book. Therefore, for example, when the Church undertook Prayer Book revision in earnest, and the various trial rites made their appearance, the result was a disturbance amounting almost to a minor convulsion."[16]

Dean of The General

Bayne had barely settled into the routine of a faculty member in the General Theological Seminary when the Dean, Sam Wylie, was elected Bishop of Northern Michigan. Stephen Bayne headed a sizable delegation to and preached at Wylie's consecration in March 1972. By then he had accepted appointment by the Board of Trustees of the seminary as Acting Dean. At a special meeting of the Board on April 26, he was elected General's eighth dean with the understanding that he would retire in 1973. The search committee for a new dean continued its work eventuating in the election of Roland Foster to succeed Bayne. The Board, as Bayne put it, "felt that it would be a helpful stabilizing factor during an interim period if the Seminary had an unqualified dean." He wrote to the alumni: "You will understand that my feelings about being asked to be Dean were very mixed. I had hoped that my time for administrative responsibility was behind me; and none knows better than I how much I lack of what a Dean here should have and be. Yet I could also see the possibility that even a very brief incumbency might be a useful interlude in the Seminary's life."[17]

Not only was Bayne once more an administrator, but he continued to teach. In addition, he maintained his position and responsibility at Trinity Church, Wall Street.[18] In late 1970, John Butler, Bayne's old friend and then rector of Trinity Church, exercised his authority, under the ancient Royal Charter that founded the parish, to appoint Stephen Bayne "Assistant to the Rector." In April, this action was ratified by the vestry. Bayne's relationship to Butler had been very close and became closer when in 1965 the churchwardens and vestry unanimously elected Bayne to be "Honorary Minister of Trinity Parish." Now, "Assistant to the Rector," it was explained, "he will perform such duties in Trinity Parish as may be developed in the future, and he will always have the right to speak for the Rector in the Rector's absence from the Parish, or in the event of the physical disability of the Rector. Indeed, he is directed to perform the duties incidental to the office of the Rector in such cases." This appointment included a much appreciated stipend. In return, Bayne preached often and was a much-used adviser. When John Butler retired, Bayne supported the election of Robert Parks as rector and did much to assist Parks in getting established as the leader of a prestigious parish.

On September 28, 1972, Bishop Bayne was installed as seminary dean, "in a very simple ceremony at Evensong."[19] The new dean gave the sermon, using as his text the parable of the Pharisee and the Publican. It was a sermon on pride and on the task of the seminary. He began: "What I think is said to us in this parable is that the main work of the Seminary is to help us to know and to confront and to be confronted by the Wholly Other — the Saving Presence." He concluded, saying that to make known this Presence is the chief task of the seminary, as it is of the Church at large.[20]

Bayne was not, however, at liberty to concentrate his efforts on the chief task, for the seminary was in the midst of a financial crisis of major proportions and required the Dean's most serious and intense attention. In January 1972, having become Acting Dean, he wrote to Professor Denton of the faculty that "we are operating on an indicated deficit of over $300,000 in this fiscal year."[21] In a report to the Board in March, Bayne reported on the preliminary proposed budget for 1973–74 and, including some items of deferred maintenance, projected a total excess of expenditure over income of $634,000. Escalating costs and decreasing enrollment were the major problems. The Dean added these comments: (1) "The Seminary is not bankrupt and nobody in his right mind thinks we ought to pack up." (2) "There is nobody to blame for our pickle.... There is no angel specially assigned to the General Seminary to keep us from having to do what most every other institution of higher learning has had to do for decades or more."[22]

In September, Bayne made known that the entering class was 17, compared with 41 the year before, and 50 ten years before that. The Seminary community was smaller than anticipated, 138 in all, with 51 seniors, 34 middlers, and 12 special students, one not yet classified, 23 in graduate courses, and 12 writing theses, and so forth. Women were now a factor, with 4 middlers, 3 juniors, and 4 special students. Bayne was concerned to understand the decrease and conferred with others about it. Many factors were involved, he thought, including "uncertainty as to the next dean, the cost and difficulty of life in downtown New York, and a swing away from the 'liberal' (social, theological et al.) reputations this and other seminaries have acquired."[23]

Regarding the financial problems, in his 1973 report Bayne pointed to the need for greater support from the Church at large, to the false assumption on the part of many that being the creature of General Convention, the General Seminary received financial aid from the convention, and to the determination of General Seminary, with its companion schools, to ask "this Convention to begin to give support

on a national basis to all our seminaries." Another avenue of exploration concerned ECTENE (the Episcopal Consortium for Theological
Education in the North East), including the Episcopal Theological
School (Cambridge, Massachusetts), the Philadelphia Divinity School,
and General Seminary.

ECTENE had been a major concern for Dean Wylie and was for
Bishop Bayne. It involved serious conversation among the three deans,
the three faculties, and the three boards. The Rev. Joseph Koci had been
retained as a consultant to the schools as they studied "the resources of
the schools in endowment, land, buildings, etc., and the limitations or
difficulties there might be in the way of closer consolidation or even
merger."[24] Various models were studied with an eye toward greater
economy and efficiency, from the reduction to two locations (involving
the merger of two schools), to specialization in two or three locations
(one concentrating on the Masters in Divinity degree, another on field
education/pastoral studies, a third on doctoral studies). In the meantime, cooperation was developing with the establishment of three special
ministries, funded by Trinity Parish and explored by the three schools.
Merger was seriously considered and did in 1974 result in the merg-
ing of the Episcopal Theological School and the Philadelphia Divinity
School on the Cambridge campus. Bayne said:

> Speaking for myself alone, I find "merger" a beguiling but also
> a misleading word; mergers can, I suspect, sometimes work to
> narrow the range of possibilities where looser and less institution-
> alized forms of united planning and action can widen the range
> and multiply possibilities; and the fundamental issue in the minds
> of most of us in ECTENE, I believe, is precisely that multiplica-
> tion. And it should be achieved through whatever model will best
> conserve resources and multiply the ways in which those resources
> can be put to work in our Lord's service. Simply to accumulate a
> larger number of Episcopalians in one place will not necessarily do
> that, nor do the ECTENE schools assume that it will.[25]

Bayne believed that a faculty many times the size of the one at General
"could not hope to meet the expectation and needs of the Church in the
New York metropolitan area alone." Nor did Bayne believe that merger
would solve anyone's financial crises.

Another matter with which Bayne as Dean had to cope was a change
in curricular style, something for which his predecessor had considerable responsibility. As Bayne explained it, "From a time-honored scheme
of required basic courses, we moved to a much more flexible arrangement within which the requirement of specific courses was dropped."
In place of the old arrangement, students knew when they matriculated
that they would be required to take four courses in each of the three

disciplines — Bible, History, and Theology — and eight in Pastoral Studies. Bayne noted: "They also know that they must pass comprehensive examinations in the four disciplines if they are to receive their degrees." With the help of syllabi and faculty advisers students were to choose the courses they would take. This placed much confidence in the maturity of the students and cultivated an understanding of what it means to exercise responsible freedom.[26]

Bayne recognized that the "free elective system" was not perfect. It did not always "work to the satisfaction of either the student or the Seminary." He also acknowledged that some people looking on from outside the seminary thought that General was relaxing its traditional high standard of scholarship. He did not believe that to be the case and invited a closer inspection on the part of doubters. He concluded: "What has been gained in flexibility and mature participation for both faculty and students far outweighs the problems caused by growing-pains and the inevitable mistaken choices."[27] The style, similar to that at the Philadelphia Divinity School, from which Richard Norris had come not too long before to join the General faculty, would appeal to Bayne with his emphasis on freedom-in-obedience and Christian maturity cultivated through making choices.

Bayne was concerned by the demands the new curriculum style and the new styles of teaching made upon faculty. "The man hours it takes to teach in imaginative new styles, to share core-groups or tutorials, to take part in the participatory governance of the seminary, to try to respond to the invitations from outside the seminary, and to stay in some kind of touch with one's colleagues in other places would have been inconceivable to the men who taught me forty years ago." The changes were exciting and inevitable, given the changes in society and the Church. But the price was high in terms of research and writing not done. He therefore argued against false economies such as would limit sabbatical leave time or give undue weight to favorable faculty-student ratios.[28]

There were other matters of note, such as the new Epiphany term; the Dean's Conference; the departure of faculty, Powel Dawley into retirement, Fred Borsch to be dean of Church Divinity School of the Pacific, Roland Cox to be headmaster of Groton; the hiring and tenure review of faculty; a letter from students and faculty protesting against Vietnam; and the continuing activity of the committee searching for a dean — eleven meetings between March and November 1972, many of them two days long.[29]

As Bayne expected, human sexuality, women and men, was a major concern in the seminary, as elsewhere. The ordination of women was endorsed by the General faculty in a statement which, as Bayne summarized, "affirmed the equality of women with men with respect to all orders of ministry." This statement was then "adopted by the faculties of the Episcopal Theological School in Cambridge, the Philadelphia Divinity School, and the Virginia Theological Seminary." The basic reason for this stand was that "the basic qualification for ordination is not masculinity but redeemed humanity.... If women are full members of the priestly body (the Church) then they cannot but have the basic qualifications for ordination to the Church's priesthood." Bayne agreed, although he stated that he "did not join in drafting or adopting the faculty's statement."[30] The reaction to the statement was strong. Bayne was flooded with letters, some praising the faculty but most opposed, "a few to the point of wishing to penalize the Seminary financially or in other ways." Bayne wrote to the alumni and friends of the seminary saying:

> The one point I try to make in response is that it is not "the Seminary" which is advocating women's right to Holy Orders. It is the faculty who have done so, and they have a perfect right as a group of priests and teachers to take that position. But to say "the Seminary" is taking the lead in pulling the Church down the road to ruin, as one friend recently did, is not the fact. The *Seminary* can't take a position unless all its estates — trustees, students, alumni, and faculty — join in taking it; and the possibility of such an action on this issue is remote, I judge, to say the least. So I keep writing the protesters to hate the faculty as much as they wish but to keep loving the Seminary, which maintains its own integrity and faithfulness within the vexing world in which it is set.[31]

Homosexuality was also an issue. One prominent rector wrote to Bayne about what he had heard of homosexuals at GTS. Bayne replied, "I do not know what your informants regard as 'rampant and uncontested homosexual activity' at the Seminary. I have observed no such activity nor would I be likely to do so.... I am sure there are men here who are homosexually oriented and actively so. This is only saying what would be true of any college or seminary at any time."[32]

Bayne and the faculty chose to deal with human sexuality at General in relation to the general topic. John Johnson prepared a series of meetings of faculty and students "to stimulate inquiry within the Seminary Community into the problems related to human sexuality and to explore the possible resources provided by the various disciplines of inquiry within the theological curriculum for a responsible, contemporary understanding of these problems. Dr. Corney lectured on Biblical insights, Dr. Shriver dealt with "Approaches to Human Sexuality in Christian History," Dr. Norris offered "Theological Reflections," and Johnson spoke on "Insights from Modern Psychology and Pastoral Concern." The Dean presided, and Susan Hiatt served as consultant.[33]

This grew out of discussions at the seminary during the spring. Another result of such discussions was a statement on Christian responsibility in the seminary prepared by Bayne at the request of the faculty. Bayne spoke of the freedom of the sons of God, freedom-in-obedience as made known by Christ. "Freedom for us," he said, "must express itself in the deepest concern for the good of other persons, of the community which we presently share, and of the Church which holds our avowed loyalty." He acknowledged that the seminary is not immune from the difficulties of the time, from "questions of authority or of the code of sexual conduct or of what constitutes 'relevance' or of change in our society." Freedom is not freedom from the strains of the times; "it is rather freedom to walk with understanding and gentleness and assurance among the perplexities."

Freedom being so, what is required? First there must be "honesty in studying and teaching." Cheating, copying "under the cloak of 're-search,'" substituting an easy opinion for a complicated truth, misusing a faculty member's authority, these are sins "against the Holy Spirit who is given us to lead us into truth." Second, there must be "respect for others' rights and necessities and avoidance of stealing, no matter how defensible." To steal a book from the library "is to put one's own self-ish wishes above the common welfare and to get in the way of another person's freedom." Third, "because we believe in the inviolability of persons in God's eyes, we are bound to stringent vigilance against the exploitation and manipulation of others. Predatory behavior, whether homo-sexual or hetero-sexual, is intolerable in a Christian Community." Fourth, there was the disciplined worship of the community and its affirmation of faith. "To play at 'church,' to mock another's search for faith, to take liberties with what is sacred to our fellows, to refuse to partici-pate in particular services because of personal grudges — these are marks of shallowness and callousness which destroy ministry."[34]

This was the way in which Bayne preferred to deal with specifics such as homosexuality in the seminary community. He was concerned for principles growing out of the gospel and for discipline, "freedom-in-obedience." To those who would say that he was idealistic, unrealistic in his expectations, he would speak of God and of God's love and support along the way.

Examinations for the Priesthood

Stephen Bayne was a bishop while dean, a bishop who had served in the highest level of leadership in the Episcopal Church, a bishop alongside being a teacher, "Assistant to the Rector" of Trinity Church, and Dean of the General Theological Seminary. Account needs to be taken of his attendance at meetings of the House of Bishops and his involvement in the work of the national church. In September 1971 Bayne wrote to Archbishop Coggan of his pleasure with life during the first year as teacher at General. He added:

> The only problem with my life here is that I am still involved in so many non-Seminary duties. John Hines gets his revenge for my defection from headquarters by making me chairman of anything he can think of. Some of it I enjoy — especially our new national board of examining chaplains. D.V. we will launch PECUSA's first national canonical examinations next January. It is a voluntary system, so I dare say a good many of my brothers will prefer to keep their own chaplains; but we are winning more support than I had dared hope.[35]

The 1970 General Convention in Houston created the General Board of Examining Chaplains and the General Ordination Examinations (GOE) for which the Board was responsible. According to Canon III.7, the Board, consisting of three bishops, six presbyters with pastoral cures, six members of theological faculties or other educational institutions, and six lay persons, was elected by the House of Bishops and confirmed by the House of Deputies. The Board was required to prepare, each year at least, an examination in the subjects listed in Canon III.5 and as requested to assist diocesan commissions in administering and evaluating the examination. A report on each person tested was to be sent to the bishop and to the dean of the responsible seminary. From the beginning and during discussions at General Convention, there was conflict as to whether the examinations were to be "content" or "situation" centered, a matter that was to be settled by the new Board in favor of the latter, largely as influenced by Bayne.

The first meeting of the Board was in December 1970 at the Trinity Institute in New York. Bayne was elected chairman and Charles Long vice-chairman. They had samples of general examinations from the Church of England and the United Presbyterian Church, U.S.A., and after discussion reached a consensus on the purpose of the examination, as well as other matters. They agreed that the seminaries were best able to judge the academic competence of their students, and the bishops and their advisers to judge the personal formation and suitability of candidates for the ministry. They went on to agree: "A third area related to, but not coincident with, those previously mentioned, involves an individual's ability to focus his faith and learning in a way responsive to the needs and demands of people in the world. It is the purpose of these general examinations to offer to the Church a partial means of assessing a candidate's capability to make this synthesis."[36] In another attempt at a statement, the Board emphasized their responsibility to test candidates in the canonical areas (Bible, Church History, Theology, Pastoral Care, Ethics, Contemporary Society, and Mission) but not in the way a seminary would test. The examinations would test a candidate's ability to reflect and to apply what he had learned. At this first meeting, they considered an examination composed of one question on authority, one on communication, and a third on ministry and mission.[37]

The second meeting was held in April at Nashotah House. A formal statement was drafted, and a sample examination was hammered out, the Board working in three groups to provide questions in three areas: authority or norms, communication, and ministry and mission. It was here that the Board recognized the necessity of their controlling the administration of the examination and also the necessity for carefully chosen readers, two for each examination. It was hoped that the readers would have different backgrounds, such as one academic and one pastoral. There began to take form the idea of readers' conferences where readers would be enabled to work collegially for an intensive period with adequate compensation.[38]

At the meeting that followed in October in Alexandria, Virginia, the Board had in hand responses to the draft statement and to the sample examination, both having been sent to bishops and seminaries. The draft examination was generally well received, although there was a suggestion from a few people that there needed to be at least a couple of content questions. As it was, the examination was issue and situation centered, not content centered. Suggestions having been received, the formal statement was amended and promulgated. Concerning the examination, it said that the seven canonical areas would be linked together in comprehensive, integrated ways, measuring "a candidate's understanding of the interrelationship of the various academic disciplines and his ability to relate such knowledge to professional practice." The Board was determined to issue the first examination in 1972.[39]

The first GOE was given to 192 persons, from January 31 to February 5. Ten were evaluated otherwise than by the Board process. One hundred eighty-two were evaluated by 72 readers, working in pairs. Most of those who took the examination liked it.[40] The major question concerned the work of the readers, which was understandably uneven. There were 269 examined in 1973, 263 of them being evaluated by 106 readers, working in pairs. Bayne noted improvement in the examination and its evaluation as a result of the first year's experience.[41]

When the process got underway, Bayne was heavily involved in the administration of the GOE, its headquarters being at the General Seminary. Bayne read many of the examinations, reviewed all evaluations, dealt with problem cases, and carried on a voluminous correspondence. He found himself longing to reassure some readers ("your evaluations — although perhaps a little brief — were on the mark"),[42] and some students ("the evaluation is cast in more negative terms than were intended. I do not feel that it was intended to be hostile.").[43] To a bishop who was concerned about one student's evaluation he wrote, after reading the examination himself: "the GOE flummoxed him; he responded to it with a superficiality of second-hand opinion; and succeeded mainly in disguising himself so that neither of the first two readers really could get any clear impression of him at all."[44] Another bishop strongly objected to the situational orientation of the examination. Bayne wrote pleading for patience and stated that it was hoped that in 1974 a set of content examinations would be issued in the seven fields for ministry commissions to use if they wished. A student also wrote questioning the exclusive use of situation-type questions. Bayne responded with a recognition of the need for variation; "some direct content questions would give a change of pace." This writer also wrote complaining about the readers. Bayne responded, saying that "in general, the readers did a fairly good job, with some spectacular exceptions."[45] To a member of the Board, he confided: "Some of the readers seem to me almost impossible in the way they characterize candidates."[46]

By 1973 the work of the Board was becoming oppressive. Bayne wrote to the Board members in March 1973:

As last year, I reviewed all the examinations which were not scored as "Satisfactory" in all seven fields. In a number of cases I added an N.B. where it seemed appropriate. In a few cases I revised the scoring suggested by the readers. In some other cases I provided for the additional reading as requested by one or another of you, and I "adjudicated" as needed.

We must also take some time to look at ways to cope better with the annual mountain of paper. After being edited here, we farmed out 125 of the most legible evaluations to two typists up in Westchester County who obliged us greatly. Peggy and Anne were here, working like beavers even Saturday and Sunday, editing and even preparing evaluations, getting the certificates, etc., ready to go and the like. They did a perfectly fantastic job, but there must be a better way to run a satellite.[47]

With the Louisville General Convention of 1973, Bayne's work with the General Board came to an end, and the Reverend Emmett Gribbin was hired to be the administrator of the GOE.

Bayne could look back on his service as Chairman of the General Board of Canonical Examiners with satisfaction. He had seen to the founding of the GOE and had done much to set the tone of the examination. The "situation theme," as he called it, was in accord not only with his pedagogical convictions but with his theological emphasis on choice, on freedom-in-obedience, and on apologetics. He would have every priest be capable of drawing upon all his learning, his theological grounding, in making judgments, judgments that would also be sensitive to people and to the contemporary scene. The GOE as originally conceived was in a sense very much Bayne's kind of exercise.

The Ordination of Women

At the General Convention in Houston in 1970 the House of Bishops referred to the House of Deputies for consideration the statement: "It is the mind of this House that it endorses the principle of the Ordination of Women to the Priesthood and of the Ordination and Consecration of Women to the Episcopate." At a subsequent meeting of the House in 1971, this was considered and referred to the Presiding Bishop for him to have appropriate committees or have a new committee review the matter with particular attention to the necessary canonical changes. A report was expected at the House's meeting in October of 1972, looking forward to action at the General Convention of 1973. John Hines appointed a committee of seven with Bayne as chairman, with two bishops known to favor ordination of women, two opposed, and three uncommitted.[48]

Bayne called the committee together at a meeting in St. Paul, Minnesota, in June, after a preliminary consultation on May 12, where the task of the committee was defined as providing leadership, not legislation, and "theological material and recommendations of a positive character which could support thoughtful and high-level debate and perhaps avert ill-considered 'band-wagon' action on any side."[49] More concretely, the committee was to prepare a report. It was recognized that it might be impossible to gain full consensus in the committee, thus necessitating both majority and minority reports, it was hoped within the one document. It was also determined not to enter into specific recommendations prematurely. Great caution was called for, recognizing the sensitivity of the matter, the deep divisions in the Church over it, and the threat of schism. Bayne knew the way things should go and were going and was with the majority, but he feared the battle that he knew would ensue and the pain for women in it as well as for others.

Some areas were identified as needing attention: "Diaconate, Priesthood, Episcopate, Biblical icons and images, Evangelism and Development, and the 'Penumbra.' "[50] The latter concerned problems that would arise with the ordination of women, or problems that people thought might arise. There was a fairly thorough discussion of the first three at the meeting, and it was agreed that the fourth, eventually renamed "Scripture, Tradition, and Images," would need to be worked upon further. Bishops Atkins, Myers, and Wylie agreed to prepare drafts for the fourth. The fifth, "Evangelism and Development," was to be drafted by Bishop Moore. Bayne agreed to draft an overall introduction, areas one, two, and three (eventually brought together under the heading "The Ministry"), and the "Penumbra."[51]

The committee met again in September at O'Hare Airport in Chicago. It was affirmed that the report would supply no specific recommendations to the House for action. Emphasis would be placed on the main issue, not on tinkering with the meaning of "man of Christian character" in Canon III.10. The draft documents were then considered. Bayne's introduction and closing were revised, Part I on Ministry was accepted as it was, "with some editorial improvement." Drafts on Scripture, Tradition, and Images by Atkins and Wylie were to be pulled together. Paul Moore's draft on Evangelism and Development was carefully considered, and Bayne agreed to work on it with help, if possible, from Bishop John Krumm and perhaps some material from Bishop Robert F. Gibson. Bayne's Part IV on the Penumbra was approved, with some amendments, "especially in view of the remarkable *motu proprio* from the Pope."[52] On September 29, Bayne informed the committee that there were then sixty women enrolled in the seminaries; that the Philadelphia Divinity School faculty statement was on hand; and that Herbert Ryan, Bayne's Jesuit friend, had read the drafts and commented on them.[53]

The "Report of the Special Committee of the House of Bishops on the Ordination of Women" was submitted to and discussed by the House, meeting in New Orleans, October 29–November 3, 1972.[54] It was a major and highly influential document. In the discussion of the ministry, the diaconate was recognized as the one order to which women could legally be ordained at that moment. The report recognized the murky character of the ministry of the deacon in the contemporary Church and went on to define the diaconate as a ministry of service "distinguished from the service to which all Christians are called simply by intensity and by the authority and accountability conveyed in ordination, of which perhaps the liturgical privilege of reading the Gospel is a token."[55] Clearly, there needed to be rethinking of common and false assumptions and a fresh and authoritative restatement of purpose.

The section on the priesthood was carefully drafted. Bayne took into account Herbert Ryan's statement concerning the draft of an earlier version, "I am aware that it is very popular today to derive the role of the ordained ministry from the ministry of the baptized — the ministerial priesthood from the priesthood of all believers. To my knowledge such an attempt lacks biblical and patristic support."[56] Bayne did not necessarily agree with Ryan, but he absorbed his point. As the report puts it, the New Testament seems to know only one priest, who is Christ; the priesthood of the Church is derivative from Christ's High Priesthood. The ministry of those ordained a priest shares in and is representative of both Christ and also the Royal Priesthood to which 1 Peter 2:9 refers. "To say, as we do, that ordained priesthood is 'representative' is to say that the priest is, in ways far beyond our understanding, acting for both the Lord and His Church. His priesthood is not derived from the Church nor has anyone a right to claim priesthood; the priest is called to receive a gift, in ordination, which comes from the Father. But his call and the gift are alike recognized and ratified by the Church; he acts for them by receiving and exercising the gift." Furthermore, the priest is not above the *Laos* but within it, "as a particular focus or symbol or effective means of Christ's action toward the Church and the world."[57] All these thoughts led Bayne to conclude that the duality of roles seems "to several of us to pose the question whether representation implied or required male-ness as a necessary attribute."[58] The same duality of representative roles was seen in considering the episcopate, and the same question was posed: "whether it can be said that female-ness is a detriment impediment to their [women's] consideration as bishops."[59]

In the next section, "Scripture, Tradition, and Images," there was an admission that Bishops Atkins and Wylie could not combine their work, therefore both papers were presented, one con and one pro.[60] The first paper found no evidence in the New Testament to support the admission of women to be bishops, presbyters, or deacons, on a regular basis. The paper concluded, "On the evidence, to admit women as bishops and priests is to overturn the practice of the New Testament church and the Catholic Church ever since." Nor is it right for "a small branch of a particular Catholic Church on its own initiative, without reference to the remainder of catholic Christendom, and I am sure, against the convictions and sentiments of a majority of its own members," to take so drastic and momentous a step.[61] The second paper admitted that the presence of women in the ministry as depicted by the New Testament is the exception and not the rule, but that did not mean that women should not nor could not ever be ordained to the episcopate/presbyterate. "If the adoption of the Canon of Holy Scripture or the threefold ministry or the conciliar faith can be defended as legitimate developments of what was implicit in the revelation of God in Christ from the beginning, there is no reason why the ordination of women cannot similarly be defended." The paper then proceeded to refute the opposition, concentrating on four particular areas, from the two accounts of Creation to the statement "God is male toward humanity; humanity is female toward God." And it concluded with the information that more than seventy member churches of the World Council of Churches admit women to all orders of ministry.[62]

There was a note appended, probably by Bayne as editor, a statement pointing out that several members of the committee wanted to note the cogency of female imagery with regard to the priesthood, as well as the fact of male imagery. They further questioned "whether it is not true that Christ's priesthood is too comprehensive to be contained by the symbolism of one sex, that in fact its variety and depth call for full sacramental feminine expression in order to represent a God who sustains both masculinity and femininity." The statement concluded: "If this be true, might we not be on the threshold of a new dimension and awareness of the unsearchable riches of Christ? Far from confusing sexual roles or affirming unisex values, might not the ordination of women assume the enrichment of our understanding of humanity in Christ by guaranteeing the presence of both its components visibly present in the offering of the Oblation which is Christ's and ours?[63]

It was in the third part, "Evangelism and Development," that attention was drawn to the women's liberation movement and its way of confronting the Church, "testing the Church's capacity to see itself and hear itself and open itself again to the cleansing judgment of God," to be purged of " 'sexist' stereotypes," cease treating women as second-class citizens, and allow women into the power centers of the Church.[64] This statement did not necessarily solve the problem of the ordination of women to the priesthood and the episcopate, but it had to be faced. "If the Church has, as the Committee unitedly believes, a peculiar mission to men and women struggling to learn how to become what they really are, the Church must seize every way it finds to re-establish lost credibility and to take the initiative and regain its capacity to serve its mission to contemporary humanity."[65]

In the "Penumbra" section, problems under four headings were considered: (1) "Questions of selection, training, deployment, and continuing education," (2) "the group of problems the Church will face in establishing the place of women in the clergy generally," (3) "the strains the ordination of women can lay on their families, if they are married, and on themselves because of the unavoidable fact of novelty, of sexual rivalry, of animosity," etc., and (4) "the ecumenical issues implicit in the main question." Bayne ended with no recommendations for action by the House, but with counsel for how the House should proceed, and with this plea: "We most deeply plead for a steady understanding of the gravity of the issue as it is perceived on both sides. This means to us that the members of this House must be the first to reach out with compassion and supportive love to those on both sides."[66]

On November 1, 1972, the House of Bishops adopted the resolution moved by Bayne, approving "the principle of the Ordination of Women to the Priesthood and to the Ordination and Consecration of Women to the Episcopate," which was the statement first considered by the Special Meeting of the House in October 1970, and instructing the Committee on Constitution and the Committee on Canons to "prepare the necessary constitutional and canonical changes to put this Resolution into effect for presentation at the General Convention of 1973."[67] That it was not possible to make further changes at that time was indicated by the results of ten small-group discussions revealing the divided mind of the House on the main question.

There was yet a long way to go before the canonical changes were made, but Bayne's report was a key step along the way. Bayne was praised by many for his chairmanship of the committee, but he was also excoriated by some. To one priest, who believed that Bayne was no longer qualified to be the Dean of the General Seminary, Bayne wrote defending his actions as chairman of the special committee. He admitted that the House of Bishops was divided on the issue, voting 75 to 61, with 5 abstaining, for the original resolution. With perhaps a sigh of relief he noted that with that action the committee went out of existence. Bayne then said: "It is perfectly true that I can see no conclusive argument against admitting qualified women to all three holy orders, and I said as much in the debate. It is also true that I am not eager for the day when they are admitted — not because I think they are not eligible but because of the bitterness and hostility they will encounter in many places in the Church. But this is their concern far more than mine."[68] In any event, he was not to live to vote in the final decision made at the 1976 General Convention.

The Ecumenical Movement

In September 1971, Bayne, whose involvement in the ecumenical movement continued in these latter years, gave at a meeting of the Anglican Council of North America in Puerto Rico an address in which he reflected upon "the Ecumenical Scene."[69] In this address he spoke of negotiations continuing for organic union, Anglican jurisdictions participating in fifteen of thirty-one interchurch negotiations then in progress. The result of this movement, beginning among the "younger" churches in Asia and spreading to the West, had been the "loss" of twenty Anglican dioceses, a calamity to some and to others a cause of rejoicing. Recently, Bayne reported, there had been a waning of such negotiations. "Among seminarians I know and teach, for instance, there is very little interest even (to say nothing of enthusiasm) in the work of the Consultation on Church Union (COCU). These negotiations — now more than ten years old — seem to them to be hopelessly slow, overburdened with institutional detail, and unresponsive to the real situation."[70]

Bayne asked: "What are the ecumenical alternatives to the dinosaur of negotiations for a United Church?" There was "instant ecumenism" — a disregard of institutions in a fellowship that is highly romantic. There were "coalitions and the like — often informal and temporary associations of churches, or church groups and agencies, around an issue, for a more-or-less specific purpose." There was "theological dialogue — most often bi-lateral, and greatly affected and, indeed, excited by the vigorous participation of the Roman Church." And there were councils of churches, intercommunion, and separatism, the latter a growing phenomenon.[71]

Bayne indicated his continuing commitment to inter- or full communion as the preferred way, saying: "Like many Anglicans, my impulse is to say that 'full communion' is about as far as I can see. If that relationship will give us the essential basis of unity, would it not be wiser to leave it at that and let the organizational and structural things grow out of it, in due course, as they may be indicated?"[72] Bayne knew that there were sound objections to this way of proceeding, the need for structures to protect minorities, and the poor record of those churches that had enjoyed full communion over a long time, but he still believed that full sacramental communion was the heart of unity.

Finally Bayne spoke "of the changes in ecumenical affairs and ecumenical directions caused by the growing awareness of the pluralistic world we live in." He had in mind the ways in which ecumenical discussions kept expanding beyond Protestants to include the Orthodox, the Roman Catholics, and the Jews. He recognized the challenges inherent in this widening beyond Christianity to dialogue with non-Christians. "Perilous or not," he said, "it is hard to see that true ecumenism, deep ecumenism, can now survive without the immense broadening of dialogue now forced upon us, I believe, by the narrow world in which we live."[73]

With all his misgivings, Bayne maintained his ties with COCU and acted as convenor for a theological colloquium held at General Seminary in June of 1971 in which the pros and cons of "A Plan of Union for the Church of Christ Uniting" were explored. Out of this meeting of nineteen persons, three of them non-Episcopalians, there came "A Sense of Waiting: A Notebook of Resources and Background for a Study of a Plan of Union for the Church of Christ Uniting."[74] The chapters of this publication dealt with whether the Plan met the requirements of the Chicago-Lambeth Quadrilateral, was theologically sound, was relevant to mission, was faithful to the gospel, and concluded with considerations of its political and human viability. This was the kind of exploration that Bayne believed necessary.

It is of interest to note that the colloquium included a serious discussion of confessionalism. Bayne had early expressed the uneasiness of Anglicans with confessionalism. But the two Presbyterian churches in COCU were confessional, and the Plan introduced an authoritative confessional statement. Anglicans generally believed that the great creeds of the Church were sufficient (as the Quadrilateral indicated), and they were fearful of confessionalism being used to exclude people. The members of the colloquium considered the positive effects of a confession, such as that proposed by the Plan of Union. Although participants were uneasy, there was a realization that the ecumenical task required wrestling with the confessional statements of churches, the ways in which they interpreted the great Christian symbols. A Roman Catholic participant quoted a scientist as saying, "The real advancement in scientific inquiry comes when there is a conceptual crisis — when a concept, so to speak, has to turn in on itself, to reflect upon itself, and then hopefully something new can arise." He then said: "It just struck me, that there may be an ecumenical equivalent to this. In other words, when one reaches a confessional crisis, this is of course dismaying, causes anguish, may be exasperating, frustrating, and so on. But it also may be the human means for advancement."[75] Bayne, who had already begun to moderate his opposition, would have taken this comment seriously. He was to indicate the extent to which his thinking had shifted in what was, perhaps, his last major statement on ecumenics.

Bayne contributed a chapter to a book called *Episcopalians and Roman Catholics: Can They Ever Get Together?*, edited by Herbert J. Ryan, a Jesuit, and J. Robert Wright of the General Theological Seminary.[76] The publication was meant to be a contribution to the Anglican-Roman Catholic International Consultation then in progress. In his chapter Bayne spoke of theological teaching and confessionalism. Anglicans had emphasized learning and teaching theology in and through liturgy (*lex orandi, lex credendi*) with *The Book of Common Prayer* providing the chief means. "It was an admirable way," he said, "to guard and teach the Tradition, to pray our theology and to cleanse and deepen our prayer. It was also a perilous way, for it tended to breed a carelessness within Anglicanism, a sometimes-frivolous feeling that we did not need to engage in the hard work of theological exploration and could remain aloof about confessional formularies and disputes."[77] The position had become untenable on two grounds: (1) the Prayer Book as a result of liturgical experimentation was not what it had been. With a variety of rites and new freedom in contents and use, it would no longer be as useful as it had been as "teacher, conservator and transmitter of the Church's faith." (2) "the Anglican distaste for confessional theology is by now hopelessly passé." Bayne wrote:

Man in contemporary society faces issues of social order, of conscience, of identity, of meaning with which he cannot cope by merely traditional statements. Great as is the danger of an attractive new confession being a terrible pseudo-solution for him, there is a greater danger in saying nothing to him except what has been hallowed and has become treasured over the years. The Anglican attitude has often been that of a free-loader on what others have done — a kind of eclecticism which disdained the hard confessional work but used the fragments which fell from the confessional table.[78]

The need now to do the hard work of drafting theological statements was recognized by Bayne. He pled for but one proviso and that was the addition of "mystery" to the list of that which must be preserved. He also wanted to restate the Episcopalian stance in positive terms: "It is not that we need not fear; it is rather that we should eagerly welcome. It is this unifying task, fruitful of such confessional statements as those on the Eucharist and the like, which ARC and ARCIC have pioneered, which are models for many areas and levels of our two churches' approach to unity."[79] This can be marked as the final point to which Bayne came in many years of thought concerning confessionalism and experience with confessionalist churches. He was in the end deeply impressed by confessional statements that came from Vatican II and from ARCIC. He had hoped that the Episcopal Church in establishing a consultative agency on the Church's teaching could contribute toward the needed work. He was seriously convinced that the Church was in the midst of a confessional crisis that could result in disaster if not attended to with the requisite hard work on both official and unofficial levels. The kind of seriously theological labor involved in drafting confessional statements was essential to the Church's continuing life and faith.

A Final Sermon

In the last years of his life, Stephen Bayne preached often, and some of these sermons were among his finest. He preached at his two appointed preaching stations, Trinity Church, Wall Street, and the General Theological Seminary. He preached at various New York churches: St. Mary the Virgin, the Church of the Incarnation, and the Church of the Heavenly Rest, among others. He preached at special occasions: a series of sermons at the Episcopal Churchwomen's Conference of the Diocese of Northwest Texas, at the consecration of Samuel Joseph Wylie as Bishop, and at the ordination of Richard Wees Wyland in the Seminary Chapel.

One of his finest sermons was given at the Cathedral Church of St. Paul, in Burlington, Vermont, just two months before his death. His son Bruce remembers the occasion well, having driven his father to Burlington for the dedication of the new Cathedral at which Bishop Bayne was to preach. The text was Isaiah 49:7, and the subject was the place of a Cathedral or any congregation of Christians in a society like ours, a society of doom and promise. He likened the Church of his day to exiled Israel but recognized the difference: "We are exiles in a society which has almost unmeasured power; we are imprisoned in an affluence unknown anywhere else in the world." As was true of exiled

Israel, our old dreams are no longer credible. Our hope for a society of peace and unity under God has run out. Even Christians are in disarray. "We do not know what is possible to believe or what is right to attempt to do in fulfillment of the trust on which our nation is built." It is to this condition that the Church must speak. Bayne drew two certainties from his text. "God is true to Himself and His revelation. God keeps the initiative; He chooses whom He will to bear witness to Him."[80]

Bayne then shifted focus to the Cathedral itself and what it might be. He confessed that he had thought on first seeing it what a perfect place it would be in which to have a sit-in, a protest against corruption in government or for sexual equality. And then it occurred to him that there would be nothing new in that for every church service — "even the most conventional — is precisely a liturgical sit-in of protest against corruption and for equality." He continued:

> The Church's title-deeds, the very basis of our existence, are given us in the sanctifying and liberating Word of God. This Cathedral is a place where people will come to celebrate the fight for purity in public life, where people will gather to proclaim that all power is of God and that the salvation of people who are stewards of His power in government, like citizens of this republic, depends on their remembering that it is His power and not ours. This is the place where, God willing, it will forever be remembered that in Christ Jesus there is neither Jew nor Greek, slave nor free, male nor female, for we are all one in Him.
>
> I only wish our solemn sacramental sit-ins had more of the passion and anger that so often is found outside the Church. We are shamed by those in our society who say what we should have said and feel so deeply what we should have felt. I pray that there may be a fire of new commitment in this place that will warm the hearts of every friend of honor and freedom, in or out of the Church.[81]

Returning to his text and meditating on the first great certainty "God is true to Himself and His revelation," which is to say that God is faithful, Bayne argued that because "God is faithful, we are free to accept the necessity of change in every aspect of life, if we are to stay alive." He was thinking of the revision of *The Book of Common Prayer* that he loved so much. He knew that revision was necessary. "The important thing is to see to it that what replaces the old is true to the faithful God. Not everything that is new is true to Him. What we need is the assurance that what we know of Him can be made known in many ways, and He guides us in our testing of the new ways."[82] Bayne was thinking too of sexuality and the sexes, acknowledging that he grew up "in the twilight of the Edwardian moral code," when women were regarded as weak and dependent, expected to obey their husbands, whereas men were viewed as robust, not marrying until they had a sufficient bank account, keeping women on a pedestal. It was all coherent and grossly unfair to both men and women and needed changing. "But," Bayne said, "it is the faithfulness of God that demands the changing; He is not denied by the changes which set men and women free from the old injustices; His faithfulness is the reason for the changes and the best guide we have in making them." He concluded:

> What I am saying is that part of the Church's essential witness in the public life of our society is to be able to tell the difference between the transitory and the unchanging, between change for the sake of change and change for God's sake. What we are taught about men and women in the first chapter of Genesis or in Paul's great argument in Galatians 3 is the faithfulness of God and the truth about humankind. How this truth is to be worked out in practice is the question before every generation, and it is not to be feared or to be evaded; God is faithful.[83]

The second certainty or assurance was that "God keeps the initiative; He chooses whom He will to bear witness to Him." Those who are chosen are called to be "faithful witnesses of the God who is ever true to Himself." Bayne reflected on the amazing story of Christianity's success in outliving, outloving, outdying the pagan world. It was, he believed, the cruelty of pagan society "which condemned it to death, and it was the glory of Christians to demonstrate to the world, in the world, the obedience to Christ from which the saving heart of pity and mercy were forgotten. And the future quite clearly lay there."[84] It is, he contended, still the "destiny of the church to beget mercy." Not the church alone, for as Isaiah said, God "shaves with a hired razor." We must join forces with others not of the Church who are concerned about our society's cruelty and prove to them, in William Temple's words, that the Church "is not mainly concerned with religion" because God is not mainly concerned with religion.

> What is He concerned with? He is concerned that all our wealth and power shall serve the community of mankind and that men and women shall not be subservient to wealth and power. He is concerned that every child of His shall know how great a thing it is to be human — how holy, how inviolable, how clothed with the glory of Christ is every one of the uncounted millions for whom Christ died. He is concerned that truth and honor and self-discipline shall be the highest dignities of human life. He is concerned that we shall celebrate life and yet not fear death. He is concerned that the human community shall not be pushed aside in the bitter rivalries of nationalism and racism and the haves and have-nots.

God is not mainly concerned with the details of worship. He is concerned that His children learn how to master and guard His great gifts in creating and redeeming us in His love. And we, foolish and weak as the church is, have been chosen to bear our witness to that in the midst of this society, at this time.[85]

In the years from the 1930s to the 1970s, through almost forty years in the ordained ministry, Bayne preached hundreds of sermons. He who disclaimed any expertise in the art of homiletics was one of the most influential preachers in the Episcopal Church. He also had taught many the rudiments of the craft and inspired others to reach greater heights in the proclamation of the gospel. He was a skillful exegete of Scripture and an adept prophet. He achieved something of the ideal of the gifted preacher being able to apply the Scripture, in which he was deeply immersed, to the issues of contemporary society.

The Death of an Apostle

Stephen Bayne carefully planned his retirement to take place June 30, 1973, arranging his affairs with the Church Pension Fund and sending on June 28 the requisite letter to the House of Bishops.[86] He planned to spend more time in Essex, in the house he and Lucie had bought in 1972. In the sermon he preached in Burlington in November of 1973 he said: "The only home my wife and I have ever owned is an old house in the village of Essex, twelve miles south of Burlington on the New York shore of the lake. Ever since I was 6 years old, for most of my boyhood summers and for many more years after, this valley, this lake, have been very dear to me."[87] The house they bought was named Drydock, and the little cottage equipped to be Bayne's study was named Plumstead. "Non-Trollopians," Bayne said, "may skip the reference."[88]

Bayne was fascinated by Anthony Trollope's *Barchester Chronicles*. In 1967, as a sort of Christmas present to his friends, he wrote a "Fragment from a Barset Journal,"[89] supposedly an authentic manuscript, which was a description of contemporary Barsetshire with critical notes and a detailed map, owing something, one supposes, to Ronald Knox. As learned schoolboys have been known to spend hours mapping and discussing the imaginative land of Tolkien's Hobbits, so Bayne found relaxation and enjoyment in exploring Trollope's Barsetshire. "Curiously," one of his notes reads, "Trollope has very little to say about the western section of the country, perhaps because there was no post-office there to justify an expense account? (but see B. Dull and O. Platitude, *Did Trollope Visit Barset?* for another possibility)."[90] In another note he wrote, "With the coming of Socialism in Britain ... the main streams of Barset have been redesigned and combined in the Southwestern Counties

Riverine Experiment (Waterpower). 'SCREW,' as it is known in British officialese, now controls more than 9 million horsepower of hydroelectric energy. Cactus and greasewood have been widely introduced in Barsetshire."[91] In discussing the name Barsetshire, Bayne refers his readers to "P. Chisholm's *A New Speculum of Early Syllableology (American Journal of Supra-Significant Research,* Vol. I; No. 1.)."[92]

Why this interest in Trollope? One might justly answer with another question, "Why not?" Bayne was a mixture of Anglophile and Anglophobe. He had from his youth a love for things English, but he also could be exasperated with the English. Trollope suited him well, with his devastating caricature of the English church and society and with his deep appreciation of the underlying character of the English people and their institutions. Bayne could identify around him the Archdeacon Grantlys, the Mr. Swopes, the Mr. Hardings, the Dukes of Omnium, and all the rest, including the vulnerable Vicar of Frameley and the tortured, pitiful Mr. Crawley. Caricatures, yes, but nevertheless real. And Bayne had a special liking for the not altogether admirable Archdeacon Grantly, naming his little cottage after Grantly's cure of Plumstead Episcopi.

It was at Essex that Bayne gathered his family, children and grandchildren, telling the story of the burning of the old nail factory at Essex[93] and preaching at the baptism of David Edward Dexter Bayne, speaking then of courage. "Courage is fear plus obedience to duty, courage is fear plus love, courage is fear transformed by our freedom which bids us to do what we must do regardless of our fears."[94] There were many happy moments the summer of 73. But Bayne was very unwell. There had been serious bouts with bronchial infections going back as far as 1970 when he was hospitalized in New York. Yet he was coping. He did not sleep well in the last two or three years of his life, made use of oxygen when he could, and was taken about in a wheelchair toward the end.

In February of 1973, he wrote to Robert Parks, rector of Trinity Church, from St. Kitts, to which Parks and the vestry of Trinity had sent Bayne, with Lucie and Lydia, for a rest. Bayne said that he was recovering his strength. "I was a lot sicker than I had known, and I think Lucie was as well." He was looking forward to retirement but was deeply grateful for his relationship to Trinity, which he hoped to continue, with some changes. He was also grateful to Foster, the new Dean of General, for the opportunity to stay on, "to teach ascetical theology and be an adviser and companion to him." This, Bayne realized, would be without pay but with honorarium and office space as the Pension Fund permitted.[95]

Bayne found it difficult to get going in the morning and requested that he not be scheduled for chapel duty before afternoon. In April he wrote to C. H. Osborn withdrawing from an engagement at the Priest's

Institute in Oregon. "After two weeks in the hospital last Christmas, I had hoped to be fully recovered by Spring and indeed I am well enough to do my duties here, except for chapel services, and to go out to some essential meetings and conferences where I have no very elaborate part to play. But it is clear that until I can manage a month or two of uninterrupted rest and exercise in the sun, I can't get off the plateau of breathlessness and weakness where I now am."[96] In October he told Tom Talley of having to ask Jim Carpenter "to celebrate for me at noon because I could not clear the congestion that plagues me...am an old Crock, no doubt of it."[97]

Though suffering from emphysema, Bayne continued to smoke. In August John Hines wrote, "I hope you've stopped smoking — and God bless you!"[98] Bayne responded, saying that he recognized the need to stop and the weakness in not stopping, but could not stop. Thinking of the General Convention, Hines' last, to be held soon, Bayne wrote, "I think I should not attempt to go to Louisville. While I am much strengthened and better able to do many things than I was last Spring, I am far from my old self. Traveling is still very complicated and exhausting, and the demands of an extended meeting call for a ridiculously heavy expenditure of energy which I think would outweigh any contribution I could make."[99]

At Christmastime Bayne was seemingly much better. A trip was planned for January, and Bayne wrote to Dean Foster about it: "Lest I violate Chapter 6, Section 3 of the Statutes of the Seminary and thereby risk the penalties of Praemunire, may I ask to be excused from residence from next January 5 to January 26, inclusive, for the purpose of going to St. Marten for sunshine, with my wife?"[100] Foster wrote in reply to "The Bishop": "Lest I turn green with envy too soon — go in peace. And think about all the beautiful snow we are enjoying while you sweat away in the South Seas!"[101]

While in the Dutch West Indies, Bayne became very ill. Lucie arranged to fly with him to Puerto Rico, where Bishop Francisco Reus-Froylan saw to it that Bayne was taken to a hospital. There he died on the morning of the January 18, 1974. The death certificate attributed his death to cardio-pulmonary edema.[102]

Bayne's death came as a shock to many. Tributes flowed into New York from all over the world. John Hines issued a statement saying, "Bishop Bayne left to this Church, and to society, a legacy of Christian ministry difficult to match. His Creator was profligate in conferring upon him talents and gifts of particular brilliance and magnitude."[103] Martin Sullivan, dean of St. Paul's Cathedral, London, wrote to *The Times*: "He was a man of warm and generous heart, and throughout the whole Anglican Communion his memory will be deeply cherished."[104]

His body lay in state Sunday, January 20 in Trinity Church, New

York, and on Monday until 2 P.M. when the Requiem began. John Butler, Robert Parks, Roland Foster, and Paul Moore, Bishop of New York,
participated in the service. The Right Reverend John M. Allin, Presiding Bishop-elect and his eminence, the Archbishop Iakavos of the Greek
Orthodox Church of North and South America, along with other bishops and many clergy, were in attendance.[105] John Hines preached the
sermon, recounting Bayne's gifts through the course of his life: parish
priest, competent scholar, exemplary bishop, exercising vital leadership
as Executive Officer of the Anglican Communion. But Hines noted, he
was not universally liked; not everybody praised his ministry.

> Stephen Bayne was too positive, too dedicated a person for that to
> happen. In him integrity was an incandescent flame. And he was
> willing to pay the price demanded by it. He had the intelligence
> and the courage to question — in the name of His Lord — time-
> worn institutions which, long ago, had failed to fulfill the humane
> purposes for which they had been created. And — like his Lord —
> he made enemies of people whose devotion to the institution out-
> ran their compassion for mankind. But he had the capacity to love
> his enemies and to hear them out, so that not a few of them heard
> the Christian Gospel anew — and were moved and changed by his
> reconciling ministry.[106]

EPILOGUE

Stephen Bayne firmly believed that humans were created by God "because He is Love; and because Love seeks an answering love, freely given, for Love's sake."[1] Freedom is not, therefore, simply a predicament, as it is for many moderns, but a condition, and a most fundamental condition of human existence. As such, freedom necessitates responsible choice and ultimately reaches its end or purpose when humans as individuals and as societies choose God, loving God above all else and one another as found in God. There are limitations to our freedom. Bayne mentions three in *Christian Living:* (1) limitations of time and space, (2) limitations of knowledge, and (3) limitations of the "divided self." This last concerns what is traditionally known as sin. We are free to choose in order that we may choose God, but instead our freedom becomes a means of pain and evil — hurting a fellow human being beyond the possibility of healing in this world, wronging others in such ways that we are the causes of incredible pain and anguish. The way out of this sinful state is through freedom.

God redeems us through our freedom, preeminently through Jesus Christ. In Christ God entered into our freedom and made choices with a purity of motive that astounds even yet, revealing the perfection of choice through sacrificial offering. This is God's self-offering, inspiring us to take responsibility for our choices and their consequences and to be penitent, repenting, exercising freedom as God meant it to be exercised in words and deeds of love. Thinking on these things Bayne wrote: "It is not accidental that penitence and holiness go together. Strange as it may look to the outsider who wonders at the depth of penitence in souls transparently good and strong, it is not strange from the inside. For the very penitence itself, arising from the knowledge of impure motives and of an evil and confused will, is the means whereby God has purified the will, unified the divided self, made more explicit the real motives so that choices more truly free could be made."[2]

Given the limitations of freedom — the inescapable reality of them — Bayne recognized the inevitability that our choices will always be less than perfect. "Our choices come to us, trailing long streamers of history behind them. They are themselves the result of other choices, made by other men. They incorporate past good and past sin. They involve other people and still other choices. They are sticky and brittle, and they cannot be molded to suit our convenience."[3] We shall, therefore, harm people as well as do them good. We may wish that we were not forced to make choices, that we did not have this freedom. But because we are made in God's image we do have freedom, and we must choose, knowing that our choices are made in the context of history and contemporary community. We must take responsibility for the choices we make and live lives of penitence and praise. Christians look to Christ as they exercise their freedom, and that is their hope and their blessing. "Truly," wrote Bayne, "we would be lost in our freedom if we did not have the constant example of Christ before our eyes, who met exactly this same sticky, imperfect world as we meet, and yet made His choices. Christianity is not example alone; it is also power. But the power comes to those who are willing to follow the example."[4]

To follow Christ is to learn the blessing and the power of obedience exercised in discipline. Bayne knew that the way lay through prayer, for it was in prayer that he was in constant communion with his Lord. Word and sacraments empower us in our creatureliness to respond to God's love with an answering love expressed not only in *Te Deums* sung out with joy in the midst of the Church's worship, but in *Te Deums* of love expressed in eucharistic living that floods the world with love and overwhelms the powers of sin and death, of tyranny and oppression, of war and injustice. Bayne knew, too, that this response to God would be made by a will both obedient and disobedient: "The only response we can make is by offering to him what we have, imperfect though it be, offering it to him in obedience. This is why, because we learn this about ourselves, that our eyes turn to Christ and we recognize in him the truth about ourselves. In this sublime self-offering, in this perfect obedience, in this complete and whole response to God, this is God's idea of what it is to be a man."[5]

Bayne spoke and wrote from the heart on the basis of his own experience. He was both ambitious and self-critical. For instance, from his youth on, inspired in part by a father who was forced to struggle out of financial poverty to achieve a sufficient degree of financial stability, Bayne strove to rise through the ranks of the Church from parish priest to bishop. In 1958 he was the choice of many of his fellow bishops to be the next presiding bishop of the Episcopal Church. He was then in the eyes of most too young, but when another opportunity came in 1964, he indicated not only his willingness to be presiding bishop but his strong desire. At the same time, however, he explained to a very close friend that he did not want the office. After the election, he acknowledged that it was best that he had not been elected, that John Hines was the ideal choice, and that he himself belonged with the Overseas Department to which he had earlier been appointed and which appointment he had accepted. One of the bishops present at the election has stated that Stephen Bayne was not elected because he appeared to be aloof, inaccessible, lacking the warmth and charm of Hines. When in seminary, some fellow students regarded Bayne as something of a snob, too readily displaying his superior intellect. They were particularly irritated as they more and more realized that he was in fact as bright as he appeared to be. He possessed a truly remarkable memory and an awesome ability to think on his feet. His colleagues in the House of Bishops could not fail to realize that at times Bayne was bored with their proceedings, critical of their ineptness, and inclined to absent himself in order to do what interested him. Yet he was highly regarded in the House, and the bishops listened carefully to him on those occasions when he felt that he had something to say.

He was made a member of the Committee of Nine and was the choice of enough of his colleagues to be presiding bishop to come within a few votes of being elected. And he loved the House; so he said time and again. In a rather lengthy description of the House of Bishops intended to initiate Oscar Carr, Bayne wrote of the members of the House: "They distrust a snow job or being preached at or shoved around emotionally. On the other hand they give a warm welcome to anybody who sincerely believes in the Christian faith and the vocation of the Church and says so simply and modestly but also with conviction.... Mostly remember that they are men who love the Church and try to be good fathers in God for it."[6] Nevertheless, there were times when he felt himself to be alone in the midst of the bishops. After the meeting of the House of Bishops at Williamsburg, Virginia, in 1953, Bayne wrote to his diocese saying that the meeting was helpful but undramatic.

> Such meetings, I must say, cause me to search my heart a little, too. Partly on personal grounds — I am not a "party" man, and in general I am out of sympathy with "parties" in the Church, but such a posture is often an uncomfortable one, and always a slightly lonesome one, and there are times when it seems very attractive to get into a caucus and vote with the organization. Also I am not a money-raiser, and it is disturbing to me to hear various success-stories from here and there, and realize I am not being a good bishop in that respect, as in many others.

He went on to speak of how the "churchiness" and the sense of Episcopalian superiority among some bishops annoyed him. "I question whether the survival of a tiny, tiny little conclave of Episcopalians is going to have much to do, one way or the other, with the salvation of the world. A little less giggling about our funny, broad ways, and a little more Gospel — a little less coziness in all being tolerant Episcopalians together among all those negroes, Roman Catholics, Communists, etc., and a little more attentiveness to the God who uses the Assyrians quite as well as He does the Episcopalians. Well, you see my point."[7]

In part, perhaps, Bayne was risking the displeasure of his colleagues by adhering to his principles. In making choices he was bound to offend one person or another. There was the possibility, as one bishop has said, that when seeming to be aloof, or distant — inattentive to those around him — his mind was intent on some deep thought or some needed strategy. He was a thoughtful man, reflective, constantly marshaling his thoughts and his arguments out of carefully structured, far-reaching theological and general knowledge. As his brother has said, he was not constitutionally aloof, but rather outgoing, capable of focusing his entire attention on the person before him.

Bayne could become irritated, even angry. In *PIE* he innocently stated:

Both the "Protestant Episcopal Standard" and the "A.C.U. News" arrive regularly (the donation of some unspecified benefaction). I read them both. What a tiresome, dreary, paranoid world their editors must inhabit! There are so few bishops they can speak to or pray with, and so little in the Church they can approve of. As for me and my house, we are just dumb Episcopalians; we like our outfit and approve of the Old and New Testaments and the Prayer Book and the Creeds and the Lambeth Quadrilateral and we don't hate anybody and we think "The New Yorker" is the best of the Church papers and the only one we really enjoy subscribing to.[8]

Canon duBois of the American Church Union cried out in protest, but Bayne would not retract. Later on they clashed again concerning policy in the American Convocation of Churches in Europe. But Bayne was on the whole remarkably controlled, especially during the harrowing years from 1964 to 1970 at the Episcopal Church Center. To one layman, disturbed by an action of the 1969 General Convention, Bayne wrote: "I have your letter of November 4th and am sorry to know of your feelings. I confess that I am surprised that a lawyer and a Churchman finds it wrong for the Church to join in empowering poor people to use the pathways of appeal which are open to more prosperous folk as a matter of course."[9] He was generally firm but moderate in dealing with what were often vitriolic letters. On another occasion, when he felt he had been grossly misinterpreted by *The Episcopalian* in a statement on liturgical revision, he was less temperate: "Your request for my comments hardly deserves any response, I think. If you were responsible for wrenching my two sentences out of the article of which they were a part and Xeroxing them within the context of Dr. Hargis' attack, I can only say that it was an unprincipled act which calls for no recognition whatever."[10]

Bayne was, however, known to many who knew him best as a loving, caring man. To those in trouble he was always supportive. To a priest he wrote: "You must not feel apologetic about having had a problem. It was an honest problem and one which you faced manfully and honestly, and I had no hesitation in going with you through it step by step."[11] There was a young woman in England, mentally ill, constantly seeking his help, toward whom he showed great sympathy and patience beyond anything that might be expected of him.[12] There was the family recently arrived from Ghana, fleeing from Nkrumah, with no money, arriving at 21 Chester Street not having eaten since breakfast (it was then 5:30 P.M.) and unable to return to their hotel, owing as much as they did for their rooms. Bayne saw to it that their needs were met and did so in such a way that their dignity was preserved.[13] There was the child to whom he was always much, much larger than life, toward whom he was gentle and kind. And there were the remarkable women around him, his mother, his wife, Ruth Jenkins, headmistress of Annie Wright Seminary, his daughter, and his administrative assistants and secretaries, all persons on whom he depended, whom he treated with respect and cared for through the years. He inspired respect and the response of love and caring from those he knew, and, he expressed his gratitude for such response. When Dave Angelica helped Mrs. Bayne decorate for Christmas in December 1973, the bishop was touched and wrote:

Raise a mighty "Bis, bis maestro" con amore to Twig
Who is not in the slightest degree ig-
Norant of the arts of hanging holly, tricking trees, lighting lims,
   etc. David
Is of many friends most favor'd
With skills, sapience, and spirit and knows it takes more than one
   glass icicle
To dress a home aright for Christmas. Michael
He is well-named as being, like his heavenly patron, intimate with
   beauty (but in no way psychedelic). A
Wassail, then, con brio (not con Brioschi) to Dave Archangelica.

There were, as we should expect, given Bayne's own account of the human condition, those who did not benefit from his care and love. The complexity of life and of human relationships in particular were ever before him. His relationship with Ned was uneven. They were, after all brothers, and one should expect some degree of sibling rivalry. There was rivalry, but much of the time there was an easy give-and-take. After Stephen Bayne's arrival in London, the relationship with Ned matured on the basis of Ned's long experience in Italy. He was able to advise his brother on things European, especially with respect to the American Convocation of Churches. There was that one difficult moment when Stephen felt that he had failed his brother. Toward the end Stephen felt remorse where his brother was concerned. Ned had dinner with his brother at the latter's apartment at General Seminary, and writes: "As I left, he walked with me to the elevator — a particularly solemn moment since I think we both knew he would be dying soon. We embraced, with particular tenderness, and he said slowly, 'I *tried* to love you...' and I believe he meant it deeply."[14] In his last days, Bayne was still traveling the way of penitence.

Something of the character of the man is revealed in his ministry as a spiritual director. As experienced by one of those whom he served in such a capacity for many years, he was both very directive and very pastoral. The sessions were usually brief. Bayne listened intently, carefully, expecting that the person before him would have prepared for their meeting. For the time they were together the person before him was all that mattered. His counsel was usually sparse, sometimes terse, drawn out of an immense storehouse of experience and experiential theology. He was always positive and supportive in what he had to say, affirming the person for what he or she was and could become. The times together were not altogether dour. There was much laughter. And there were memorable statements: "It hurts so much to grow up, doesn't it?" "I have something to tell you. I have to tell you how good God is and how He leads us and how good obedience is and how nourishing." He was often paternal, openly regarding those who came to him as his children. Toward the end he had to let those children go, and it was painful for them and for him. And in all and through all there was prayer, unceasing prayer.

Bayne was both a happy extrovert and an unhappy introvert, but also at times an unhappy extrovert and a happy introvert. Arthur Livingstone remembered the rector of Saint John's, Northampton, riding around town "in his Ford phaeton with the top down and the car loaded with college students and other young people." He also recalled that "he would sit in his office and sing as he worked....He also loved to walk in snowstorms. The two of us would walk in them for an hour. He had a nickname for everything. He called his second-floor office 'the angel's roost.' The storage space in the boiler room was 'the glory hole.'"[15] At seminary there were giddy, light moments. Bishop Sherman writes:

> I well remember "The Levites" (the annual show produced by the Student Body in which we endeavored to help the members of the Faculty to see themselves as the students saw them): on one occasion we had a meeting of the Old Testament Department in which Ed Welles appeared as Dean Fosbroke; your humble servant as Dr. Batten; and Steve hilariously as Dr. Shepherd. It might have been this same year when we had the "Quartet" from "Rigoletto," with Steve debating and protesting the innocency of Gomer bath Diblaim. One of Steve's most endearing traits was his love of music and of Gilbert and Sullivan in particular.[16]

And there was the letter he wrote to John Butler as from Dundant, Mundi, and Smirk, Attorneys at Law: "R. E. Dundant, S. Mundi, P. Jorative Smirk," that is, "*In re* New Testament-in-the-original-Greek Chowder and Marching Society v. B. G. C. Bayne et al."[17]

There were other times of darker hue. In his own mind they seemingly were related to a recurrent experience of anxiety or depression. He himself wrote of this pointing to a beginning when as a young deacon he stood in the sacristy of the Chapel of the Intercession in New York preparing to preach and there encountered for the first time "the deep vein of anxiety — stage fright — which never left him." He learned to "live with the misery of it, and even to understand something of the fear of exposure which was being expressed."[18] There were glimpses of him in the midst of depression, weeping in seclusion. There were times when he had to realize his limitations and rest from his grueling regimen. In July 1964 he wrote to Archbishop Coggan to explain why he was unable to attend a conference at which he was expected. "My physique is adequate to most needs; but I have had a cumulative burden this Spring, accelerated by almost incessant travel; and I began to notice the danger signs (for me) of sleeplessness and sudden faintness. I have learned long since that then I must get on top of my time and anxieties, and was very grateful for the three days respite and the chance to be in my office and my home and catch up with a mountain of things and begin sleeping again."[19]

There were moments of confession in the letters he wrote to Lucie while he was traveling, such as the letters from Detroit where he went in 1961 to deliver a set of lectures intended for publication. "They (the McMath lectures)," he wrote, "are a burden and a slogging job and nothing was less joyful than today's desultory writing. I just don't have it anymore I guess." The lectures began, and in the midst of them he wrote: " 'Sacrifice' last night...I thought it was very raggedly written, and I was ashamed of it, but it was delivered in the usual Bayne pontifical style so nobody understood it anyway and thought it was fine." When they were over he wrote: "The lectures ended disappointingly, I thought. I was wordy and involved without being communicative last night. Wednesday night ('Offering') was the best, everyone seemed to feel. But there is a vast amount of rewriting to do before they could possibly be published, and at the moment I'm not very excited. But everybody was most polite."[20] Such self-deprecation was seldom seen by anyone outside the family, and even then it was not often apparent to those closest to him. Bayne was, as one of his friends has said, a very private man. He suffered quietly and out of his suffering came wisdom, the ability to empathize with those suffering around him, and a sense of contrition that left him open to the workings of grace.

Bayne was a strong man whose strength was revealed in his ability to suffer, and in suffering to love and to share in many ways the grace he received — in ways that at times seemed brusque but often in ways that demonstrated tenderness. He was all this and experienced all this as he did because he lived in Christ, the Lord who suffered upon the Cross and through His suffering made it possible for us to love with a penetrating, healing, strong, and tender love. The parish priest, the university chaplain, the diocesan bishop, the first Anglican Executive Officer, the First Vice-President of the Executive Council of the Episcopal Church, the seminary professor, the seminary dean was above all and through all a Christian man who offered all that he had to the service of God, and through God, Father, Son, and Holy Spirit, to the world that God loves enough to endure the suffering of the Cross.

In the sermon he preached at Oxford in 1960 on "The Triumph and Glory of the Kingdom," Bayne expressed his deepest conviction:

> If we would know what the triumph and the glory of the Kingdom of God is it would not be enough, it would not even be true, to think of it merely in the most exalted terms of divine being. If we would see the triumph and glory of the Kingdom, we see it in the heart and will of the man, the woman, who brings to Christ's feet the best things we have, not because we think they are perfect, not because we even think they are good. They are all we have; bringing to his feet, day after day, what time we have, what gifts we have, what thoughts we have, asking Christ to offer these things with his offering. And it may be that any one day we have very little to give. It may be that in the whole of a man's life there is not very much to give. Still it may be all that we have to give. It may not look like very much to us, no more than a piece of bread or a cup of wine. But when we put these things, and ourselves, in the hands of Christ and ask him to offer them with his offering to the eternal Father, then suddenly there is a dignity and a beauty about life that I should want to call the Triumph and the Glory of the Kingdom for now. Who knows what it will *be* like. What we know now is the radiance and the power of God's transforming love that takes what little we are and what little we have and uses them if we will put these things in his hand. Therefore, in the center of our religion is the Eucharist, and the center of our life is the Eucharist, the offering in thanksgiving, the offering of our createdness as the best response that free people can make to the loving God who brought them into existence. This is the triumph, this is the glory of the Kingdom. Look for it in the lives and hearts of your fellowmen, for here is where you see most clearly the thumbprints of God, the saving work of Christ.[21]

NOTES

References to "Drawer" in the notes indicates the file drawer number in the Bayne Archives at the General Theological Seminary, New York. The number following the drawer number is to the file number and the lower case letter to the specific item in the file. The numbers preceded by upper case letters refer to the items as found in the Bayne *Bibliography* (privately printed).

Preface

1. Stephen Bayne, *The Optional God* (Wilton, Conn.: Morehouse-Barlow Co., Inc., 1980), pp. 112–13.

One: Beginnings

1. Privately circulated manuscript by Stephen Fielding Bayne, Jr.; copy in Bayne archives.

2. See Helen Kipp to SFB, January 18, 1966; Drawer #5, 32e; *Trinity Parish Newsletter* 12, no. 1 January/February 1965; Drawer #5, 17e. Also of interest are letters from Kenneth Boggs to SFB, July 13, 1970, C. F. Seibel to SFB, May 15, 1972, and SFB to C. F. Seibel, May 29, 1972; Drawer #5, 32e.

3. E. A. Bayne to J. Booty, Feb. 16, 1985.

4. Preface to Rabbi R. H. Lavine's *Holy Mountain: Two Paths to One God* (Portland, Ore.: privately printed, 1953), pp. xiii–xv, B4.

5. "To Imagine, To Believe, To Hope, and To Build," *Pacific Northwest Library Association Quarterly* 24 (January 1960), C37.

6. Foreword to Dora P. Chaplin, *The Privilege of Teaching* (New York: privately printed, 1962), B20.

7. Ibid.

8. Minutes of 113th Annual Convention, Theta Delta Chi, August 26, 1960, Drawer #5, 38e.

9. The Episcopalian 128, no. 8 (August 1963), p. 11, Drawer #5, 5b. See "What Is the Responsibility of the Press in the Scientific Age?" 11th Annual Service, Allied Daily Newspapers, University of Washington, August 8, 1958, D42.

10. See K190, H2, 3, and G. R. Elliott to SFB, Amherst, June 6, 1933, Drawer #5, 3e.

11. A. L. Kinsolving to SFB, October 24, 1929, January 15, 1930, February 14, 1930; Drawer #5, 2e.

12. William Manross, "Growth and Progress Since 1960," *Historical Magazine of the Protestant Episcopal Church* 5, no. 3 (September 1936), p. 223.

13. Introduction to *God in the Heart of Things, Hughell E. W. Fosbroke,* ed. Edward French (Greenwich, Conn.: Seabury Press, 1962), p. 4, B22.

14. K191 and *God in the Heart of Things,* p. 7.

15. *God in the Heart of Things,* pp. 6–7.

16. Ibid., pp. 7–8.

17. Ibid., p. 9.

18. E5; January 17, 1932. See also F. S. Fleming to SFB, The Purification 1932, E6.

19. "The Church's Mission to the Despairing," an address before the Origen Society, New York, November 10, 1931, D2.

20. "What the Church Can and Cannot Do in Social Reconstruction," a paper delivered during the Church League for Industrial Democracy Convention, Boston, Mass., February 20–22, 1932?, D4.

21. "Worship as a Dynamic for Social Reconstruction: An Apologetic," a paper delivered during the Tri-Seminary Conference, New York, December 1931.

22. Edward R. Welles to the author, January 10, 1985.

23. Jonathan G. Sherman to the author, April 20, 1986.

24. Howard C. Robbins to SFB, New York, April 24, 1933, Drawer #5, 3e.

25. See Drawer #5, 6e.

26. E27, K112.

27. Untitled sermon on the Christian Life as Adoration, St. Bernard's Church, Bernardsville, New Jersey, May 14, 1934, E39, K118.

28. Untitled sermon on God as the Center of the Christian Life, Chapel of the Intercession, New York, July 3, 1932, E8, K104.

29. Untitled sermon on the Nature of Progress, 1934?, E44, K122.

30. K197.

31. "The Kingdom and the Church: An Essay in the Historical Origins of Christian Ethics," STM Thesis, General Theological Seminary, New York, April 1, 1934.

32. K197.

33. Ibid. and H21, 22.

34. K104.

35. K68.

36. A. L. Tui Kinsolving to SFB, November 13, 1933. For this and other letters of inquiry, see Drawer #5, 4e.

37. K125.

38. Ibid.

Two: Parish Priest

1. Untitled address honoring Bishop Will Scarlett, delivered May 6, 1935, D6. See K58.

2. JVB to SFB, November 12, 1934, Drawer #5, 2e.

3. S. C. Frampton to SFB, August 2, 1934; Drawer #5, 7e.

4. *The Episcopalian* 128, no. 9 (August 1963); Drawer #2, 5b.

5. W. Scarlett to SFB, Drawer #5, 7e.

6. JVB to SFB, March 2, 1935; Drawer #5, 2e.

7. Published as "Liturgical Reform" in *The Living Church* 99 (January 2, 1937), pp. 17–20, C1. See D7.

8. Untitled sermon on Jesus as Gospel, Trinity Church, October 6, 1935, E86.

9. Untitled sermon on a Life of Eucharist, Trinity Church, 1935, E91.

10. Untitled sermon on the Sacraments, Trinity Church, 1935, E93.

11. K127.

12. Unpublished sermon on Preaching in a World Teeming with Grace, Trinity Church, 1935, E89, K147.

13. Untitled sermon on the Joy of the Christian Life, October 7, 1934, E53, K126.

14. Untitled sermon on the Restlessness of the Human Heart, Trinity Church, November 4, 1934, E57, K127.

15. Untitled sermon on the Peace of Christ, Trinity Church, October 28, 1934, E56.

16. Ibid.

17. Untitled sermon on God's Way and the Commonplace, Trinity Church, October 14, 1934, E55.

18. Untitled sermon on Faith, Love, and Action, Trinity Church, November 25, 1934, E60.

19. Untitled sermon on the Bible, Trinity Church, December 9, 1934, E61.

20. Drawer #5, 11e. Bayne was a Fellow at the College from September 30 through November 25, 1936.

21. Drawer #5, 7e, January 23, 1935.

22. Delivered to the Church School League, St. Paul's Church, Overland, Missouri, May 26, 1937, D8, K59.

23. Untitled sermon on Learning Faith, Trinity Church, January 19, 1936, E96, K150.

24. G1, January 1937, K184.

25. March 1937, G1.

26. Untitled sermon on the Presence of Jesus, Trinity Church, April 21, 1935, E77.

27. Untitled sermon on Dogma and the Ship of Faith, Trinity Church, January 5, 1936, E95, K149.

28. Untitled sermon on God's Presence in the World, Trinity Church, June 16, 1935, E82.

29. Untitled sermon on Faith and Knowledge, Trinity Church, January 6, 1935, E65.

30. Untitled sermon on the Costs of Faith, Trinity Church, January 13, 1935, E66.

31. Untitled sermon on a Personal Relationship with Jesus, Trinity Church, January 20, 1935, E67, K132. This sermon was subsequently preached at the College of Preachers, Washington, D.C.

32. Untitled sermon on Faith and Faithlessness, Trinity Church, 1935, E90.

33. *Why Have Pastors?* Problem Paper No. 16 (West Park, N.Y.: Holy Cross Press, 1937), p. 3, A1.

34. "Pastoral Care," in *The Holy Fellowship: The Ancient Faith in the Modern Parish,* ed. E. R. Hardy, Jr., and N. Pittenger (New York: Morehouse-Gorham Co., 1939), p. 118.

35. Ibid., pp. 120–24.

36. Ibid., p. 129.

37. Untitled sermon on the Priesthood, December 16, 1934, E62, K129.

38. Ibid.

39. Ibid.

40. Untitled sermon on Refreshment of Spirit, Trinity Church, May 19, 1934, E79, K142.

41. Untitled sermon on the Nature of the Christian Parish, Trinity Church, November 11, 1934, E58, K127.

42. Untitled sermon on Christian Freedom and Growth, Trinity Church, October 31, 1937, E110.

43. "Lost Freedom." Lenten Series on Freedom (1), Trinity Church, February 14, 1937, E105.

44. Untitled sermon on Christian Obedience, Christ Church Cathedral, St. Louis, January 1, 1935, E64.

45. "Not Alone," Trinity Church, May 26, 1935, E80.

46. Untitled sermon on the Church as Climate for Personal Growth, Trinity Church, June 9, 1935, E81.

47. "Freedom in Worship." Lenten Series on Freedom (2), Trinity Church, February 21, 1937, E106.

48. "The Enemies of Freedom." Lenten Series on Freedom (3), Trinity Church, February 28, 1937, E107, see E92.

49. Lenten Series on God, Man, and Mankind, Trinity Church, March 17–April 14, 1935, E71–76.

50. "Pathways to Freedom." Lenten Series on Freedom (4), Trinity Church, March 7, 1937, E108.

51. "Christ Is King." God, Man, and Mankind Lenten Series (6), Trinity Church, April 14, 1935, E76.

52. "The Coming of the King." Faith of a Modern Man Lenten Series (6), Trinity Church, April 3, 1936, E102.

53. "The Good Will and the Good Heart," Trinity Church, September 26, 1937, E109.

54. *The Tractarian,* January 1938, G1.

55. Ibid., November 1937, G1.

56. Ibid., January 1938, G1.

57. Drawer #5, 7e. Fleming to SFB, Sr.

58. Drawer #5, 2e.

59. Drawer #5, 7e.

60. K162.

61. Untitled sermon on the Church and the Parables of Salt and Light, St. John's Church, October 15, 1939, E119.

62. *The Episcopalian,* 128, no. 8 (August 1963), p.12; Drawer #2, 5b.

63. K162.

64. Mary Ellen Chase to SFB, March 5, Drawer #5, 2e.

65. Untitled sermon on the Present Reality of the Resurrection, St. John's Church, April 9, 1939, E118.
66. *Prologue,* 1, no. 7 (All Saints 1941), G2.
67. *Prologue,* 2, no. 3 (June 1942), G2.

Three: The College Chaplain During World War II

1. K165.
2. *Report of the Chaplain of the University* (New York: Columbia University Press, 1947), p. 8, F1.
3. K165.
4. *Report of the Chaplain,* p. 5, F1.
5. K165.
6. *The Episcopalian* 128, no. 8 (August 1963), p. 12.
7. *St. Paul's Chapel Bulletin,* no. 13, p. 4, G3.
8. K165. See F1, pp. 6–7.
9. K11. See *Forward Day by Day,* Lent 1943 (Cincinnati: Forward Movement Commission, 1943), A3.
10. *Gifts of the Spirit* (New York: Women's Auxiliary to the National Council, 1943), pp. 11–12, A4. See K1.
11. Untitled sermon on Skepticism. Lenten Series on Science and Religion (1), St. Paul's Chapel, March 14, 1943, E130.
12. Untitled sermon on the Faith and Hope of the Believer. Lenten Series on Science and Religion (2), St. Paul's Chapel, March 21, 1943, E131.
13. Untitled sermon on Becoming What We Are. Lenten Series on Science and Religion (3), St. Paul's Chapel, March 28, 1943, E132.
14. Untitled sermon on the Truth in the Theory of Projection. Lenten Series on Science and Religion (4), St. Paul's Chapel, April 4, 1943, E133.
15. See G3 and K186.
16. *St. Paul's Chapel Bulletin,* December 8, 1946, p. 4, G3.
17. Ibid., May 4, 1947, p. 4, G3.
18. Ibid., December 16, 1946, p. 4, G3.
19. Ibid., May 25, 1947, p. 40, G3.
20. "Education in the Post-War World," *Barnard College Alumnae Magazine,* 33 (Summer 1944), p. 3, C4.
21. Ibid., pp. 3–4.
22. Ibid., p. 5.
23. Ibid., p. 11.
24. Untitled baccalaureate sermon on Being Capable of Greatness. No indication of where or when given in 1943. E135.
25. "Make Room for Man." Baccalaureate sermon preached at Earl Hall, October 28, 1943. E 136.
26. "Freedom, Man, and Belief." Baccalaureate sermon preached at St. Paul's Chapel, May 30, 1943, E134.
27. *St. Paul's Chapel Bulletin,* G3, no. 10, G3.
28. K171.
29. "The Meaning of Advent," St. Paul's Chapel, November 29, 1942, E126.

30. Untitled sermon on Saint Paul and the More Excellent Way, St. Paul's Chapel, January 24, 1943, E127.

31. "A Soldier's Faith," E120.

32. SFB to Mr. Frackenthal of Columbia University, December 2, 1943, Drawer #5, 10e. Most of what follows is derived from letters, clippings, and official documents contained in a single letter file at the Bayne Archives, not specifically labeled or catalogued.

33. "On Christian Vocation," *Action* (May 1947), p. 8.

34. SFB to Capt. Robert D. Workman, ChC, U.S.N., director of the Chaplain Division, Bureau of Naval Personnel, June 15, 1944.

35. SFB to the Rt. Rev. Henry Knox Sherrill, Army and Navy Commission of the Episcopal Church, January 11, 1945.

36. "In Defense of the Proposed Marriage Canon," *The Living Church* 113 (July 21, 1946), pp. 16–19.

37. Untitled sermon on Human Nature, St. Paul's Chapel, October 6, 1946, E138.

38. Untitled sermon on Human Dignity, St. Paul's Chapel, October 20, 1946, E139.

39. "Man and the State," *The Witness* 30 (April 17, 1947), pp. 8–9, C6.

40. *The Church and Economics.* Delivered to the Church Club of New York (New York: Library and Publication Fund of the Church Club, n.d.), pp. 1–19. The talk was given on February 4, 1947.

41. K62.

42. K63.

43. "The Vocation of Our Church," *Bulletin of the General Theological Seminary* 33 (December 1947), p. 3.

44. Ibid., p. 5.

45. Ibid., pp. 5–6.

46. Ibid., p. 8.

47. Ibid., p. 12.

48. Ibid., p. 15.

49. "Duty, Passion, and Holiness." Baccalaureate sermon preached at St. Paul's Chapel, June 1, 1947, E140.

Four: The Bishop of Olympia

1. *The Episcopalian* 128, no. 8 (August 1963), p. 12.

2. In Thomas Edwin Jessett, *Pioneering God's Country: The History of the Diocese of Olympia, 1853–1953* (Tacoma, Wash.: Church Lantern Press, 1953), p. 51.

3. K183.

4. Drawer #5, 12e.

5. Ibid. See *The Living Church* 114, no. 25 (June 22, 1947), p. 5.

6. Ibid.

7. Untitled sermon preached on the occasion of the consecration of Richard S. Watson as Bishop of the Missionary District of Utah, Cathedral Church of Saint Mark, Salt Lake City, May 1, 1951, E153.

8. Untitled sermon preached on the occasion of the consecration of John Pares Craine as Bishop Coadjutor of the Diocese of Indianapolis, Scottish Rite Temple, Indianapolis, April 29, 1957, E155.

9. "A Good Work." Sermon preached on the occasion of the consecration of Daniel Corrigan as Bishop of the Diocese of Colorado, Cathedral Church of Saint John-in-the-Wilderness, Denver, May 1, 1958, E157.

10. *The Episcopalian* 128, no. 8 (August 1963), pp. 12–13.

11. Bishop's address, May 17, 1957, *Journal of the Forty-seventh Annual Meeting of the Convention of the Diocese of Olympia*, p. 52, D36.

12. *Prayers of the Diocese of Olympia,* n.d., p. 2. Courtesy of Ruth Jenkins and the Reverend Professor Holt Graham.

13. Ibid., p. 26.

14. See the files on these committees and boards in the Olympia Archives. Bayne was very active in all these affairs, as the files prove.

15. Bishop's address, May 20, 1959, *Journal of the Forty-ninth Annual Meeting of the Convention of the Diocese of Olympia*, p. 49, D45.

16. Bishop's address, May 24, 1953, *Journal of the Forty-third Annual Meeting of the Convention of the Diocese of Olympia*, pp. 25–26, D26.

17. Bishop's address, May 23, 1948, *Journal of the Thirty-eighth Annual Meeting of the Convention of the Diocese of Olympia*, pp. 30–31, D15.

18. Bishop's address, May 22, 1949, *Journal of the Thirty-ninth Annual Meeting of the Convention of the Diocese of Olympia*, p. 56, D18.

19. Bishop's address, May 7, 1950, *Journal of the Fortieth Annual Meeting of the Convention of the Diocese of Olympia*, p. 23, D19.

20. Ibid., p. 25.

21. Bishop's address, May 28, 1955, *Journal of the Forty-fifth Annual Meeting of the Convention of the Diocese of Olympia*, p. 44, D28.

22. See note 17 above. D15, p. 47.

23. K88.

24. See note 17 above. D15, p. 40.

25. See note 16 above. D26, p. 27.

26. Bishop's address, May 23, 1954, *Journal of the Forty-fourth Annual Meeting of the Convention of the Diocese of Olympia*, pp. 43–44, D27.

27. See note 11 above. D36, p. 55.

28. Ibid.

29. Bishop's address, May 20, 1956, *Journal of the Forty-sixth Annual Meeting of the Convention of the Diocese of Olympia*, pp. 40–41, D34.

30. Bishop's address, May 16, 1958, *Journal of the Forty-eighth Annual Meeting of the Convention of the Diocese of Olympia*, p. 50, D43.

31. Ben Bryant, Don Trendgold, David Ritter, Judy Austin to the Faculty, January 17, 1956, Olympia Archives, "Faculty Study Group."

32. *Seattle Times,* February 26, 1955, and "Notes on 'The Bishop's Evenings' 1955," by SFB. Olympia Archives.

33. I am indebted to Ruth Jenkins for her reminiscences.

34. SFB to James W. Kennedy, September 14, 1953; SFB to C. A. Simpson, April 2, 1958, with Simpson's paper, "Thoughts on Christian Baptism in the Light of the Old Testament," *PIE*, November 22, 1953. Olympia Archives.

35. Report to the Committee of Nine presented to the House of Bishops meeting in San Francisco, 1949; file on Committee of Nine, Olympia Archives.
36. Thomas N. Carruthers to SFB, September 25, 1954; file on Anglican Congress 1954, Olympia Archives.
37. Untitled address on the rite of Confirmation. Delivered during the Lambeth Conference, August 1948, D16. See K66 and C12.
38. K68. See D20–22 and B2.
39. See the booklet outlining the "Service of Witness," March 28, 1957.
40. Drawer #5, 13e.
41. See note 11 above. D36, p. 51.
42. Ibid.
43. *The Living Church* 117 (September 12, 1948), pp. 18–19, C12.
44. K66.
45. D16.
46. A6, K14.
47. *The Living Church* 137 (July 27, 1958), p. 7, C23.
48. *Lambeth Letters* (Tacoma, Wash.: St. Matthew's Church, July 23, 1958), A11. See C29 and K189.
49. Ibid., August 11, 1958.
50. Ibid., August 10, 1958.
51. "The Anglican Communion and the World Mission of the Church," *The Episcopal Overseas Missions Review* 3 (May 25, 1958), p. 1.
52. Ibid., p. 8.
53. *Lambeth Letters,* September 3, 1958, A11.
54. "Bishop's Diary: Russian Interlude," *Seattle Times,* September 22, 1958, C29.
55. "Five Questions About Soviet Russia," The Monday Club, November 3, 1958, D44, K75.
56. Bishop's address, May 20, 1951, *Journal of the Forty-first Annual Meeting of the Convention of the Diocese of Olympia,* pp. 23–24, D23.
57. K188.
58. *PIE,* May 29, 1955, G5.
59. Ibid., March 20, 1955, G5.
60. Ibid., December 11, 1955, G5.
61. Ibid., November 30, 1958, G5.
62. Ibid., November 23, 1958, G5.
63. See note 30 above.
64. Bishop's address, May 20, 1959, *Journal of the Forty-ninth Annual Meeting of the Convention of the Diocese of Olympia,* p. 54, D45.
65. Ibid., p. 57.

Five: The Bishop as Theologian

1. *The Episcopalian* 128, no. 8 (August 1963), p. 13.
2. K2. See file on *The Optional God* in the Olympia Archives for letters to and from Wilbur Ruggles of Oxford University Press and for reviews.

3. Stephen F. Bayne, Jr., *The Optional God* (Wilton, Conn.: Morehouse-Barlow Co., 1980), p. vii.

4. Ibid., p. xiii.

5. Ibid., p. viii.

6. Ibid., pp. 14–15.

7. Ibid., pp. 24–25.

8. Ibid., p. 25.

9. Ibid., pp. 49–50.

10. Ibid., p. 72.

11. Ibid., pp. 76, 85.

12. Ibid., pp. 85–86.

13. Ibid., p. 97.

14. Ibid., p. 101.

15. Ibid., pp. 112-113.

16. Ibid., p. 130.

17. K72. See C19–21 and D37–39.

18. "Creation," *Official Publication* (Hobart and William Smith Colleges) 54 (December 1957), p. 9, C19.

19. Ibid., p. 10.

20. Ibid.

21. G. R. Elliott to SFB, October 17, 1953, Olympia Archives.

22. *Church Times,* n.d., Olympia Archives, file *The Optional God.*

23. K3.

24. Ibid.

25. *Christian Living* (Greenwich, Conn.: Seabury Press, 1957), pp. 3, A9, 7, 24.

26. Ibid., p. 47.

27. Ibid., pp. 52, 56.

28. Ibid., pp. 91, 114.

29. Ibid., p. 243.

30. Ibid., p. 284.

31. Ibid., pp. 323–24.

32. K3.

33. D40. Published in *This Church of Ours. The Episcopal: What It Is and What It Teaches About Living,* ed. Howard Johnson (Greenwich, Conn.: Seabury Press, 1958), pp. 13–30. See K28.

34. K29.

35. In *The Essentials of Freedom,* ed. Raymond English (Gambier, Ohio: Kenyon College, 1960), p. 179, B12. See C18, D35.

36. Three untitled addresses on Freedom, p. 3, D46. June 1959.

37. Report of the Committee on the Family in Contemporary Society, in *The Lambeth Conference 1958: Resolutions and Reports,* Part 2, pp. 142–71. See also B11 and the Introduction to *The Family Today — The Report of Committee Five of the Lambeth Conference 1958* (New York: The National Council, 1960).

38. See *Time,* September 8, 1958 (Drawer #1, 2a) and correspondence between SFB and Maria Luisen Cisneros of *Time,* regarding misreporting of

the Committee's statement concerning methods of family planning, September–
October 1958, Olympia Archives, file "Lambeth 1958."

39. Drawer #1, 6a. See *The Living Church* 137 (November 9, 1958), pp. 18–
19, C30.

40. *Pi Lambda Theta Journal* 28 (December 1949), pp. 93–97, C16.

41. K27.

42. "God Is the Teacher," in *The Christian Idea of Education,* ed. Edmund
Fuller (New Haven, Conn.: Yale University Press, 1957) pp. 255–65, B6, D31.

43. *The Living Church* 118 (June 26, 1949), pp. 10–11, C14.

44. Bayne edited *The Faith, the Church, and the University: A Report of
a Conversation Among University Christians* (Cincinnati: Forward Movement
Publications, 1959), A16, K27.

45. "The Spiritual Aspects of Play," *Recreation* (January 1953), pp. 445–
46, C17.

46. "The Household of Faith," an address to the Lafayette Lodge, Seattle,
October 7, 1948, D17, K67.

47. "Free Enterprise and Leadership — Privilege and Duty," *Pacific States
Year Book, 1948,* pp. 21–22, 42, 44–46, C10, K65.

48. Address to the Monday Club, Seattle, Washington, April 30, 1956,
D33, K71.

49. Delivered at Bruton Parish Church, Williamsburg, Virginia, February
1958, D41, K73.

50. D42, K74.

51. K90.

52. *The Dialogue of the Word* (Seattle: The Diocese of Olympia, 1959),
pp. 11–12, A15. See A18, D32.

53. Ibid., pp. 24, 12.

54. Ibid., letter at beginning.

55. Ibid.

56. E141–51, A12–14. See E162–74.

57. Appendix A906, January 31, 1958.

58. E156.

59. Untitled sermon on God's Partners and Companions in the World's Work,
June 7, 1959, E161.

60. Printed in Seattle by Dogwood Press, 1967, for circulation to the clergy
of the Diocese of Olympia. Also in *Selected Sermons,* December 25, 1974 (New
York: Seabury Press, 1974).

61. K4.

62. *In the Sight of the Lord* (New York: Harper & Brothers, 1958; London:
Faith Press, 1958), p. ix, A10. Bayne recounted strong criticism from Charles
Edward Berger, who accused him of being too conservative in matters of biblical
criticism. See CEB to SFB, March 27, 1958; SFB to CEB, April 15, 1958; CEB
to SFB, April 19, 1958. Olympia Archives.

63. K13. See A5.

64. *The Living Church* 118 (February 20, 1949), p. 12, C13.

65. "The Eucharist and the Church," in *The Eucharist and the Liturgical*

Renewal, ed. Massey H. Shepherd, Jr. (New York: Oxford University Press, 1960), p. 5.

66. E158.
67. "The Eucharist and the Church," p. 17.
68. *The Optional God,* p. 130.
69. Ibid., p. 131.

Six: Anglican Executive Officer

1. Drawer #1, 44a.
2. See letters from Abp. Fisher and Michael Adie to SFB, December 3, 1958; Drawer #1, 44a.
3. SFB to Abp. Fisher, November 16, 1958.
4. SFB to Abp. Fisher, March 5, 1959, in *Anglican Turning Point* (hereafter *ATP*), pp. 9–10.
5. Abp. Fisher to SFB, March 13, 1959, in ibid., p. 11.
6. SFB memorandum, March 21, 1959; Drawer #5, 34e.
7. *ATP,* p. 11; also Drawer #1, 44a.
8. SFB to "My dear companions," April 19, 1959; Drawer #2, 3b, p. 3.
9. *ATP,* pp. 14–16.
10. "First Steps to Fulfillment," *The Living Church* 138 (June 21, 1959), pp. 8–9, 12–13.
11. "Anglican Unity," *Prism* 3 (July 1959), pp. 2–4.
12. *"Discerning the Lord's Body," Anglican World* 2 (November/December 1962), pp. 23–27; *ATP,* pp. 267–73. See E189.
13. *ATP,* p. 99.
14. "Anglican Mosaic," in *Anglican Mosaic,* ed. William E. Leidt (Toronto: Anglican Book Centre, 1962), p. 23, B19.
15. Ibid.
16. Ibid., p. 25.
17. A memorandum prepared for the World Council of Churches Consultation at Geneva, October 2–5, 1963, F23; *ATP,* pp. 101–2.
18. Ibid., p. 5. See John Howe, *Highways and Hedges* (Toronto: Anglican Book Centre, 1986), pp. 76–77.
19. Ibid., p. 6.
20. See Howe, *Highways,* p. 85.
21. *ATP,* pp. 17–19.
22. Ibid., pp. 19–20.
23. "A Map Is More than Paper and Pins," *The Episcopalian* 125 (April 1960), pp. 35–39, C39; and Drawer #2, file 9b, containing schedules, guest lists, letters, etc., all concerned with this trip. There is also a detailed account in Bayne's "Diary" (mostly memos and excerpts from letters concerning his overseas journeys from 1960 through 1965), in the keeping of the bishop's son, Duncan Bayne.
24. *ATP,* pp. 25–27.
25. Ibid., pp. 31–32.
26. Ibid., pp. 28–29.

27. Ibid., p. 29, K22; *Ceylon, North India, Pakistan: A Study in Ecumenical Decisions,* ed. SFB (London: SPCK, 1960), A17.

28. *ATP,* p. 30; see ACC Archives, "Anglican World," memo September 23, 1964.

29. Ibid., pp. 34–37.

30. On Bayne's engagement with the Strategic Advisory Committee, see Drawer #1, 19a.

31. *ATP,* p. 39.

32. I am indebted to John Furness, Esq., the producer of The Brains Trust, for this information.

33. *ATP,* p. 47.

34. Ibid.

35. Ibid., p. 49.

36. Ibid., p. 56.

37. Ibid., p. 57.

38. Ibid., p. 58.

39. Ibid., pp. 59–61; see relevant sections of "Diary."

40. There is a closely detailed and personal account of Bayne at the Seattle World's Fair in the "Diary," August 1–18, 1962.

41. *ATP,* pp. 63–66.

42. Ibid., p. 67.

43. Ibid., pp. 68–69.

44. Ibid., p. 72.

45. Ibid., p. 73.

46. Untitled sermon following the death of John F. Kennedy, Christ Church Cathedral, Oxford, E201, B32, K38; untitled address following the death of John F. Kennedy, delivered during the Requiem Eucharist for John F. Kennedy, Saint Peter's, Eaton Square, D77.

47. *ATP,* pp. 78–79.

48. Ibid., p. 83. See *Latin America: The Report of the Consultation on the Anglican Communion and Latin America,* Cuernavaca, Mexico, January 20–24, 1963. ACMS 63/1 (London: SPCK, 1963), F7. For full details see ACC Archives.

49. *ATP,* p. 87.

50. Ibid., p. 91.

Seven: Bayne's Growing Triumphs

1. See correspondence, Drawer #2, file not numbered, called "Faith and Order Conference, Montreal, 1963. Correspondence."

2. Minutes, July 29, 1963, ACC Archives, file box, "Missionary Executives Meeting," July 1963.

3. ACMS Minutes, August 5–8, 1963, p. 2.

4. Ibid.

5. Ibid., Appendix B.

6. Ibid., p. 14.

7. See *ACMS Structure.* ACMS 63/4 (London: SPCK, 1963), F10; *ATP,* pp. 159–69.

8. Minutes, Lambeth Consultative Body, August 8–10, 1963, F22, pp. 13–14.

9. Ibid., p. 15.

10. *Anglican Congress 1963, Report of Proceedings,* ed. E. R. Fairweather (Toronto: Anglican Book Centre, 1963), pp. 15–16.

11. Ibid., p. 118.

12. Ibid., p. 122.

13. *ATP,* p. 92. See letter to *The Times* (of London) from C. Murray Rogers in Asia, c. April 1–14, 1964, in ACC Archives, complaining of lack of ecumenical concern. Answered by the Dean of Windsor and John Wilkinson, Editorial Secretary of the SPG, April 15, 1964. For a critique by persons deeply involved in missions in the P.E. Church of the U.S.A., see *Overseas Mission Review,* Epiphany 1964, pp. 1–15, and Michaelmas 1964, pp. 1–6.

14. "Mutual Responsibility and Ecumenical Responsibility," *Prism,* no. 80 (December 1963), p. 29, C123.

15. *Anglican Congress 1963,* pp. 129–30.

16. *ATP,* p. 93.

17. "A Pilgrimage and a Process," *The Living Church* 147 (December 15, 1963), pp. 21–22.

18. *Regional Directories Interim Review,* no. 3 (September 30, 1964), pp. 2, 6–7.

19. Minutes, Lambeth Consultative Body, St. Augustine's College, Canterbury, England, April 17–20, 1964, p. 14, F27; copy in ACC Archives also consulted.

20. See A. C. Lichtenberger to SFB, November 22, 1960; Drawer #1, 4a.

21. In a letter to Abp. Fisher, May 8, 1963, Bayne spoke of "perhaps 5,000 baptized persons in the civilian chaplaincies and close to forty thousand in the military." ACC Archives.

22. SFB to American bishops, January 3, 1964; Drawer #2, 24b. See also Drawer #2, 30b.

23. Ibid.

24. Convocation *Newsletter;* Lent 1963, Drawer #2, 28b.

25. Letter from SFB to clergy of American Convocation, March 23, 1960.

26. SFB to F. A. McDonald, July 26, 1961; Drawer #2, 33b; I am indebted to Canon McDonald for granting me an interview. See Bayne's "Diary" for further detailed accounts of his visitations.

27. Letter from SFB to clergy, March 23, 1960.

28. See "Diary" for September 10, 1962.

29. Drawer #2, 21b.

30. "Church or National Club?" *The Living Church* 141 (August 21, 1960), p. 11, C47.

31. "Envoi," *Anglican World* 3 (July/August 1963), pp. 26–27, C117.

32. *ATP,* p. 112.

33. See note 30 above, p. 26.

34. Ibid.

35. Ibid., p. 27.

36. Ibid.

37. Ibid.

38. "Advent and Anglicanism," *Anglican World* 1 (December 1960/January 1961), pp. 21–23, C57.

39. "Internal Divisions Sap Our Missionary Effort," *Church Times,* March 3, 1961, p. 15, C63.

40. Ibid.

41. "Advent and Anglicanism," p. 23.

42. "Is the Church a One-Way Street?" *The Episcopalian* 127 (January 1962), pp. 28–31.

43. Untitled address on Mission, delivered during the Hong Kong Diocesan Association Annual Reunion, Hoare Memorial Hall, Church House, Westminster, England, June 20, 1962, D71.

44. Ibid., pp. 311–13.

45. SFB to BS, January 4, 1963; Drawer #1, 41a.

46. "The Family in Contemporary Society," Central Hall, Westminster, October 4, 1960, C55.

47. "Enemies of the Family," *Church of England Newspaper,* March 25, 1960, p. 9, C38.

48. "Family Planning and Public Policy," *Worldview* 3 (January 1960), pp. 5–6, C36.

49. "This Particular Revolution," *Kenyon Alumni Bulletin* 28 (July/September 1960), pp. 5–6.

50. "The Christian Witness of the Church's Schools," *The Church's Schools in a Changing World,* ed. Clarence W. Brickman (Greenwich, Conn.: Seabury Press, 1961), p. 16, B14, K31. See also Bayne's "Understanding Europe from the Inside," *Schools and Scholarship: The Christian Idea of Education,* ed. Edmund Fuller (New Haven, Conn.: Yale University Press, 1962), pp. 15–31, B26.

51. Ibid., pp. 18–19.

52. Ibid., p. 20.

53. Ibid., pp. 21–22.

54. Ibid., p. 42.

55. Ibid., p. 25.

56. "The Triumph and the Glory of the Kingdom," preached at the University Church of St. Mary the Virgin, Oxford, June 12, 1960, p. 1, E177.

57. Ibid., p. 2.

58. Ibid., p. 3.

59. Ibid.

60. K5.

61. K6. See his "Diary" for April 15–21 for his own highly critical remarks as he was giving the lectures. See also SFB to RSM Emrich, May 3, 1961, ACC Archives.

62. *Enter With Joy* (Greenwich, Conn.: Seabury Press, 1961), p. 49, A18.

63. *Mindful of the Love* (New York: Oxford University Press, 1962), pp. 23, 39, 49, A20.

64. SFB to Charles Ross, July 8, 1960; Drawer #5, 13e.

65. SFB to Harold Shefelmann, August 5, 1960; Drawer #5, 13e.

66. Glyn Jones to SFB, September 17, 1961; SFB to G. Jones, September 25, 1961. Drawer #2, 8b.

67. See SFB to the Convocation of American Churches, January 17, 1961, in which he wrote of the shock he experienced on learning of Fisher's retirement. See also press release of May 24, 1961, on the presentation of a silver crozier to Fisher by the Primates of the Anglican Communion, arranged by SFB. ACC Archives.

68. SFB Memorandum, January 13, 1961; Drawer #1, 44a.

69. SFB to A. M. Ramsey, January 11, 1962; Drawer #1, 43a.

70. Letters concerning SFB and Abp. Coggan at the Borthwick Institute and at Bishopsthorpe, York, consulted with the Archbishop's permission, especially SFB to Coggan, October 8, 1962, and Bp. R. Stopford to Coggan, October 31, 1962.

71. Fisher to SFB, November 27, 1962.

72. SFB to Coggan, March 18, 1963; Drawer #1, 42a.

73. Coggan to SFB, March 26, 1963; Drawer #1, 42a.

74. SFB to Coggan, August 14, 1963. Drawer #31, 42a.

75. Riddle from Paris to SFB, October 10, 1963. Drawer #3, 6c.

76. Johnson to SFB, November 7, 1963. Drawer #3, 6c.

77. Lesser to SFB, October 9, 1963. Drawer #2, 20b.

78. Brown to SFB, October 7, 1963. Drawer #2, 20b.

79. *Christian Century,* October 23, 1963, p. 1294.

80. McDonald to SFB, November 22, 1963. Drawer #2, 36b.

81. Michael Ramsey in Church Assembly, November 3, 1964. ACC Archives.

82. Ramsey to SFB, September 25, 1965. Drawer #1, 42a.

83. ACC Archives.

Eight: A National Leader in a Time of Turmoil

1. See William Crittenden, Bp. of Erie, Chairman of the Nominating Committee, to SFB, September 8, 1964; SFB to Crittenden, Sept. 17; Crittenden to SFB, Sept. 23; Lichtenberger to SFB, April 6, 1964; Drawer #1, 4a.

2. Drawer #1, 21a, July 4, 1964.

3. This account of the voting and the following reflections are from SFB's memorandum in the Bayne Collection, Drawer #5, 26e.

4. SFB to Crittenden, October 26, 1964; Drawer #5, 26e.

5. Sewanee, Tenn., June 10, 1965, D80; see K81.

6. Ibid.

7. "Overseas Department Responsibilities and Emphases," January 30, 1967, by SFB; Drawer #3, 7c.

8. Ibid.

9. "The Question About Domestic Districts," April 12, 1966; Drawer #3, 7c.

10. See note 6 above, esp. p. 5.

11. "Projects for Partnership, 1965–1966. A Directory of Projects in Mutual Responsibility. Issued by the Executive Council in Conformity with the Resolutions of General Convention. September 1965." Introduction by SFB; Drawer #1, 22a.

12. Ibid., pp. 2–5; Drawer #1, 22a.
13. *Mission Is Response.* MRI Resource Book 2 (New York: Seabury Press, 1966); see K8, D79, and D81.
14. April 16, 1968, D87.
15. SFB to Frederick Warnecke, October 11, 1965; Drawer #1, 22a.
16. See C131, 132, 138, and B33, pp. 36–37.
17. *Church Times,* May 27, 1966, editorial entitled "MRI in Trouble."
18. Ibid., June 10, 1966, letter to editor entitled "MRI Not in Trouble."
19. Roberts to SFB, June 6, 1966; SFB to Roberts, Drawer #1, 22a.
20. Webster to SFB, June 10, 1966; SFB to Webster, June 14, 1966, Drawer #1, 22a.
21. See John Booty, *The Church in History* (New York: Seabury Press, 1976), p. 240.
22. "Dear Nephew," July 25, 1967; Drawer #3, 8c.
23. The evidence is in Drawer #5, 20e. He indicated his willingness to let his name stand for the Diocese of Colorado, but not before 1969.
24. *Dogma and Reality* (New York; Trinity Church, 1964), p. 3.
25. Ibid., p. 5.
26. Ibid., pp. 4–5.
27. William Stringfellow and Anthony Towne, *The Bishop Pike Affair* (New York: Harper & Row, 1967), pp.198–99. The documents are printed in this section of the book.
28. Ibid., pp. 199–200.
29. Ibid., p. 200.
30. Ibid.
31. Ibid., p. 223.
32. *Theological Freedom and Social Responsibility,* SFB Chairman. Report of the Advisory Committee of the Episcopal Church (New York: Seabury Press, 1967), pp. 3–4, A29.
33. Stringfellow and Towne, *The Bishop Pike Affair,* p. 247.
34. Ibid., p. 249.
35. *New York Times,* August 15, 1967, p. 1.
36. *Theological Freedom,* pp. 31–32.
37. Ibid., p. x.
38. Ibid., p.21.
39. November 28, 1967, Bayne Archives, GTS, Drawer #3, 8c.
40. *Church Times,* September 8, 1967, p. 13.
41. Ibid.
42. Address delivered at the Rector's Class, Christ Church, Bronxville, New York, December 22, 1968, D89, K84. The reference is to *Stephen Bayne: A Bibliography* (Privately printed, 1978), and the work as found in the Archives.
43. SFB to J. D. Shulthess, August 20, 1969, Drawer #4, 10d.
44. "Dear Nephews," November 2, 1967; Drawer #3, 8c.
45. "Report of the Executive Council," in the *Journal of the Special General Convention II 1969,* pp. 264–65, F30.
46. Ibid., p. 265.
47. Ibid.

48. *Footnotes,* November 1967, p. 3; Drawer #3, 8c.

49. SFB to William Moore, December 13, 1968; Drawer #3, 50c.

50. SFB to Mrs. J. F. M. Stewart, November 17, 1969; Drawer #3, 19c.

51. SFB to Ivol Curtis, February 18, 1969, the famous "Dear Ivol" letter; Drawer #4, 12d.

52. Ibid.

53. New York City, April 24, 1969, D91, K86.

54. See Drawer #1, 3a. Letters to all bishops, May 7, May 14, May 27, June 2, July 22, November 14, and December 22, 1969.

55. Ibid.

56. SFB to EAB, May 19, 1969; Drawer #5, 35e.

57. Ibid.

58. Memorandum, May 18, 1969; Drawer #1, 5a.

59. *New York Times,* September 8, 1969; Drawer #4, 10d.

60. Ibid.

61. SFB to Mrs. J. F. M. Stewart, November 17, 1969; Drawer #3, 19c.

62. *Trinity College Magazine* 10 (Summer 1969), pp. 23–24. The sermon was preached on June 1, 1969. The text was 1 Cor. 4:1.

63. SFB to R. S. M. Emrich, April 19, 1968; Drawer #l, 3a.

64. March 9, 1970; Drawer #1, 20a.

65. SFB to T. H. Fraser, Jr., December 16, 1969.

66. SFB to "my Province Companions," June 12, 1970.

67. SFB to the Executive Council, December 9, 1969; Drawer #3, Memoranda, C69.

68. SFB to JEH, March 18, 1970; Drawer #4, 1d.

69. SFB to R. H. Gooden, April 1, 1970; Drawer #4, 13d.

70. SFB to Ivol Curtis, February 25, 1970; Drawer #1, 3a.

71. SFB to M. H. Shepherd, Jr., and to A. T. Mollegen, October 28, 1969; Drawer #1, 16a.

72. SFB to John Krumm, May 3, 1971; Drawer #1, 16a.

73. Draft report, July 2, 1969; Drawer #1, 16a. See also SFB to JEH, April 18, 1969, and June 25, 1969; Drawer #1, 5a.

74. Drawer #5, 24e.

75. St. Bartholomew's Church, New York, E222. See a sermon preached at St. George's Church, Schenectady, New York, April 4, 1969, E233.

76. Trinity Church, New York, June 9, 1968, E226. Bayne was paraphrasing Weil.

77. Report on a Consultation on Stewardship held at the Episcopal Church Center, New York, June 25, 1969, written by SFB; Drawer #1, 20a.

78. SFB was active on the Advisory Committee on Christian Marriage of which Bishop Spears of Rochester was chairman; see Drawer #1, 7a.

79. See SFB to R. F. Gibson, Jr., February 6, 1969; Drawer #1, 12a.

80. "What the Proposed Liturgy Should Proclaim," *The St. Luke's Journal of Theology* 12 (May 1969), p. 24.

81. SFB, response to a questionnaire, May 1970; Drawer #1, 25a.

82. SFB to EAB, March 18, 1969; Drawer #5, 35e.

83. *The Episcopalian* 131 (April 1966), pp. 8–11, C134.

84. See SFB to Robert Metcalf of Concerned Presbyterians, Inc., January 30, 1967; Drawer #1, 36a. See the *McCormick Quarterly* 20 (March 1967), pp. 201–6.

85. SFB's foreword to *A Diocesan Service Book: Services and Prayers for Various Occasions*, ed. L. S. Hunter (London: Oxford University Press, 1965), p. v.

86. December 8, 1969; Drawer #1, 5a. See Drawer #3, 10c.

87. *Washington Daily News*, Friday, March 28, 1969. The article was syndicated and appeared in a number of other papers including the *Atlanta Journal*, March 15, 1969, where it was headlined, "Bishop Bayne Comes to Power." This was the copy that SFB first saw.

88. See Drawer #4, 6d, for the "comments" and A. P. Stokes to Lester Kinsolving, April 17, 1969.

89. John Leffler to SFB, December 13, 1969; SFB to Leffler, December 22, 1969; Drawer #3, 10c.

90. June 25, 1970; Drawer #5, 20e.

91. See note 80 above.

92. Ibid.

93. SFB to T. H. Fraser, Jr., December 16, 1969; Drawer #3, 10c.

94. Ibid.

95. See note 80 above.

96. January 29, 1970; Drawer #1, 20a.

97. See SFB to John Coburn, and essentially the same to Robert Rodenmayer, November 12, 1969; Drawer #3, 10c.

98. SFB to Donald Coggan, June 15, 1970; Drawer #3, 10c.

Nine: The Last Years

1. *Pan Anglican* 15 (July 1970), pp. 31–32, C144.

2. Ibid., pp. 32–33.

3. Ibid., p. 33.

4. Ibid., pp. 33–34.

5. Ibid., p. 34.

6. Address on "The Future Church," for the ecumenical panel at the centennial celebration of North Presbyterian Church, Geneva, New York, November 3, 1970, pp. 3–4.

7. Ibid., p. 6.

8. SFB to Sam Wylie, January 17, 1971; Drawer #3, 14c. The course was recorded on twelve cassette tapes that are now in the Bayne Collection.

9. Lecture notes, syllabus, et al., Drawer #3, 12c.

10. Lecture notes, syllabus, et al., Drawer #3, 13c.

11. December 6–10, 1970.

12. *St. Luke's Journal of Theology* 15 (September 1972), pp. 3–18. The address was given on December 12, 1970, C148, 9b.

13. London, Ontario, November 25, 1970, D95.

14. Address given at the Episcopal Theological Seminary of the Southwest, October 18–19, 1971, D100.

15. "The Condition of Spirituality in the Church," delivered to Trinity Institute, Trinity Church, New York, December 30, 1970, published in *The Anglican* 2 (Autumn 1971), pp. 5–12, and excerpted in *The Episcopalian* 137 (January 1972), pp. 6–7, D97, C147.

16. Ibid., p. 3, D97.

17. *General Dynamics* 2 (May 1972), p. 1, Drawer #3, 17c.

18. See Drawer #5, 28e, 29e, 31e.

19. *General Dynamics* 2 (September 1972), p. 1, Drawer #3, 17c.

20. *Bulletin of the General Theological Seminary* 58 (November 1972), pp. 4–5, C149, E265.

21. SFB to RD, January 28, 1972; Drawer #3, 16c.

22. SFB to Members of the Board of Trustees, March 8, 1972, Drawer #3, 10c.

23. *General Dynamics* 2 (September 1972); Drawer #3, 17c.

24. *General Dynamics* 3 (January 1973).

25. 1973 General Convention Report, F34, p. 6.

26. Ibid., p. 5.

27. Ibid.

28. Ibid., p. 4.

29. See Drawer #3, 17c.

30. *General Dynamics* 2 (November 1972).

31. Ibid.

32. May 26, 1972; Drawer #3, 17c.

33. Document on "Working Group on Human Sexuality," signed by SFB; Drawer #3, 28c.

34. Draft document dated August 16, 1972; Drawer #3, 17c.

35. SFB to Abp. Coggan, September 10, 1971; Drawer #1, 42a.

36. SFB to all bishops, January 11, 1971; Drawer #3, 40c.

37. See minutes of the first meeting, December 2–4, 1970, and "Interim Report to the House of Bishops," October 24, 1971.

38. See minutes of April 15–17, 1971, meeting, April 22, 1971.

39. See minutes of October 14–16, 1971, meeting, and the "Interim Report"; Drawer #3, 40c.

40. See report to the House of Bishops, October 30, 1972.

41. See the document "The General Board of Examining Chaplains," 1973, p. 6.

42. March 21, 1972; Drawer #3, 48c.

43. Ibid.

44. March 28, 1972; Drawer #3, 44c.

45. April 28, 1972; Drawer #3, 48c.

46. April 5, 1972; Drawer #3, 48c.

47. SFB to GBEC board members, March 26, 1973; Drawer #3, 49c.

48. JEH to SFB and others, February 3, 1972; Drawer #1, 12a.

49. SFB to members of House of Bishops' committee in an "Aide Memoire" of June 1972, p. 1; Drawer #1, 12a.

50. Ibid., p. 2.

51. Ibid., p. 4.

52. SFB to the Committee on the ordination/consecration of women, September 18, 1972; Drawer #1, 12a.

53. SFB to the Committee, September 29, 1972; Drawer #1, 12a.

54. House of Bishops document 72165; F33.

55. Ibid., p. 2.

56. SFB to the Committee, September 29, 1972; Drawer #1, 12a.

57. House of Bishops document 72165, p. 3.

58. Ibid., p. 4.

59. Ibid., p. 5.

60. Ibid.

61. Ibid., p. 10.

62. Ibid., p. 16.

63. Ibid., p. 17.

64. Ibid., p. 18.

65. Ibid., p. 19.

66. Ibid., p. 24.

67. House of Bishops document 72166.

68. SFB to KEA, December 4, 1972; Drawer #1, 17a.

69. September 18, 1971, D99.

70. Ibid., pp. 2–3.

71. Ibid., p. 4.

72. Ibid., p. 9.

73. Ibid., p. 12.

74. Report of the Joint Commission on Ecumenical Relations (New York: Ecumenical Office of the Episcopal Church, 1971), F31.

75. The speaker was John Ford, see B39, p. 28.

76. *Episcopalians and Roman Catholics: Can They Ever Get Together?*, ed. Herbert J. Ryan and J. Robert Wright (Denville, N.J.: Dimension Books, 1973), pp. 20–36; B39.

77. Ibid., pp. 26–27.

78. Ibid., pp. 27–28.

79. Ibid., p. 29.

80. November 11, 1973, pp. 2–3, E272.

81. Ibid., pp. 3–4.

82. Ibid., pp. 4–5.

83. Ibid., p. 5.

84. Ibid., p. 6.

85. Ibid., pp. 7–8.

86. See Drawer #5, 20e.

87. E272, p. 1.

88. Bayne to the GTS faculty, August 3, 1972; Drawer #3, 19c.

89. "Fragment from a Barset Journal," 15.

90. Ibid., p. 6.

91. Ibid., p. 7.

92. Ibid., p. 10.

93. On tape, belonging to Mr. Duncan Bayne, copy in Bayne Collection.

94. August 12, 1973, E270.

95. SFB to R. Parks, February 22, 1973; Drawer #5, 18e.
96. SFB to C. H. Osborn, April 26, 1973; Drawer #5, 20e.
97. SFB to T. Talley, October 16, 1973; Drawer #5, 20e.
98. JEH to SFB, August 1, 1973; Drawer #1, 5a.
99. SFB to JEH, September 16, 1973; Drawer #1, 5a.
100. SFB to R. Foster, November 20, 1973; Drawer #3, 9c.
101. R. Foster to SFB, n.d.; Drawer #3, 9c.
102. Commonwealth of Puerto Rico, Dept. of Health, Division of Demographic Registry and Vital Statistics, Vol. 42, folio 77, Certificate 77.
103. Diocesan Press Service, 74010, January 18, 1974.
104. *The Times* (of London), January 26, 1974.
105. *The Episcopal New Yorker,* January 1974, p. 8; *Trinity Parish Newsletter,* March–April 1974, p. 4.
106. *Bulletin of the General Theological Seminary* 60, no. 1 (February 1974), pp. 3–4.

Epilogue

1. *Christian Living,* p. 324, A9.
2. Ibid., p. 20.
3. Ibid., p. 21.
4. Ibid., p. 23.
5. "Thy Kingdom Come," a sermon preached in the University Church of St. Mary the Virgin, Oxford, June 12, 1960, E177.
6. SFB to Oscar Carr, September 27, 1971.
7. "Notes on the Meeting of the House of Bishops, Williamsburg, 1953." Olympia Archives.
8. *PIE,* III Epiphany, January 24, 1954. Olympia Archives.
9. November 12, 1969; Drawer #3, 57c.
10. March 24, 1972.
11. December 12, 1960; Drawer #5, 19e.
12. March 25, 1962–April 4, 1964; Drawer #2, 23b.
13. SFB to P. L. Brock, August 22, 1961; Drawer #2, 23b.
14. EAB to JEB, February 16, 1985.
15. *The Boston Daily Globe,* May 21, 1959, p. 27.
16. J. G. Sherman to JEB, April 20, 1986.
17. October 29, 1970; Drawer #3, 20c.
18. K104.
19. From the correspondence of Archbishop Coggan in the Borthwick Institute, York, dated July 2, 1964.
20. Journal, April 21, 26, 28, 1961.
21. E177; see note 5 above.

INDEX

Adie, Michael, 92
Africa, Anglican churches in, 106
Alianza grants, 158, 159, 166
Allen, Clara, 11
Americans in Europe, 119–122
American society, 46–48, 58, 128
   American Christians, 22
   changes in, 139, 148–150
   and the Church, 149
Amherst College, 4, 5
Angelica, Dave, 198
Anglican Cycle of Prayer, 106–107
Anglican Exchange, 109
Anglican World, 104, 106, 109
Anglicanism, 6, 49–50, 55–56,
   122–126
   churches, worldwide, 96–97, 100
   communion, 63, 96–100
   history of, 123–124
   spirituality of, vii–viii.
   See also Episcopal Church
Anne Wright Seminary, 60, 89
Aquinas, Thomas, 37
Argentina, Anglican Church in, 97
Aristocracy and Justice (Paul Elmer
   More), 4
"Art of Living, The," (radio program),
   88
Atkins, Stanley (bishop of Eau Claire),
   180, 181
Australia, Anglican church in, 96, 97
Ayres, Harry, 34

Baines, H. W. (bishop of Singapore),
   113
Bard College, 32
Barrett, George W. (bishop of
   Rochester), 146
Batten, Loring W., 199
Bayne, Bruce (son), 61, 187
Bayne, Charlotte (sister), 3

Bayne, David Edward Dexter
   (grandson), 191
Bayne, Duncan (son), 32, 45, 61
Bayne, Edna Mabel (Ashley) (mother),
   1, 2, 52
Bayne, Edward (Ned) (brother), 3,
   102–103, 155–156, 163, 198
Bayne, Frances (great aunt), 1
Bayne, George Gladstone
   (grandfather), 1, 2
Bayne, Lucie Culver Gould (wife),
   4–5, 11, 16, 31–32, 134, 200
Bayne, Lydia (daughter), 32, 45
Bayne, Mary Elizabeth Yonge
   (grandmother), 2
Bayne, Philip (son), 13, 45, 61
Bayne, Stephen Fielding, Jr.
   Advisory Board of the Seattle
      Council on aging, member of,
      54
   Advisory Board of the Seattle
      Research Foundation for
      Alcohol, member of, 54
   and the Advisory Committee on
      Christian Marriage, 162
   Advisory Council on Missionary
      Strategy, responsibility for, 94
   and the Alianza grants, 158, 159,
      166
   on American Christians, 22
   on American society, 46–48, 58,
      128
   Andrewes, Lancelot, influence of,
      77
   on Anglican communion, 63,
      96–100
   as Anglican Executive Officer,
      93–111
      appointment as, 69, 93
      problems of, 131–133
   on Anglicanism, 6, 49–50, 55–56,
      122–126